The Road to Santa Fe

GEORGE CHAMPLIN SIBLEY
Reproduced by permission of Lindenwood College

The Road
to Santa Fe

The Journal and Diaries of George Champlin Sibley

AND OTHERS
*Pertaining to the Surveying and Marking
of a Road from the Missouri Frontier
to the Settlements of New Mexico
1825–1827*

EDITED BY KATE L. GREGG

PREFACE BY MARC SIMMONS

University of New Mexico Press
Albuquerque

LIBRARY OF CONGRESS CATALOGING-IN-PUBLICATION DATA

The road to Santa Fe:
   the journal and diaries of George Champlin Sibley /
   edited by Kate L. Gregg : preface by Marc Simmons.
   —2nd paperbound ed.
        p.   cm.
   Includes bibliographical references and index.
   ISBN 0826315674 (paper)
   1. Santa Fe Trail. 2. Sibley, George Champlin—Diaries.
I. Sibley, George Champlin. II. Gregg, Kate Leila.
F786.R63   1995
978'.02'092—dc20
   {B}   94-45893
                                              CIP

PREFACE © 1995 BY THE UNIVERSITY OF NEW MEXICO PRESS

Contents

Journal of George C. Sibley

Report of the Commissioners

Appendix

Footnotes

Bibliography

Index

Preface

"One of the basic books on Santa Fe Trail history" was how the late bibliographer and southwest bookman Jack D. Rittenhouse characterized Kate L. Gregg's *The Road to Santa Fe: The Journal and Diaries of George Champlin Sibley*. The work first appeared in 1952 and was reprinted in clothbound and paperbound editions in 1968 by the University of New Mexico Press. Out of print now for a quarter century, the book fittingly is being made available to a new generation of readers, on the occasion of the 174th anniversary (1995) of the formal opening of the Santa Fe Trail by pioneer merchant William Becknell in 1821.

For this volume, Dr. Gregg collected and edited documents pertaining to the United States government survey of that trail, a congressionally funded project initiated in 1825 and concluded in 1827. Of the three commissioners selected to direct the survey in the field and treat with the Indians, George C. Sibley of Fort Osage, Missouri, emerged as the acknowledged leader. He was the only one of the trio to cross, with a scaled down mapping crew, the international boundary, which was then located on the Arkansas River in southwestern Kansas, and continue on to Taos and Santa Fe in the Mexican territory of New Mexico.

Kate L. Gregg was professor of English Language and Literature at Lindenwood College, St. Charles, Missouri from 1924 until her retirement in 1946. George C. Sibley had been a cofounder of Lindenwood, and copies of his personal papers remained with the college. Dr. Gregg became custodian of his collection and, consequently, developed an intense interest in the Santa Fe Trail survey. After the publication of her book, some Sibley papers were transferred to the Missouri Historical Society in St. Louis.

Many readers have assumed that *The Road to Santa Fe* contains the majority of significant documents dealing with the survey, although Gregg herself was careful to make no such claim. In her introduction, she mentioned specifically the field notes of the surveyor Joseph C. Brown, which were published by the Kansas Historical Society in 1911 and 1912 and which she therefore excluded from her own work.

Another missing document, of whose existence Dr. Gregg seemed to have been unaware, was the "Diary of Colonel Thomas Mather, Santa Fe Road Commissioner." Its entries begin on July 16, 1825, the day before the party set out from Fort Osage and conclude on the following September 17 at the Arkansas River boundary. This diary, containing details not recorded in other sources, is preserved by the Newberry Library in Chicago, along with several pieces of Mather correspondence.

In the appendix to her book, Gregg printed an assortment of fourteen letters that deal with various phases of the enterprise. Much additional correspondence is known today: for example, more letters to and from Sibley resting now in the Mexican Archives of New Mexico at Santa Fe and in the Ritch Collection of the Huntington Library in San Marino, California. Finally, Craig Crease of the Santa Fe Trail Association, after a recent examination of Sibley materials in the Missouri Historical Society in St. Louis, reports the existence of a set of field notes unrecorded by Dr. Gregg.

Although not a trained historian, Kate L. Gregg won respect and wide acclaim for her competent handling of manuscript sources. She had almost completed the editing of *Prairie and Mountain Sketches* by Matthew C. Field, another prominent figure of the Santa Fe Trail, when she died suddenly on July 9, 1954 at her home in Chehalis, Washington. That book, which was published posthumously, and her earlier *The Road to Santa Fe* firmly secured Dr. Gregg's reputation in the field of western history.

Public and scholarly interest in Santa Fe Trail history has climbed steadily in recent years. In part that interest can be traced to the road's elevation to the status of a National Historic Trail by Congress in 1987. The action brought the old road to Santa Fe under jurisdiction of the National Park Service for purposes of interpretation and marking.

With a spotlight suddenly on the trail, new books have begun to appear, helping to illuminate neglected or shadowy chapters in the story. At the same time older, solid works such as Dr. Gregg's volume are being dusted off and appreciated again. Clearly, *The Road to Santa Fe* is one of the key foundation blocks in the edifice of Santa Fe Trail studies. Aficionados of the subject will welcome its reappearance.

MARC SIMMONS

Foreword

In editing these diaries, I have kept the capitalization used by the writers except that, where there was no capital letter at the beginning of a sentence, I have supplied one. The punctuation is as written except when it interfered with the flow of the sentence or with the meaning. In all cases I have substituted the period for the dash at the end of sentences.

My grateful acknowledgments are due to many—first of all to Mr. Buford Rowland of the National Archives, who notified me that George C. Sibley's Journal, lost for over a hundred years, had come to light in a Senate Committee room, and that I might have a photostatic copy for publication; to Lindenwood College for giving me access to the original diaries of Sibley and permitting their publication; to Dr. Floyd C. Shoemaker of the State Historical Society of Missouri for permission to use the valuable material in the Leonard Collection; and to the Missouri Historical Society of St. Louis for access to Sibley manuscripts and direction to sources. I am also deeply indebted to the Huntington Library, to the Bancroft Library, to the Historical Societies of Massachusetts, Oregon, Kansas, Illinois, and Wisconsin; to the American Antiquarian Society, the Congregational Library in Boston, the Harvard-Andover Theological Library at Harvard, the Library of Congress, and officials of the War Department and the Office of Indian Affairs. Special thanks are due Miss Lillian Rasmussen for her work on the map; and to Mr. John F. McDermott of the Historical Documents Foundation of St. Louis for his interest in publication of these diaries.

KATE L. GREGG

Chehalis, Washington
January 30, 1952

The Road to Santa Fe

INTRODUCTION 1

Road to Santa Fe

Whether one considers the road to Santa Fe in terms of the "manifest destiny" of Anglo-Saxons, or more prosaically in terms of calico, whiskey, mules, beaver, and desirable hard money, the causes for the survey and marking of the road from the frontier of Missouri to the boundary of Mexico lead far back, are complex, and not always apparent.

Within the second month after Fort Osage was christened on November 10, 1808, George C. Sibley, government trader at the new post, pointed out in a letter to his brother that if the United States should go to war with England, and if Spain should enter, "it is likely this will be a rallying post from whence to attack Santa Fee; we could march there and seize their rich mines in less than 20 days. And I have no doubt if we have a war, but seize them we shall."[1]

Young Sibley was not spinning idle theory. He had his knowledge of the route first hand from Dr. John H. Robinson, whom he had known at Fort Bellefontaine—the Dr. Robinson who had marched to Santa Fe with Lieutenant Zebulon Pike in 1806, and who had mapped the country and the route as he went. Presently Dr. Robinson would come to Fort Osage as deputy Indian Agent. The young factor would board with the Robinsons, and interesting would be the after-dinner conversations about the country to the southwest and how to get there and why.

Back of the dinner table of the Robinsons and over it loomed the spirit of Thomas Jefferson, whose right hand does not betray what his left hand was up to even now after a hundred years. George C. Sibley, appointee of Jefferson and stationed at Fort Osage on the extreme western frontier in 1808, was the oldest son of Dr. John Sibley, who, one remembers, was exploring Louisiana at the time that the Louisiana Purchase was made and who now, like his son, was an Indian Agent on the western frontier. The literary skill which Dr. John Sibley had for-

1

merly wielded on the *Fayetteville Gazette* in North Carolina he now applied in description of Louisiana and the country that lay west of it, and mailed his findings post-haste to the federal capitol. George C. Sibley also, before the War of 1812 made travel impossible, had done his bit of exploring toward the Southwest and written descriptions of salt plains for the same master. How much Dr. Sibley was involved in Dr. John H. Robinson's filibustering west of Nachitoches still remains a teasing riddle. The movement toward Santa Fe, one cannot but feel, had some of its origin in the heads of certain eminent gentlemen who did not scatter papers carelessly: Thomas Jefferson, General James Wilkinson, Lieutenant Zebulon Pike, Dr. John H. Robinson, Dr. John Sibley—fascinating figures all, and all with eyes toward Santa Fe.

Another reason for the road—developing trade with northern Mexico—has been set forth in government documents, magazine articles, and books. Beginning in 1821 with William Becknell and his little party of three or four, their $300 worth of goods packed on the backs of horses, the Santa Fe trade by 1824 had reached proportions sufficient to engage Congressional attention. How much of the evidence submitted to Congress as reasons for speedy action in surveying and marking a road rose out of the real need and how much out of the ambition of Thomas Hart Benton is another problem. William Becknell observed in his "Journal of Two Expeditions from Boon's Lick to Santa Fe," published in the *Missouri Intelligencer*, Franklin, Missouri, April 23, 1823: "An excellent road may be made from Fort Osage to Santa Fe. Few places would require much labor to render them passable; and a road might be laid out as not to run more than thirty miles over the mountains." So far as I have been able to glean, this is the only mention of a *road* to Santa Fe in the *Missouri Intelligencer* previous to 1824, the year in which Benton laid his groundwork for introduction of the bill to survey the route and make treaties with Indians for a right of way.

The *Intelligencer* is full of stories of the Santa Fe trade—caravans leaving or returning; the amount of merchandise carried out; the gold, silver, mules, furs brought back; attacks from marauding and murdering Indians. From reading the files of this frontier newspaper, one gathers that the need of the hour was protection of the trade from Indians. Abolition of government trading posts in 1822 had removed a salutary check on the behavior of the tribes of the plains. The unfettered individualism and open competition that the fur companies were now to enjoy extended coincidentally to the red man. What the Indian had formerly bought from the government trading houses with beaver skins and other furs, he now had opportunity to seize on the open prairies for nothing; and, greatest boon of all, he now had an opportunity to mount himself on a swift horse or mule, the better to escape punishment, the sooner to fall upon another caravan. The government threat, "Behave, or the Great White Father will not trade with you or let traders come among you," had lost its power. Brigandage on the high plains paid better than hunting and trade, especially since progressive removal of tribes from east to west of the Mississippi had quickened competition for hunting fields. Extension of trade and freeing of the Indian to prey upon it coincided with greater need why the Indian should prey upon it.

Thomas Hart Benton organized his political machinery to meet this exigency. In 1824, the Congressional delegation from Missouri worked as one man to extract from various parts of the state petitions relative to the need of a protected route to Mexico. As letters turn up in various collections it becomes apparent that such a deluge of petitions from Missourians to their congressmen must have had intelligent prompting from a master mind, the more so because their purport is largely identical and the language unmistakably Bentonian. On April 27, 1824, Alexander McNair, governor of the state, pointed out in a letter to the federal Secretary of State the benefits of a lively trade with Mexico and listed six points that ought to be considered[2]—the very points embodied in the bill that Benton drew up nearly a year later or presented in arguments for the bill. On May 12, John Scott, representative from Missouri, brought in a resolution that the President of the United States be requested to communicate to the House any information that he might have on Mexican trade, a motion that brought McNair's letter into the open.[3] On August 19, Captain Alphonso Wetmore, in compliance, he wrote, with the wishes of Mr. Scott as expressed during his stay in Frank-

3

lin, transmitted all the information that he could procure in relation to internal trade between Missouri and Santa Fe.[4] In October, sundry inhabitants of Missouri petitioned Senator Benton upon the same subject in winged words and rhythmical phrases.[5] On January 24, 1825, Senator David Barton wrote Abiel Leonard that he had received and presented a petition from Boone County concerning where forts ought to be built along the route.[6]

And now on January 3, 1825, almost a year having gone into education of his constituency, state colleagues, and fellow congressmen, Senator Benton rose in the Senate and stated that he had received a paper which he took the liberty of presenting. It was a statement of facts in relation to the origin, present state, and future prospects of trade and intercourse between the valley of the Mississippi and the internal provinces of Mexico. The reporter of Congressional Debates missed nothing of the true spirit of the great man and caught the rhetorical phrases as they fell from his lips:

"Intending, for a year past, to bring this subject before the Senate, and to claim for it a share of the national protection, Mr. B. said that he had felt the necessity of resting his demand upon a solid foundation of facts. With this view, he had addressed himself, during the last summer to many inhabitants of Missouri, who had been personally engaged in the trade; among others, to Mr. Augustus Storrs, late of New Hampshire, a gentleman of character and intelligence, every way capable of relating things as he saw them, and incapable of relating them otherwise. This gentleman had been one of a caravan of eighty persons, one hundred and fifty-six horses; and twenty-three wagons and carriages, which had made the expedition from Missouri to Santa Fe (of New Mexico) in the months of May and June last. His account was full of interest and novelty. It sounded like romance to hear of caravans of men, horses, and wagons traversing with their merchandise the vast plain which lies between the Mississippi and the Rio del Norte. The story seemed better adapted to Asia than to North America. But, romantic as it might seem, the reality had already exceeded the visions of the wildest imagination. The journey to New Mexico, but lately deemed a chimerical project, had become an affair of ordinary occurrence. Santa Fe, but lately the

4

Ultima Thule of American enterprise, was now considered as a stage only in the progress, or, rather, a new point of departure to our invincible citizens. Instead of turning back from that point, the caravans broke up there, and the sub-divisions branched off in different directions, in search of new theatres for their enterprise. Some proceeded down the river to the Passo del Norte; some to the mines of Chihuahua and Durango, in the province of New Biscay; some to Sonora and Sinatoa [sic] on the Gulf of California; and some, seeking new lines of communication with the Pacific, had undertaken to descend the Western slopes of our continent, through the unexplored regions of the Multnomah and Buenaventura. The fruit of these enterprises for the present year amounted to $190,000 in gold and silver bullion and coin, and precious furs; a sum considerable in itself, in the commerce of an infant State, but chiefly deserving a stateman's notice as an earnest of what might be expected from a regulated and protected trade. The principal article given in exchange is that of which we have the greatest abundance, and which has the peculiar advantage of making the circuit of the Union before it departs from the territories of the republic—cotton—which grows in the South; is manufactured in the North, and exported from the West."[7]

With which all-embracing appeal Senator Benton rested his case and moved that the statement of Mr. Storrs be printed for the use of the Senate and referred to the Committee on Indian Affairs.

The bill authorizing the President to cause a road to be marked out from the frontier of Missouri to the boundary of Mexico was reported from the Committee on Indian Affairs on January 11, and came up for consideration in the Senate on January 25. Senator Benton reminded the Senate of the petitions which had already appeared before them, and reported that the people of Missouri had also asked for appointment of consuls to Santa Fe and Chihuahua. He pointed out that the land route was free from obstructions and abounding in subsistence for men and horses. He repeated the cotton argument. For senators apt to be swayed by such considerations he pointed out the missionary possibilities of the road: "The consolidation of their [the Mexican] republican institutions, the improvement of their moral and social conditions, the restoration of their lost arts, and the development of their national resources, are among the grand results which philanthropy anticipates from such a commerce." He recited a list of Indian atrocities, beginning with that at Chouteau's Island. He presented "the republics against the world" argument. And then, most interesting of all, he came to the question of precedents in governmental road-building and laid foundations for continuation of the road from the boundary to the settlements of Mexico:

"I had," he said, "always been opposed to the boundary line of 1819; and I liked it less when I found it a stumbling block in my road to Mexico, and a protecting barrier to the cruel Comanches who kill and rob our citizens. It is true, I could see no reason for not continuing the road, with the consent of the Mexican Government, through the unoccupied territory of that Power, but the novelty of the thing was appalling; and gentlemen might call for a precedent, although they should find it impossible to start an argument against it. Well, sir, I have a precedent: . . . I speak of a road from Georgia to New Orleans, in the year 1807, under the administration of President Jefferson. The first part of the road lay through the territories of the Creek Indians; the second, through the dominions of the King of Spain."

For this precedent, Benton went on to say, he was indebted to Jefferson himself. "It was on the evening of Christmas day that I called upon Mr. Jefferson. The conversation, among other things, turned upon roads. He spoke of one from Georgia to New Orleans, made during the last term of his administration."[8] And Benton held up for inspection of the Senate a map showing two hundred miles of road in blue ink through the dominions of the King of Spain.

To make a long story short, the bill authorizing a road to the Mexican boundary seemed to be undergoing a metamorphosis into one authorizing a road to be surveyed and marked to the Mexican settlements. The Mexican government should be asked to coöperate, though Benton well knew, as he told the Senate, that he expected no coöperation—the people were too ignorant. "We are not to expect anything more from them than the privilege to mark out the way."

On March 3, just before James Monroe stepped out of the White House to make way for John Quincy Adams, he affixed his signature to the bill and it became a law. It provided $10,000 for surveying and marking the road—little enough, one thinks, to make what Senator Benton called "a highway between nations"—and $20,000 for treating with the Indians for a right of way.

2 *The Commissioners*

On March 16, 1825, President Adams appointed the three Commissioners: Benjamin H. Reeves of Howard County, Missouri; Pierre Menard of Kaskaskia, Illinois, who resigned and whose place was filled by Thomas Mather, also of Kaskaskia; and George C. Sibley of Fort Osage, Missouri.

The appointment of Reeves was to be expected. After some experience as a legislator in Kentucky, he had taken a prominent part in Missouri politics from the time of his arrival in that state in 1819. In 1820 he had been a member of the first Constitutional Convention; in 1821, state auditor; in 1822-24, state senator; in 1824, an Adams elector; and in 1824 had been elected lieutenant-governor, an office he resigned to accept his appointment on the Santa Fe Road Commission. He was undoubtedly the most influential citizen of Howard County, which had become the center of the Santa Fe trade.

Sheer prominence seems likewise to have dictated the appointment of Pierre Menard. On each successive frontier his life had touched, he had been a man of affairs. At the age of twenty-three he had accompanied his employer, Colonel Francisco Vigo, to consult with George Washington for proper defense of the Indiana frontier. Two years later (1791) found him in Kaskaskia, Illinois, setting up in a small way the business that eventually gave him a wide reputation as a merchant and trader. As a partner in the St. Louis Fur Company, and later in the Missouri Fur Company, he had had his full share in tapping the rich beaver regions of the upper Missouri. By 1825 he had had nearly all the honors his state had to offer—Major of militia, Lieutenant-Colonel of militia, judge of the Court of Common Pleas, state senator, president of the senate, and lieutenant-governor of the state, the last an honor that necessitated a change in the state constitution. It is small wonder that when a new frontier in the Southwest was opening that the President, prompted by Senator Benton, should think of Pierre Menard. Whether his capital was already at work in Santa Fe trade is a question. Certain facts are apparent: Kaskaskia had had its connection with Santa Fe trade ever since the Morrison venture with Baptiste Lelande; and before very long Pierre Menard's grandson, Lucien Maxwell, would give his name to the largest land grant in New Mexico.

Pierre Menard could not serve. "Although I am," he wrote the Secretary of War, "profoundly penetrated with a sense of my incapacity, still I would hope to supply the deficiency by extraordinary zeal. But my private affairs claim my undivided attention, and forbid, unless at the risk of great sacrifice, my acceptance of the appointment. The long and still continued absence of my Partner together with my late visit to Washington has produced an accumulation of claims upon my time and attention, wholly inconsistent with the duties pertaining to the station to which the President has appointed me. I therefore beg you to consider this my resignation and be assured, that they are no ordinary obstacles, which prevent me from accepting an office so flattering."[9]

Whereupon Thomas Mather was appointed in his place. Though a younger man than Menard and of less eminence, he qualified as a representative of Mississippi trade interests through his mercantile association with James L. Lambe in Kaskaskia. He was a member of the lower house in Illinois, and had the social advantage of being a lineal descendant of Cotton Mather.

The appointment of George C. Sibley was a surprise even to him. Stationed as government factor at Fort Osage since 1808, he knew the Osage and Kansas tribes with whom the Commissioners would treat for right of way, and for four years he had seen the trade with Santa Fe stream by his door. Naturally, he wanted to have a part in that trade. A letter from Sibley to his brother-in-law, Senator Josiah S. Johnston of Louisiana, reveals his deep interest: "Having lately engaged in that Trade, & intending to embark in it pretty extensively (provided I can see a pretty clear prospect ahead) I feel considerable solicitude about it, and hope Congress may afford it Such aids as are necessary to afford Security to those who are, or who may hereafter be engaged in it."[10] He went on to recommend a consul at Santa Fe, a military post and agency between the Arkansas and the mountains, and a treaty with Mexico. He recommended Paul Baillio, his partner, for consul, and Major William Bradford for the Arkansas Agency.

Captain Alphonso Wetmore in his memorable statement and petition had emphasized the need that one of the Commissioners should be a practical man—one who had been to Santa Fe and knew the perils of the way—and that one should be a gentleman of literary attainments who would be able to describe the activities of the Commissioners and the country through which the expedition moved. He named Captain Benjamin Cooper outright as the man of practical experience who should be included, but refrained, perhaps through modesty, from naming the gentleman of literary skill. One wonders if on that significant Christmas evening when Benton and Jefferson discussed the road, whether the question of who ought to be the literary Commissioner came up for consideration, and if the aged Jefferson remembered the writing and reporting skill of the Sibleys.

In any event, inasmuch as George C. Sibley from the start took the initiative in the work of the Commission, wrote the history of the project, made the government report—in truth saw the surveying and marking through to a finish when his colleagues long since had grown tired of dust, heat, prairie flies, and buffalo meat and refused longer to bother themselves with Benton's road to Santa Fe—it would be perhaps not amiss to inquire into the history and character of the man.

His twenty years as an Indian factor had given him no special eminence. His little savings of half a lifetime, invested in Missouri land, were in desperate jeopardy. He had underwritten for the trading firm of Sibley, Baillio, and Boggs the purchase of the Indian goods at Fort Osage when government trading ceased in 1822 and, any day, judgment in the courts might sweep away everything he possessed. His lack of importance, however, combined with certain strains in his character, gave him qualifications not possessed by either of his colleagues. First of all, he had an unusual passion for government service. Something of the English Tory's devotion to public affairs, a holy zeal to immolate himself on a government altar, to do some enduring work for the common weal, some memorable work in which his name should not perish, burned in him steadily. And in all justice to him it must be said that his devotion to government service transcended devotion to the public payroll. He saw in his appointment to the Road Commission the greatest honor of his life. His hour had come for memorable service and, Heaven helping him, he would put through the survey and marking of the road to Santa Fe with all the thoroughness that Benton urged.

Persistence and endurance were his heritage. The Sibleys for nearly two hundred years had been pushing back the American frontier toward the west and south. Landing in New England in 1629, they had by successive stages reached western Massachusetts before the Revolutionary War, and in the three decades succeeding had migrated into western New York, the South Atlantic and Gulf States, the Old Northwest, and the Louisiana Purchase. Some of them were outstanding figures. Dr. John Sibley of North Carolina and Louisiana was distinguished as publisher of the *Fayetteville Gazette,* as author of early reports to Jefferson, as an Indian agent, and as a legislator. His most eminent descendant was, probably, his grandson, General Henry Hopkins Sibley of the Confederacy, inventor of the Sibley army tent. Dr. John's daughter, Ann Elizabeth, however, merits more than a passing word, for as the widow of Henry D. Gilpin of Philadelphia, she highly endowed the Historical Society of Pennsylvania, the American Philosophical Society, and the Chicago Historical Society. From Stephen, Asa, and Benjamin, brothers of Dr. John, have sprung the Sibleys of New York and Ohio, the most distinguished of whom have been Mark Hopkins Sibley of Canandaigua, and Hiram and Harper Sibley of Rochester. From Cyrus and Origen, nephews of Dr. John, who early engaged in the mercantile business on Mobile Bay, have descended the Sibleys of Alabama. From Josiah Sibley of Georgia—banker, railroad builder, and mill-owner—and from his brothers Amory and Royal, have sprung the Sibley's whose descendants claim such an unusual percentage of space in the current *Who's Who in America.* Solomon Sibley of Detroit, a cousin of Dr. John, must for brevity's sake be the last of this list, though his importance in the history of Michigan is rivaled only by that of his son, Henry Hastings Sibley, in that of Minnesota.

11

In George Champlin Sibley the energy of these men of action blended with the intellectualism of his mother's family, the Hopkins. Dr. John Sibley, when he returned to Great Barrington, Massachusetts, after two years' service in the Revolutionary forces, married Miss Elizabeth Hopkins, daughter of Dr. Samuel Hopkins—he who was known as the friend of Jonathan Edwards and Ezra Stiles, and who goes down in theological history as the father of Hopkinsianism, a belated attempt to liberalize Calvinism. In making this alliance, Dr. John Sibley bestowed on his eldest son a countenance of surprising likeness to that of Henry Hopkins, brother of Mark; some of Dr. Samuel Hopkins' persistence in following spiritual gleams; and a piety that surely Dr. John Sibley never possessed. Why Peggy Hopkins passed over the name of her father Samuel and the name of her husband John to fix upon her first-born the name of George Champlin of Newport is a baffling mystery. Surely more was involved than merely the fact that he was a first citizen of Rhode Island in shipping, finance, and patriotism. Was it George Champlin who was able to get the Hopkins family safely out of Newport when the British hovered off shore previous to stabling their horses in Dr. Samuel Hopkins' Congregational church? Or was it Champlin who rallied to the Hopkins family in some one of those dark hours after they returned to Newport to find church ruined, congregation impoverished, and support problematical? So far no record has revealed the story.

At any rate, born at Great Barrington on April 1, 1782, George Champlin Sibley came into a Massachusetts sorely unsettled, indeed so out of joint that his maternal grandfather did not get around to baptizing him for two or three years, and he had no place that he could call his home until he was six years old. Elizabeth and her two sons lived until 1786 in the home of her father; then for a time with an uncle David Hopkins in Baltimore; and then with another uncle, Stephen Sibley, in Great Barrington.[11] Finally, in 1788, Dr. John Sibley sent for his family to join him in Fayetteville, North Carolina, where he had set up the *Fayetteville Gazette* and was urging reasons for the adoption of the Federal Constitution.

Fayetteville, at the head of navigation on the Yadkin, was an outfitting post for frontiers that lay beyond. The population was predominantly Scotch-Irish, so Scotch that the burr of the Highlander, we are told, could be heard upon its streets well into the nineteenth century, and so Presbyterian that it remains a stronghold of the faith until this day. The two young Sibleys who returned to Fayetteville three years after the death of their mother in 1790—Dr. Sibley in the meantime having married Mary White Winslow—could read in the *Gazette* of parties of emigrants departing for the Cumberland Gap, and could see on the streets buckskin-clad hunters and trappers making ready for another bout with the wilderness.

As nearly as one can judge, the abiding influences upon young George came from four years in the Pittsborough Academy of Dr. William Bingham, and from two years in Fayetteville Academy under the tutelage of Dr. David Kerr. Six years under the instruction of two such famous teachers fixed upon young Sibley for life, habits of high rectitude and a lofty code of honor. To these were added an obligation to be acquainted with literature, history, and government, and the consciousness that he should be able to express himself correctly and fluently. Several years in the mercantile house of John Winslow introduced him to the world of trade and gave him ability to wrestle with the long government reports that lay ahead. If to a later day he sometimes seems over-righteous and lacking in a sense of humor, one must recall the anxieties of his pillar-to-post childhood, the death of his mother when he was eight years old, the years of separation from his father, his guardianship of the younger brother, and over all—the dour Presbyterianism of the time and place.

In 1800, when George was eighteen years old, the *Fayetteville Gazette* burned to the ground. Yearning for another frontier took possession of Dr. John Sibley and he boarded a boat for New Orleans, leaving the care of his second wife and children to young George and Samuel. Again he seems to have been a long time getting settled to receive his family. Not the least of George's responsibilities was his carefree, open-hearted, open-handed father.

In 1805, on appointment of Thomas Jefferson, George C. Sibley entered government service as assistant factor in the Indian trading post at Fort Bellefontaine, newly established eight miles from St. Louis.

Beaver skins, buffalo robes, shaved deer skins, and bear grease came over the counter to the trader; and blue beads, red calico, shoddy blankets, tomahawks, and scalping knives went over the counter to Sac, Fox, Piankishaw, Missouri, and Osage Indians. Sibley bought himself a frying pan, a kettle, and so on, resolved to save his salary and pay back the money that John Winslow had been kind enough to lend him for his transportation. He also bought a copy of Webster's *Dictionary*.

The thorn in Sibley's side in these early days at Bellefontaine was the irregular bookkeeping of the chief factor, Rudolph Tillier, who either ignorantly or innocently thought that everything he took out of the business for the use of his wife and five children ought to be entered on the credit side of the ledger. Differences on this matter came to a head on the day when Tillier fired young Sibley outright, charging him with an improper attitude toward a superior. Thereupon the young Galahad took a horse to Washington, laid the whole matter before John Mason, Superintendent of Indian Affairs, was exonerated and promoted. It was decreed that Rudolph Tillier's factory should be broken up, that part of his goods should go up the Mississippi to the new trading house to be established above the Lemoin, and part should go to the new trading establishment up the Missouri, where George C. Sibley should be chief factor. The Superintendent of Indian Affairs, having equipped Sibley with money and credit, sent him out to buy goods for the new factories.

The position of a government trader was not a pleasant one. He walked a slippery plank between necessary extension of credits to Indians for their hunts, and a respectable balance sheet at the end of the quarter. He worked in a sphere where authority was divided between the man who ran the factory and the military who guarded it, and few indeed were the posts where clashes did not occur between these two arms of government service. As a government factor, buying furs and skins for more than private traders could pay and selling goods for less, he met with little or no favor from traders in general. He was likely to sink into the savagery which he was supposed to control, and in such degeneration think he could wield a stronger influence and perhaps the more surely emerge from a trying hour with his scalp intact.

Moreover, as a public servant sworn not to engage in trade for himself, he grew restless as he saw opportunities passing him by.

Into this maze of difficulties George C. Sibley entered in the fall of 1808 when he assumed his new position at Fort Osage; and so skillfully did he walk his slippery planks that he was still in charge when government trading was abolished fourteen years later. Not one trial of the public trader did he escape. There was a clash with Capt. Eli Clemson in command of the garrison at the fort, all of it echoed in recriminations still filed away. There was continuous undercover bickering with the Chouteaus for control of the Osage trade. Yet with nice discrimination he walked the line between mercy and the balance sheet, preserving friendship with the Indians and presenting for imitation the rare spectacle of a government factory that more than paid its way.

Something from Dr. Samuel Hopkins; something from his mother Elizabeth; something from his second mother, Mary Winslow, whom he loved; something perhaps from his shrewd old father, or from the teachings of Dr. Bingham or Dr. Kerr—who can tell—enabled George Sibley for twenty years to live on the Indian frontier without descending to the savagery around him. He pondered over Montesquieu's *Spirit of Laws;* he chortled over the cleverness of the *Salamagundi Papers;* he kept up his subscription to the *National Intelligencer;* he began his perfect file of Niles' *National Register;* and in season and out wrote letters and essays for whoever would publish. Insatiable desire for self-expression made him a voluminous correspondent of the Indian offices both in St. Louis and Washington, filled columns in local and national newspapers, and sometimes gave him the rare pleasure of seeing his name over a magazine article. He was the perfect son of Dr. John Sibley in making every occasion yield its quota of newsprint.

In 1815 he married Mary Smith Easton, fifteen-year-old daughter of Rufus Easton, first postmaster of St. Louis, and thenceforward had the advantage of her educational gleanings from Lexington, Kentucky, the "Athens of the West," and the tinklings of her piano with its drum and fife attachment to beguile his leisure hours.

Such was the least important of the Commissioners with his great opportunity upon him.

INTRODUCTION 3

The Surveyor and Secretary

JOSEPH C. BROWN, SURVEYOR

The Commissioners made no mistake in selection of their surveyor. Joseph Cromwell Brown loomed head and shoulders above all others of his profession in Missouri and, when selected for survey of the road to Santa Fe, had a notable list of surveys behind him.

He was born of Scotch-Irish stock, "before morning light," the family Bible says, on January 29, 1784, in Prince Edward County, Virginia.[12] He accordingly grew up in the Presbyterian heritage of the Reverends John Caldwell, Samuel S. Smith, John Blair Smith, Drury Lacy, Archibald Alexander, and Moses Hoge. Scant wonder is it therefore that in his maturity he was described as "a man of genuine piety." His granddaughter, Miss Laura Brown of the School of the Ozarks at Hollister, Missouri, was sure that he was reared and educated near Charlotte Courthouse.

He came to Missouri at the end of the War of 1812, riding thither on horseback, so descendants say, in the company of Nathaniel Beverley Tucker. And if Tucker's book, *George Balcombe* is as autobiographical as some aver, they were "bravely caparisoned as became Virginia gentlemen with new saddles, capacious saddlebags, and horses that showed good breeding." The cross-country trip seems to have been accomplished in the summer of 1815, for by October 27 of that year, Brown had entered as deputy surveyor upon the first of his notable surveys—determination of the base line of the Fifth Principal Meridian, which with survey of the twenty-ninth township engaged him until the fifth of December.[13]

In 1816, from August 15 to October 16, he surveyed the Osage Indian line from Fort Osage to the Arkansas River, Archibald Gamble assisting.[14] It was, the Commissioners reported, a task not devoid of danger, for the Osages at last realized that they had sold the bones of their fathers and the heritage of their children for less than nothing. They were in an ugly mood.[15] On March 24, 1820, Archibald Gamble filed Brown's Survey of the Incorporated Limits of St. Louis, the first ever made.[16] In 1823, Brown made two other important surveys—determination of the western boundary of Missouri south of the Kansas River, and determination of the Missouri-Arkansas line.[17]

He had, moreover, held various public offices in St. Louis county and city—deputy sheriff, sheriff, collector of revenue,—and at the time he was appointed by the Commissioners to survey the road to Santa Fe, he had been elected a member of the upper house in Missouri. Out of about two hundred applications for the positions of surveyor and clerk, "Mr. Brown was," recorded Sibley, "preferred to all his competitors without a moment's hesitation, as being in the opinion of the Comm[issione]rs best qualified in all respects. Mr. Gamble's pretensions for Sec[retar]y were thought at least equal to those of any other applicant; and he was preferred because he was accustomed to the business of surveying with Mr. Brown."[18]

Joseph C. Brown's determination of the north line of Missouri in 1837 became the basis for an interstate controversy that was ended only by decree of the Supreme Court of the United States on February 13, 1849. And though Brown's line was the one for which Missouri contended through twelve years, and though the Supreme Court in working out a compromise between the claims of the two states rejected his line, the court appointed him one of the two surveyors to run and mark the new line.[19] This was the last great survey on which he ever engaged, for death claimed him before it was finished.

His life is significant in another respect. A talent for responsibility, heightened by a superior education, made him the leader and center of the Brown family migration from Virginia to Missouri.[20] Trained judgment and wide travel as a surveyor enabled him to hit upon desirable lands. New Madrid certificates, relinquished pre-emptions, forced sales at courthouse doors, and immediate access to land transactions as surveyor, sheriff, or deputy sheriff, enabled him to acquire them. Thus he settled Russell Brown, Clement J. Brown, and Burril B. Adams on the Missouri bottom at Point Labbadie; David Adams and Edmund

F. Brown on the Merimac; and Henry Brown on the Bayou in Franklin County.

Captain James Brown, his uncle; John Kelso Walker, who married his niece Lavinia Russell; and James B. Walker, who had married Lavinia Brown, were all close neighbors of Joseph C. Brown and Nathaniel Beverley Tucker on the Halls Ferry Road in St. Louis County. And there with the Bissells and Gibsons for neighbors they built up a little Virginia very like the one that developed on Dardenne Prairie in St. Charles County. Investigation of relations of some of these drives one into Damon-Pythias Jonathan-David figures of speech. In the intimate affairs of life—weddings, funerals, and the administrations of estates, securities and bonds—they stood by each other like brothers. What Tucker thought of Brown he is said to have written into Sheriff Green in *George Balcombe*: ". . . a tall, strong, middle-aged man, of a serious but benevolent and intelligent countenance," of "manly frankness," and, that irradicable mark of a gentleman, "the tones, the modulations, and inflections of the voice."

The warmest friendship of his life, however, he gave to John Kelso Walker. Their mutual Virginian background, their closeness as neighbors and kinsmen on adjoining farms in the Maline Creek settlement, and their years of courthouse association in almost continuous office-holding, were fused by an inner unity of the spirit rarely found in two men each so capable and so independent. Perhaps the key of their oneness politically, financially, and sympathetically is to be found in the Scotch-Irish Presbyterianism of which both were props and pillars. Each of them, often in the same session, served as elders to both the First Presbyterian church of St. Louis and to the Maline Creek church on the Halls Ferry Road.

On April 26, 1827, Joseph C. Brown married Miss Martha Nash Stephenson, descendant of that Colonel John Nash who wrote himself deeply into the annals of Prince Edward County.[21] She was born on September 30, 1802; was educated near Charlotte Courthouse; and after the wedding ceremony came to Missouri by horse and buggy, a trip that took six weeks. Of their children, Ellen, born on August 30, 1828, died in infancy; James Henry, born on August 14, 1829, died on

September 14, 1854, at the age of twenty-five. Joseph Thomas Brown, born on January 14, 1832, lived to maturity, attended Westminster College at Fulton, Missouri, afterward studied medicine and became a practising physician. On March 22, 1860, he married Miss Virginia Conway, daughter of Joseph Conway of the Conway Road in St. Louis County, and from this marriage were born the sole descendants of Joseph C. Brown.[22]

When Joseph C. Brown died of pneumonia on February 21, 1849, the *St. Louis Republican* summed up his life as follows: "As an honest man and competent surveyor, he had no superior if an equal. His superior capacity caused nearly all important and complicated Government surveys to be confided to him."[23] He was buried in the Maline Creek Church cemetery, now this long time since converted into a cabbage patch. The Maline Creek Church, its cemetery, and his dwelling called "Glen Allan" are now gone. His best and most enduring monument is in the Missouri lines he established and in the survey of the road to Santa Fe.

The Field Notes of his survey of the western boundary of Missouri south of the mouth of the Kanzas river, and part of his Field Notes of a survey made in Illinois and Missouri in 1833 are in the Missouri Historical Society in St. Louis. The Field Notes of his survey of the road to Santa Fe are in the Topographical Division of the War Department in Washington. They were published in 1911-12 by the Kansas State Historical Society as a part of the Eighteenth Biennial Report.

ARCHIBALD GAMBLE, SECRETARY

Archibald Gamble, secretary of the Commissioners, was of English-Scotch-Irish stock from Virginia. He was born in Winchester, Virginia, on January 14, 1794, the son of Joseph Jr. and Anne Hamilton, his wife. He left the parental roof when he was twenty-one and must have headed west soon thereafter, for he was assistant surveyor to Joseph C. Brown in 1816, when he established the Osage boundary line. Their Virgina background, their Presbyterian religion, their association on surveys and in office-holding became the basis for a deep friendship between Gamble and Brown. In 1822, for instance, Archibald Gamble appeared with Nathaniel Beverley Tucker as bondsman for Joseph C. Brown; and in 1836 as one of the executors of his will.

After clerking for a year in the St. Louis Bank, Gamble became a member of the Virginia contingent of city and county office-holders by becoming a deputy clerk of the Circuit Court. A year later he became clerk of the Court, an office he held for eighteen years. Then ensued years as judge and presiding judge of the County Court. On July 3, 1821, he married Miss Louisa Easton, third daughter of Rufus Easton, who had been the first postmaster of St. Louis, territorial delegate in Congress, and attorney-general of Missouri. The marriage made him a brother-in-law of George C. Sibley and gave rise to the accusation that relationship with Sibley had been one of the reasons for his appointment as secretary of the Commission.

Family relationship and the Presbyterian religion became the basis for close friendship between Archibald Gamble and George C. Sibley. When the latter's farms were knocked down to highest bidders, Gamble bid in "the beautiful scite of Fort Osage," and on it laid out a town which he called Sibley in honor of the man who had spent so many years there. On January 1, 1838, Archibald Gamble came to St. Charles to enter his two daughters in Mrs. Sibley's Lindenwood School for Young Ladies, and gave further proof of his interest in the project by appearing at the examinations in the following March. When the Lindenwood School for Young Ladies was incorporated as Lindenwood College in 1853, the name of Archibald Gamble headed the list of trustees.

This was not his only educational interest, for he served for many years as lawyer for the St. Louis school system. He died in September, 1866, having outlived Brown by seventeen years and Sibley by three. Many children and grandchildren survived him.

His autobiographical sketch, written in 1858 and supplemented in 1863 and in 1864, is the basis for most of the above account. I have my copy of it from Miss Jennie Ruth Gamble of Dahlgren, Illinois, a granddaughter of Archibald Gamble's eldest son, Joshua Barton Gamble.

4

The Rank and File

Another interesting phase of this survey of a road to Santa Fe lies in the personalities of the men selected by the Commissioners to accompany them. Those chosen were the pick of the frontier in hardihood, character, daring, and experience. To recite their names is to suggest the history of the western movement from the Missouri border to the Pacific.

Stephen Cooper, pilot of the expedition, had fought in the War of 1812 in Missouri, been several times to Santa Fe, and before two decades should pass, would join the emigration to the West and, with George Yount, give the first Fourth of July dinner in California in 1846.

William Sherley Williams, more familiarly known as "Old Bill," was the interpreter for the Commissioners. Santa Fe was for him the jumping-off place into the remoter West where place names are his best memorial—Williams Peak, Williams Fork, Williams River, and Williams, Arizona.

Joseph Reddeford Walker, who was hunter and chainman on the expedition, is the Capt. Walker of Irving's *Adventures of Captain Bonneville,* the man who made the famous trip through the Sierras in 1833, traversed the wonders of the Yosemite, and gave name to Walker's Lake, Walker's Pass, and Walker's River. Guide of fur trappers, traders, and emigrants, pathfinder like Bill Williams for Benton's son-in-law on his way to California—surely no greater figure emerges from the hundreds of mountain men than Joseph R. Walker.

Joel P. Walker, Joseph's brother, who according to Bancroft, brought the first Anglo-Saxon family to California in 1840, was also one of the men on the survey. Andrew Broadus, hunter and guard, became in the very next year, 1826, subject of that harrowing prairie amputation described in Kit Carson's *Autobiography.* Dudley Dedmon and Daniel East disappeared into the West with Nathaniel M. Pryor but they did not emerge with him in California. George West, interpreter and wagoner, went toward Chihuahua with Mr. Douglas. Benjamin Majors is the father of Alexander Majors of the Overland Express; and Andrew Carson is an older half-brother of Kit, whom the expedition returning in 1826 might have passed on his first trip west.

Through old Ben Jones who had gone with the Astorians in 1811, the survey is linked with the past; and through such figures as are mentioned above it is tied with the future in westward expansion. And through the pages of the diaries flit the names of Ewing Young, Antoine Robidoux, Samuel Chambers, James Baird, and many another whose name is history.

5

The Survey

Out of the many letters, the several diaries, the journal, the Report of the Commissioners, and Brown's Notes, now for the first time brought together, appears a more dramatic story than has hitherto been known concerning the survey of the road to Santa Fe. The general outline of the work has long been familiar to readers of Chittenden, Inman, and Duffus. That the Commissioners, having appointed Joseph C. Brown surveyor and Archibald Gamble secretary, moved with their assembled outfit from Fort Osage on July 17, 1825; that they surveyed and marked as they proceeded, made treaties with the Osage nation on August 10, and with the Kansas on August 16, arrived at the Mexican boundary on September 11 and there waited until the twentieth for permission of the Mexican government to move across the line and continue the survey; that then the expedition divided, one part under Reeves and Mather returning to Missouri, and the other under Sibley continuing to Taos and Santa Fe to await word from Mexico; that the permission at last arrived in the summer of 1826, and Sibley and Brown finished the survey under the restrictions set by the Mexican government; and that at the finish of their labors they filed maps, journal, and field notes with the United States government—these facts have been known for years.

But the human drama involved—the connection of personality and national tendency—the struggle of the human will to achieve an end—becomes apparent only when the documents are assembled. It emerges from detail which is the essence of life and history and tells its own story, a complicated one and not the same for all who read. In some lights it looks like a drama modeled on the pattern of Job, featuring a zealous, patriotic soul beset by negative colleagues and sickening delay, and thwarted finally in its high purpose only by the lightning bolts of

Heaven. In some aspects the smitings of circumstance appear to be deserved afflictions for one of God's fools. To some the story will be one of national aggression in which the Job-like protagonist looks more like the pliant tool of Machiavelli Benton intent on despoiling a weaker republic.

On one conclusion, however, all will agree. George C. Sibley, whether interpreted as hero, fool, or villain, emerges as chief of the Commissioners. The story of the survey is his, not only because he wrote it, but also because his was the will that carried it through. Whether it stopped short of its perfect goal because of human frailty, outward circumstance, or a fateful mingling of both, each will have to judge for himself. The diaries, journal, and letters reveal a complicated interplay of the inner and the outer—a complexity heightened by individual and political differences and given a certain largeness by its relation to national tendency.

On the afternoon of an April day in 1825—the twelfth, to be exact—the slight figure of George C. Sibley jogged along on horseback across the prairie that stretched west of Arrow Rock. He lifted his eyes but seldom to the beauties of the grove-dotted plain. He had too much to ponder over. How to meet interest payments on $9,000 due the United States Government and whittle down the mounting principal—an obligation he had assumed in underwriting his partners for purchase of the trade goods at Fort Osage in 1822—nagged at him consciously by day and subconsciously by night. It looked as if his venture in Indian trade with Paul Baillio and Lilburn W. Boggs would wrest from him every acre he had accumulated in his twenty years of government service, and he would in his forty-third year have to start again from scratch. He would talk with Richard Graham in St. Louis—maybe he could put off the collection of the judgment. He would write another letter to his brother-in-law, Senator Josiah S. Johnston of Louisiana—treasury officials had to listen to senators. Maybe Thomas L. McKenney of the Indian department could do something to avert the destruction hovering. Perhaps spring returns from Baillio in Taos would bring a temporary relief.

Perhaps—perhaps—! It was all a sickening anxiety. What of the

24

rumors that had within the past few days come to him? Could it be true that the President had appointed him one of the Commission to survey and mark the road to Santa Fe? Could financial ruin and a great honor walk side by side? He would find out in St. Louis.

So engrossed was he in despair and hope that he failed to notice a horseman approaching until he was almost upon him. The recognition was simultaneous. Thomas J. Boggs, where was he going?[24] And, "By Jove, it's Sibley!"

Boggs had reason to be glad. Meeting Sibley on the prairie saved him the rest of his journey to Fort Osage. Having heard in Franklin that Benjamin H. Reeves of Fayette, Pierre Menard of Kaskaskia, and George C. Sibley had been appointed Commissioners for the survey of the road to Santa Fe, he had set out that morning to urge his election as secretary to the Commission. After visiting Reeves, he wanted to know now whether Sibley also would favor his application.

Sibley, confused by the implications, fumbled for an answer. If he had been appointed—and he had no official reason to think that he was—he didn't know yet whether he could accept. But if he had been, Mr. Boggs could rest assured that he would have no objection to considering him for secretary. He was surely well qualified, etc. But of course before making any definite answer he would have to know the truth about the appointment. With that, Thomas Boggs turned around, and the two traveled along to Franklin together.

A slight uneasiness seems to have crept into Sibley's mind while he slumbered. The next morning he wrote a brief note to Benjamin Reeves, "in haste from the tavern with a most intolerable pen."

> I am now on my way to St. Louis for my family, & have concluded not to listen to any application 'till I decide whether I am actually appd. & whether I shall accept, & not then, 'till I confer with you & Col: Menard.
>
> I shall be glad to hear from you at St. Louis, if you should receive any official communication from Washington. I beg leave to suggest to you not to give any positive encouragement to any applicant 'till we all confer together on the Subject: Altho' I am not yet decided to accept this Service (if offered) I am rather of

the opinion I shall do so. I shall soon decide when I reach St. Louis.[25]

With this note to Reeves begins the initiative of Sibley on the Commission. With the application of Thomas J. Boggs begins the counterplot of "Mr. Santa Fe."

By April 25, Sibley had in his hand the official appointment made in Washington on March 16. Whatever hesitation he had ever felt over accepting the honor—and in all justice, there may have been some rising out of the matter of suitable emolument and the more pressing question of whether collection of the judgment could be postponed—that hesitation had given place to feelings of responsibility. He had also in hand the instructions of Thomas Hart Benton,[26] penned on the very day Sibley had met Mr. Boggs on the prairie. The master mind observed that in making the road, Sibley would have an opportunity to become intimately acquainted with the intervening country and suggested the propriety of his keeping a journal for noting geographical details and hinted that it might be published among the government documents and be a lasting monument. Sibley wrote from St. Louis to Benjamin Reeves:

> It is very desirable that the Commissioners on the Road to N. Mexico, should have a meeting here as Soon as practicable. Col: Menard is to be here in course of the day, as I am informed, and I hear that you may be expected soon. We ought to meet for business early in May; say by the 3d. As the principal outfits must necessarily be made at this place, our meeting should of course be here. Much preparation is requisite for our trip which ought to be made without delay, if we commence our duties this Summer, which I see no Reason to prevent. I am much importuned by applicants for appts. under the Commission, & being alone here, feel very desirous to see and consult with you & Col: Menard.[27]

The delays that characterized the work of the Commission began at the outset. Reeves did not leave Franklin until May fifth. The two Commissioners met in St. Louis on May 10, one week later than Sibley had suggested, and on the next day wrote the Secretary of War that they had appointed Joseph C. Brown surveyor and Archibald Gamble secretary and expected to leave the frontier by the middle of June. "We hope no delay will be necessary at the boundary line of the United States."[28]

No sooner had the two principal appointments been made than criticism began—a gale of contrariness which during the life of the Commission was never dead and which, one must believe, had its part in shelving the report and maps of the Commission at last in an oblivion of a hundred years. To modern minds, used to government spending in millions and billions, the importance of this $30,000 to be expended on the Missouri frontier in 1825 is well nigh beyond comprehension. "I do not suppose," wrote Sibley, "that if the Comm[issione]rs had half a million at their disposal, they would be able to satisfy all the good men (to say nothing of others) who would apply for service."[29] There were two hundred applications for the positions of surveyor and of secretary. Wilson Price Hunt recommended René Paul for the surveyorship; Silas Bent Jr. and William Clarkson Jr. also applied. James Logan, who had fought with General Anthony Wayne, would have been glad to go in any capacity. His letter of application is worth quoting:[30]

> Jackson 25th May 1825
>
> Dear Col
>
> After my Particular Respects to you and a Desire for the wellfare of your family me and mine is well I would be verry glad to see you and of all things to accompany you on your route to St afee if there is time and your Company not made up write to me Stateing In what way I shall go and with what Equipage and I will Come on with out fail if nothing occurs more than I know of the woods is my Home and the forest my own.
>
> Give my Respects to my friend Collo. Burkhartt and Receive them your Self
>
> James Logan

Thwarted ambition expressed itself in newspaper scurrility. "Santa Fe" in the *Advocate* accused the Commission of having made the two principal appointments on the basis of friendship and relationship. Archibald Gamble and Sibley had married sisters. Brown and Gamble were members of the same church and had been associated on previous surveys. "Texas," who probably was Dr. Robert Simpson, replied in the *Missouri Republican:* "I think better apptmts. could not have been made, if we regard the qualifications of those gentlemen."[31] The same writer a week later in the *Republican* begged the pardon of those gentlemen whose names had been dragged before the public by "Santa Fe." "Worth and integrity so signal as to attract notice and procure emolument are with him unpardonable sins, utter disqualifications for future office."[32] Sibley wrote a long letter to Reeves in which he regretted very much to find Mr. T. Boggs had so forgotten what he owed to his standing as to indulge in some very unnecessary & exceptionable remarks in his Letter to the Editor of the *Advocate*.

> In that letter Mr. B. permits himself to assert in the most unqualified manner, that I gave him my promise to support him for the appt. of Secy. &c.—which assertion I aver most peremptorily is not true; & I am sure that Mr. B. has greatly missed the mark, when he suffered his angry feelings to get the better of his reason so far as to charge me publicly with violating a promise to him—when a moment's reflection must have convinced him that he *may* have been mistaken . . . it is certain that I had not the most distant intention of pledging myself, nor can I for one moment believe that I gave the slightest reasons to M: B. to think so.[33]

The resignation of Pierre Menard and necessary delay in appointment of his successor threw the burden of all preparation for the survey upon Reeves and Sibley. They early decided on their division of labor. Sibley was to assemble what necessarily had to be procured in St. Louis— wagons, supplies, horses to pull the wagons, and wagoners to drive them; while Reeves was to purchase horses and mules in the upper country, assemble a party of chainmen, hunters, and guards, and select someone to captain the men and act as pilot. He seems to have returned to Howard County almost immediately, for Sibley five days after the meeting on May 10th wrote him that he had made arrangements for the construction of the six wagons.[34] They were to be ready by June 12th under a penalty of $500, by which time Sibley was sure he would have everything ready to load and start without a moment's delay.

As to whether the Commission could in some cases pay more than $20 a month for hunters, guards, etc., Sibley was of the opinion that hundreds of the most suitable were available at that price. Several young men of the first respectability had applied, and he had no doubt that he should offend many by refusing them. "We do not want a party of

Gentlemen Coffee Drinkers, who cannot even cook their own Victuals or Saddle their own Horses." He deemed it highly important that every man should be a rifleman and hunter, but at the same time be qualified to serve as chain bearer, axeman, etc., and above all, be able to submit cheerfully to all the necessary privations of the trip. Every man ought to understand that from the moment of entrance into his duties, he was to be subject to such regulations as the Commissioners might deem necessary. He must understand that the thirty hands were to form their own messes distinct and separate from that of the Commissioners, were not to be supplied with groceries unless in cases of sickness, and especially were not to look for a constant and regular supply of bread. If it were made perfectly plain to the men from the start that they were not to have access to the stores and tents of the Commissioners, those in charge of the expedition might be saved from many unpleasant difficulties.

Although the appointment of captain and pilot was wholly in the hands of Reeves, Sibley hoped that Ira Emmons of Franklin would be considered, for he had been twice to Santa Fe, once in command of a party, and had given general satisfaction. This, however, was only a suggestion, "for I leave the selection of this officer entirely to yourself; and am persuaded that I shall concur with you whether you appoint Mr. Bynum or Mr. Emmons."

By June 9, it was apparent that neither of these was available. Gray Bynum could not go; Ira Emmons had already left for Santa Fe; and Reeves had engaged Stephen Cooper as chief of the working party, "whose knowledge of the country," he wrote, "will make him highly useful as pilot."[35] In answer to Sibley's letter of May 15th, Reeves wrote that as soon as he could see the men he had engaged he would have them subscribe to an article for the faithful performance of their duties. He believed that his colleague would be pleased with his selection. "They are men who have not participated largely in the dainties & Luxuries of life—has lived and led a life of enterprise & Industry, and in my opinion of a noble dareing."

Six men had been selected by Sibley: Benjamin Jones,[36] experienced traveler and hunter; Benjamin Robinson,[37] Mr. Jones' stepson, a good rifleman, waggoner, etc.; James Wells, son of a respectable farmer near

St. Louis; Daniel Murphy,[38] who had been a surveyor; and Harvey Clark, a good rifleman and hunter, son of another respectable farmer. "All young men," wrote Sibley, "except Mr. Jones, all good Riflemen & of good families. Mr. Jones is a great acquisition; he is the man who piloted W. P. Hunt & party from the heads of the Yellowstone to Ft. Osage, & was formerly the compeer & favorite of the celebrated trader and Indian fighter, Robt. McClellan. I have selected the six men just named after very strict inquiry, from a list of more than a hundred applicants; and have given offence to many good but silly men; who *conceived themselves* best qualified, and best entitled to the preference."[39]

There was a hitch in getting away from St. Louis. On June 5th Sibley wrote Reeves that the wagons would be ready on June 12th as promised; he had his horses and harness all ready; shoeing of the horses would be completed within the next two days, and he hoped to have his party in St. Charles by the fifteenth.[40] Inasmuch as L. H. D. Chauvin ferried seven wagons for him at St. Charles, it looks as if he had more goods than his new wagons could hold and had been compelled to add a second-hand one—the kind he had said in the beginning he could not trust for the long journey—and to find another team of horses and George West to drive them. The wages of Ben Jones and other wagoners began on June 20. It took two days to load and they were off on Wednesday, June 22—"seven strong light wagons (painted light blue)—2 of them drawn by 4 horses each and 5 by 2 horses."

The *Missouri Republican* observed: "The hot weather, the number of flies and the difficulty of getting their wagons through a tractless [sic] country will oblige them to travel slow, and it will be sometime before they complete the work. The Commissioners say twelve or thirteen months."[41] The *Republican* was right. Heavy rains, break-down of one of the wagons (perhaps the second-hand one), repairing, and waiting their turn at the ferry made progress of the wagons slow. They were barely out of St. Charles when Sibley arrived there on Saturday. It had taken the wagons three days to go twenty miles.

Joseph C. Brown paid ten dollars for Dr. John H. Robinson's map of Mexico, bought five dollars worth of material for maps and notes, and with Archibald Gamble joined Sibley at St. Charles on Sunday.

"Everything," wrote Sibley to his friend Owen Simpson, "combined to render my departure from St. Charles by far the most painful and distressing of the kind that I ever endured."[42] Suffering from a bilious fever, he hoped like Dr. Josiah Gregg that an extended tour of the prairies would improve his health. Saying farewell to wife and friends was a melancholy duty, for he was pretty well convinced that he might never return from the hazardous expedition.

Sibley, Brown, and Gamble left St. Charles on Monday and that night lodged at Mrs. Bailey's near the site of the old Pond Fort, twenty miles toward the west. In spite of the heat of the season and pestering flies that prevented their traveling by day across Loutre and Grand Prairies, the wagons reached Franklin, 165 miles from St. Louis, on July 2, and there were held up for two days by repairs, alterations, and celebration of National Independence. "A Committee of Arrangements waited on me," recorded Sibley, "& requested that Mr. Brown, Mr. Gamble, & myself would join the citizens of Franklin at a Public Dinner in honour of the day, which polite invitation we were bound to accept."[43] For as Nathaniel Patten observed in his *Intelligencer,* "Our citizens are beginning to derive some advantage from the operations of the Mexican Road Commissioners. Their guard of riflemen have been taken from among us. This is an employment not only congenial with the tastes of our young men, but sufficiently lucrative to enable each of the persons engaged in this service to pay for a tract of land on their return."[44]

National tendency—the spirit of westward expansion—found utterance in the toasts of the day. The vice-president of the occasion toasted "The two Westward Expeditions; one up the Missouri, the other across towards New Mexico: May success and our country's aggrandizement be the result of each." Benjamin H. Reeves, who had joined the expedition at Franklin, drank to "Our Country—It advances to its brilliant destinies under the auspicious reign of Liberty and Law." Sibley honored Howard County: "A few years since I saw it a trackless wilderness; now it is the *left arm* of the State." And Captain Archibald Gamble offered a toast to "Daniel Boone, the pioneer of the west: his descendants may yet see the Seat of Empire in the recent trackless desert."[45]

Reeves and Sibley found time somewhere in the festive day to write the Secretary of War of their progress—they expected to reach the Mexican boundary early in September, where they hoped they would not be detained for want of authority to proceed through New Mexico.[46]

The high light of the journey between Franklin and Fort Osage was the violent storm that descended on the party in the midst of the crossing of the Missouri at Arrow Rock. Most of the horsemen, and the Commissioners, but only two of the wagons had reached the west bank when the wind became so violent that William Becknell could no longer run his ferry. Those on the west bank found cover at Reece's, but where the rest of the party found protection the record does not say. The next morning, however, the rest of the wagons crossed safely and Sibley could then write, "and now our whole party is assembled ready to move on to the work assigned us.[47] The men who had joined in Howard County were: Hendley Cooper, Richard Brannin,[48] Edward Davis,[49] Joe Davis,[50] James Davis,[51] G. Patrick,[52] Bradford Barbee,[53] Joe Reynolds,[54] Bird Pyles,[55] S. Smith, Reuben Cornelius,[56] Levi Cornelius,[57] Neriah Todd,[58] Samuel Givens,[59] William Givens, Thomas Adams,[60] Singleton Vaughn,[61] Daniel East, Dudley Dedmon, and Andrew Broadus.[62]

By Tuesday, July 12, the whole party had reached Fort Osage. Thomas Mather and Benjamin Reeves had arrived at Fort Osage on the evening of July 11, and were now enjoying some of the hospitality that made Sibley's "Fountain Cottage" memorable on the frontier. The men, encamped in a grove at the edge of Fire Prairie, were engaged repairing wagons and shoeing the horses which had been purchased in Jackson County. Five more men here joined the party—Joseph Reddeford Walker,[63] John Walker,[64] John S. Davis,[65] Andrew Long, and Daniel Bohon. The expedition now, including a negro servant of Sibley and one of Thomas Mather, numbered forty persons. There were fifty-seven horses and mules, seven baggage wagons, a good supply of provisions, tools, and ammunition. All were in good spirits and ready for a service that Sibley was persuaded was "fraught with difficulties, privations, and hazards innumerable."[66]

On Sunday, July 17, the expedition began the survey from its camp near Fort Osage, the surveyor having been instructed to note all the courses very exactly and to measure as he proceeded. "The main idea," wrote Benton to Sibley, "is thoroughness for it is not a County or State road which they have to mark out but a highway between Nations."[67]

Sibley, having private business to attend to—probably details of his farm work and his voluminous correspondence—planned to overtake the working party later. "The weather," he wrote, "is very warm, & the flies still very troublesome." On July 25, he wrote to Senators Benton, Barton, and Josiah S. Johnston, and to John Scott, representative from Missouri, stating his opinion of the inadequacy of the sum appropriated to complete the road, and recommending an additional appropriation of $12,000.[68] On July 27, Colonel Marmaduke and James Moore arrived straight from Santa Fe with an account of how their caravan had been robbed of 120 horses and mules by a party of Osages near the mouth of the Little Arkansas, and otherwise badly treated. They had met the surveying party seventy miles west of Fort Osage, going on pretty well considering that they had had to do a great part of their travel at night on account of the prairie flies.[69]

Sibley and his servant Abram started in the late afternoon of July 29, accompanied by John S. Davis, and lodged that night eighteen miles from Fort Osage where Joel P. Walker and John Young were erecting houses. On the morning of August 3, Sibley and his companions came up with the road party before they were out of their beds. They were encamped on Elk Creek (now 142 Mile Creek), a branch of the Marais des Cygnes. They had been there for two days, allowing their jaded horses to rest and waiting the return of Archibald Gamble who had gone to invite the Osages to counsel with the Commissioners at some convenient point on the road farther west.

Two days later, having arrived on the main branch of the Neosho where there was excellent pasturage and a beautiful grove of fine timber, they settled down to await the arrival of the Osages. "As we propose to meet the Osage Chiefs in council here, to negotiate a Treaty with them for the Road &c. I suggested," wrote Sibley, "the propriety of naming the place 'Council Grove' which was agreed to, & directed Capt. Cooper to select a suitable tree, & to record this name in strong and durable characters—which was done."[70]

On the evening of August 8, Archibald Gamble arrived with fifty of the principal chiefs and warriors of the Great and Little Osages and with them William S. Williams (Old Bill) as Interpreter. At the council on the ninth, the Commissioners explained that they proposed to give $800 for the privilege of marking the road through the land of the Osages and for the free use of it forever. At the final council on the tenth the treaty was signed; the Indians were given $300 worth of goods in hand and an order on A. P. Chouteau, a trader in their village, for $500 more to be taken out in ammunition, knives, etc. Sibley wrote letters to his wife and friends, enclosed them in a packet and gave them into the keeping of Belle Oiseau, who promised to deliver them to Lilburn W. Boggs, Sibley's partner, in the trading house on the Marais Des Cygnes.

The Osages in departing expressed their entire satisfaction with the visit, "all except a few inferior individuals," wrote Sibley, "who had their chiefs to blame for an unequal distribution of the presents." The Indians might very well be satisfied, thought Sibley, for their right was at best a doubtful one if the treaty lately signed by them in St. Louis were ratified and confirmed by Congress.

Bill Williams, whom the Commissioners hired to accompany them throughout their journey as interpreter, runner, hunter, etc., set out immediately to invite the chiefs and warriors of the Kansas tribe to a council at some convenient place east of the Arkansas. On the evening of August 14 he returned with two of the Kansas tribe and word that fifty more of the principal warriors would overtake them the next day. On the Sora Contsa two days later the Commissioners and the Kansas chiefs and warriors signed a treaty very like the one made with the Osages. The Indians received $300 worth of goods in hand and an order for goods to the value of $500 on Curtis and Eley, who had a trading house at the mouth of the Kansas.

The next event of importance was arrival on the Arkansas at the point where, cut by the 100th degree of West Longitude, it became the Mexican boundary line. There, grass and fuel being plentiful, the party settled down on September 11 to await permission from Washington to continue the road through Mexican territory. Some contrariety having sprung up among the Commissioners as to the proper course to pursue, they met at Sibley's suggestion on the fourteenth, Colonel Reeves presiding, and decided first not to continue the survey until they had received further instructions.

"Upon this point," wrote Sibley, "I differed in opinion with Cols. Reeves & Mather. I thought we might safely proceed with the survey without any violations of our instructions, or of Mexican sovereignty; tho' I did not believe we could properly go on to *Mark* the Road without further orders from our Government." He thought they should remain where they were, recruiting the horses and laying in a supply of dried beef, until at least the first of October, when if no further instructions arrived, twenty men and four wagons should go on to Santa Fe, surveying, measuring, and examining as heretofore, and there spend the winter.

The Commissioners compromised on how long they should wait for further instructions. Mather and Sibley being of the opinion that October 1 would be a proper dead-line and Reeves being convinced that delay beyond September 15 would be hazardous, the three agreed to wait until September 20th. Sibley, however still opposed to returning until the survey was complete, gave notice that at the next meeting of the Commissioners on September 17, he would propose another plan: that the Commissioners, having sent back to Missouri part of the wagons and men, should proceed to Santa Fe with the rest of the expedition and there await instructions. Under this plan no surveying was to be done until authorized.

At the meeting on September 17, Sibley moved that they wait where they were until the twenty-sixth, and then proceed as outlined at the previous meeting. "This proposition was accompanied with some very minute estimates and calculations that I had prepared with great care, and upon good data; all going to shew that the fund already at our disposal would be sufficient to meet all the expenses, and to complete the work about two months sooner than if we return home again from this place." At request of Colonel Mather the question was divided. Fixing the date for departure was postponed until the twentieth, and the second part of the plan was voted down. Sibley requested that his reasons for the plan proposed be entered in the journal.

On the twentieth, the Commissioners were of the same opinion as to a date for their departure. Sibley and Mather held out for October 1, but Reeves was convinced that they had already waited long enough, if not too long. Desirous that all three should agree upon some plan, Sibley then proposed that *one* of the Commissioners with surveyor, interpreter, nine men, and two wagons should go on to Santa Fe. The upshot of the discussion was appointment of Sibley as the one to go. "It was then decided that Cols. Reeves & Mather are to join me at Santa Fee, as early as they can next summer (if the whole road is to be completed) that I am to wait for them 'till the 1st of July and then if I hear nothing from them or the Government to justify longer delay I am to return to Missouri as soon as I can."

The returning party pulled out for Missouri on the afternoon of the following day. The two diaries that chronicle their adventures are brief and incomplete but fortunately complementary. That of Joe Davis, assistant surveyor, of which only the second volume is extant, begins on October 1 with their attempt to shorten the route between the Arkansas and Cottonwood Grove and relates with fine detail their dramatic and fortunate meeting with Captain William Becknell, carrying mail for the Commissioners. The diary of Benjamin H. Reeves begins a week later on an anxious note: "our Horses appear as if they must fail before we get in." Its few pages are rich in detailed description of the country—a perfect fulfillment of Benton's admonition to observe carefully.

On October 12, Colonel Mather, Captain Becknell, and Hendley Cooper left the expedition near Cottonwood Grove to hurry back to the settlements and bring fresh horses for relief of the party. A pleasant moment it must have been nine days later when Reeves lifted his eyes and saw the "seasonable relief" advancing slowly toward him across the burnt prairies—Becknell, Cooper, and Joe and Joel Walker bringing oxen, horses, beef, and salt.

Though the weather on the whole had been kind to them, the return had not been pleasant. Failing and dying horses, decreasing game, dangerously diminished supplies, and enforced delays before advancing winter sharpened anxieties. A happy man was Benjamin Reeves when he came in sight of the house of John Young, "The first white Man's Habitation which I saw since 18th June." . . . Both diaries end on October 25 with arrival at Fort Osage.

Sibley's advance to Taos and Santa Fe and his winter in New Mexico are the best documented part of the expedition, for in this case one of the diaries is extant on which he based his journal and another carries on where the journal leaves off. The three are a perfect revelation of the undefeatable Commissioner. Once the returning party with two of the Commissioners had disappeared over the eastern horizon Sibley exulted in his unhindered freedom to achieve, and, with infinite satisfaction, ticked off day by day difficulties overcome.

To strengthen his small party of twelve, he had, as soon as he knew that he was going to Santa Fe, dispatched Bill Williams on a good horse to overtake Nathaniel M. Pryor's party with word that he was coming, so that the two groups could pool their strength against possible attack by Pawnees. Pryor and men, however, were traveling fast. After Williams had gone fifty miles without overtaking them and discovered that they had crossed the Arkansas and had already entered upon the Cimarron desert, he deemed it prudent to return. They must go on without Pryor.

The two wagons were too heavily loaded; but, said Sibley, "I must now go on with them. As the weather is cool & the horses fresh, I mean to push on pretty briskly, with the view of getting 100 miles or so on my journey in this month."

He pushed up the Arkansas forty-four miles, crossed to the south side and traveled up as far as the east end of Chouteau's Island, whence he struck south through the sand hills and high plains to the Lower Spring of the Cimarron. After the sand hills were "passed with ease"—though they made only nine and one-half miles that day—he wrote "So much for this bugbear." After he had reached the Cimarron, he recorded: "a most excellent road, the greatest distance without water twelve miles." The trip was surprisingly uneventful. Sometimes they dug in the sand for water, sometimes they burned buffalo dung for fuel, and nearly every day Sibley commented on his failing horses. They sighted and steered by successive natural landmarks—the Rabbit Ears,

Mount Dora, Mount Clayton, the Point of Rocks, and Taos Gap. From the top of the Point of Rocks, Sibley and Brown marveled at the sublimity of the Shining Mountains.

On October 19, having reached the South Fork of the Canadian a little north of Taylor Springs, Sibley sent two of his men to San Fernando to bring back ten pack mules and a guide. He reasoned thus: "If I had attempted to reach Santa Fe by the way of San Miguel, my horses must nearly all have failed, and many of them been lost. If I attempt to haul the wagons over the mountains, loaded as they are, the horses must necessarily fail, and probably the wagons be lost entirely. If I hire mules to pack my baggage &c. over to Taos, I believe I shall be able to get the empty wagons over the mountains, and thus at a small expense save all my horses and wagons, & prove the existence of a wagon route over the mountains into the Valley of Taos; and I determined, upon all these considerations, to adopt the latter plan."

In Santa Fe, to which Sibley and Brown moved on November 29 after settling men and horses in Taos, Sibley's main objective was to get coöperation of the Mexican government in respect to the road, and, as a secondary and subsidiary interest, to investigate opportunities in Santa Fe trade and to profit by them if possible. The judgment against Sibley was suspended while he was on the survey. Only cash in hand could keep the axe from falling once the survey was finished.

As soon as he had arrived in San Fernando he had written Narbona, governor of New Mexico, of his mission and made inquiry as to whether permission had yet come from Mexico City. At the same time he had written to Senator Benton and to J. K. Poinsett. Once arrived in Santa Fe he entered upon the happiest of relations with the governor. Narbona called on Sibley; Sibley called on Narbona; Sibley dined with Narbona; he attended Narbona's fandangos; he sent Narbona a map of the road for the Mexican government. No courier departed for Mexico City but Sibley sent inquiries and arguments to Poinsett; no courier arrived but Sibley inquired of Narbona whether word had yet come. He waited with something of the patience of oaks and glaciers. On February 26, he received Poinsett's letter of December 3; no action yet—maybe something could be done after change of the administration. Sibley pointed out in reply that unless word by way of Washington could get to his colleagues early in May, they might decline coming to join Sibley in June. "If this assent can be communicated to me here by the 20th of June, or even by the 15th of July, I might perhaps, be able to obviate the most of the above difficulties & finish the road by the setting in of winter, whether my colleagues join me here or not.[71]

How much of Sibley's resolution to put the survey through to a successful finish was strengthened by the exigencies of his own business affairs is a fascinating and complex problem. All the correspondence shows the public servant resolutely bent on carrying out successfully the purpose of the Congressional Act as Benton had conceived it. The correspondence and the diaries show also one who intended to profit by Santa Fe trade if opportunities were available. They reveal his pressing need for money to stave off execution of the government judgment against him.

The campaign of vituperation against him which raged in the fall of 1825 while all three Commissioners were still in the wilderness brought forth loyal friends who warmly defended him. One E. F. of Cooper County, in the *Missouri Intelligencer* of August 19, belabored Senator Barton for having appointed on the Commission "one who was a public defaulter for upwards of $12,000."

"Indeed they say that this appointment was given in discharge of a debt for those able essays that appeared in your paper last fall, over the signature of 'Missourian.' Be this as it may, have no doubt the citizens of this state do believe there were a number of applicants for this appointment, not public defaulters, equally deserving, and as well qualified as the individual who has it."

Dr. Robert Simpson of St. Louis, replying in the *Missouri Intelligencer* of September 16, pointed out that Sibley had been appointed not by Barton but by the whole Missouri delegation—Benton, Barton, and Scott. Moreover, Mr. Sibley was not a public defaulter. The judgment against Mr. Sibley was to secure to the United States government payment from Paul Baillio & Co., for which Mr. Sibley was responsible, either as security or as a partner. "This debt will be duly paid either by Paul Baillio & Co. or by G. C. Sibley, who, in making himself personally and directly responsible, has been governed by those principles of honored integrity which have uniformly influenced him in his public and private concerns. And I will further remark, that this debt of Paul Baillio & Co. was contracted with an agent of the U. S. after Mr. Sibley ceased to be a public agent; and that he has made a large payment towards this debt from his private funds, and made arrangements to meet the balance of the claim." He believed that while Mr. Sibley was absent in exercise of an important public trust, his reputation should be "shielded from the depredation of disappointed ambition and malignant detraction." Following this letter to the editor is one from Edward Bates substantiating Simpson's statements.

The *Missouri Intelligencer* of September 23 and of September 30 gave further space to the acrimonious and disgruntled. The best result of the whole controversy was a letter from Edward Bates on December 3, 1825, to George Graham, Commissioner of the General Land Office, in which he makes a clear statement of Sibley's affairs:

> Mr. Sibley is now in Santa Fee (being one of the Road Commissioners) & will not return till some time next year. On leaving this last summer, he proposed to make payments from time to time to the credit of the judgment, and I, in return, told him that I should issue no execution in his absence, unless by order of my superiors. . . .
>
> I consider Mr. Sibley a solvent man; and yet were his property (the most valuable part of which is land) hastily brought to the hammer, in his absence, I fear he would be ruined, & a good part of the debt remain unpaid; but with some indulgence, I believe he can & will pay the whole.[72]

Though Reeves and Mather had been persuaded into letting Sibley await in Santa Fe permission of the Mexican government for continuance of the survey and had promised to meet him there if it arrived, expectation that they would have to make the long and hazardous trip did not remain a constant quantity. The first communication from the War Department—a letter from C. Vanderventer, Aug. 6, 1825, brought out by a small party of twenty traders whom the returning Commissioners met at Walnut Creek—tallied with Sibley's belief that permission might come by way of New Mexico. Mr. Poinsett had been instructed to get authority from Mexico as soon as possible for the survey to proceed beyond the boundary line.[73] Reeves and Mather wrote Sibley by the caravan that they expected the government permission to come by way of Santa Fe, and said, moreover, that they would have opportunity to come out the following spring with some of these same traders.[74] Archibald Gamble in his report of the survey written for the *Missouri Republican* of October 4, 1825, wrote that Major Sibley and the surveyor with ten men had been sent to Santa Fe to winter, with a view to obtain information of the country and to make arrangements with Mexican commissioners for completion of the road in the spring.[75]

A second letter from the War Department, dated September 19, 1825, was not encouraging. Mr. Poinsett had not been able to make any progress with the Mexican government relative to continuation of the road beyond the boundary line, and the Commissioners would therefore confine operations to the United States side of the line agreeably to the first section of the Congressional Act of March 3rd last.[76] Reeves, in a personal letter to Sibley, accompanying a copy of the letter from James Barbour, expressed uncertainty: "Should we not join you in the spring which is believed to be doubtful I would be glad if you would examine the Route from the lone Hackberry & mound or mark as you return that being the only part of the route that needs or requires much marking."[77] And in a joint letter the Commissioners told Sibley that if nothing favorable was heard from Mr. Poinsett, Sibley had better come home, so the report could be made.[78]

Sometime in the winter of 1825, Reeves wrote Gamble that he could not say anything at the time relative to construction of work beyond the United States border: "I am informed that the Mexican government is somewhat jealous about this little matter of the Road & will not consent to its survey without haveing it mixt up in the general treaty (if I may so express myself) of amity & friendship between the two governments which will require time & deliberation to effect but that it was hoped the arrangement would be entered into in time to Recommence our labours early this spring. This tho is only hope . . ."[79]

In a letter of February 7, Sibley wrote Reeves that he was sending home six of his men and some mules to cut down expenses. He thought the road ought to turn south at or near the old Caches. "I shall look for you early in July, and with the most restless anxiety."[80] A month later he wrote Poinsett: "Unless the consent of the Mexican Government is obtained in season to reach my colleagues in Missouri via the City of Washington, early in May, I should be very apprehensive that they may decline coming to join me here in June agreeably to our arrangement. . . . If this assent can be had and communicated to me here by the 20th of July, I might perhaps, be able to obviate the most of the above difficulties, and finish the Road by the setting in of winter, whether my colleagues join me *here* or not."[81]

Reeves in reporting to the War Department robbery of the six men sent in by Sibley concluded his letter with these words: "Mr. Sibley is still at St Fee and confidently expects to be joined this spring by the other Commissioners to continue the survey of the road beyond our line. Should the negotiations with the Mexican government have progressed so far as to induce a belief that such will be the result, if not incompatible with the state of the negotiations, I would be highly gratified to be informed."[82]

Thomas Mather, on his return from Washington, whither he had gone with the Indian treaties made by the Commissioners, wrote Reeves that the day before he left the capitol, the Secretary of War had told him that there was no prospect of arrangements being made in time for them to join Mr. Sibley in the spring, and therefore they had better write him to return.[83] On May 12, Reeves wrote Sibley that in view of what the Secretary of War had said he hoped for Sibley's speedy return with as little delay as possible.[84]

On the very next day, May 13, 1826, S. Camacho, Secretary of War for Mexico, wrote J. R. Poinsett that the President of Mexico had instructed the Governor of New Mexico to permit George Sibley to examine the western part of the road, but to make no cutting or marking, or establish any work of any sort whatever. It was inconvenient to send Mexican representatives with Mr. Sibley. He hoped that no objection would be made by the United States government when similar examination was desired of the eastern part of the road.[85] On May 20, Sibley at

Taos wrote Reeves and Mather that as yet he had had no word from the Mexican government.

"There will be three mails from Mexico to S[an]ta Fee before the 1st of June, to wit, one on the 28th of this month, one on the 13th, and another on the 28th of April. I shall expect you to arrive here early in July, but as it is not very probable that we can set out upon our journey homeward sooner than the 15th, there will still be another prospect of hearing from Mr. Poinsett by the mail of the 13th, if it should so happen that his letter does not arrive sooner. . . . I give it as my opinion that the U. S. Commissioners ought to meet here as early in July as practicable, and that they have good reason to believe the assent of the Mexican government will be communicated to them in time to enable them to complete the Road before the setting in of the next winter."[86]

On June 14, Antonio Narbona, governor of New Mexico, wrote Sibley that he had permission to proceed with the survey as the Mexican government specified.[87] Sibley in Taos, five days later acknowledged receipt of the permission and wrote that he then was awaiting arrival of the other Commissioners.[88] All the rest of June Sibley waited. All of July he waited. Twenty-three days of August he waited. Pedro Martinez, alcalde *pro tem* of Rancho de Taos, who tried to detain Sibley to explain why one of Sibley's men had knocked down a Mexican who was endeavoring to keep the horse he had stolen from the surveying party,[89] received the peppery letter that fixes the date of Sibley's departure:

> In answer to your note to me of yesterday, in which you require my personal appearance before you that you may communicate to me certain orders from the Governor of this Territory.
>
> I have to say to you Sir, that I deem it proper to decline altogether a compliance with your extraordinary demand. It is well known to you Sir, that I am here on business for my Government, and you ought to know that whatever official intercourse I may have in this country must be with the superior authorities, & not with you.
>
> The Governor is already apprised of every circumstance in relation to my business, and I am in possession of his authority to examine & survey a road from here to the Arkansas agreeably to the permission granted by the President of Mexico. I shall com-

mence my operation tomorrow, in conformity with that permission, with an escort of armed men.

With due respect, I am
Yr. Obt. Svt.
G. C. Sibley.[90]

Sibley's diary of the survey on Mexican soil has to this date not been found. His findings are undoubtedly embodied in Brown's Field Notes. We know that he started on August 24 from Taos, that he reached Walnut Creek on September 23, and by October 12 was safely back in Missouri, though there had been rumors that he had been cut off by Indians. In July, Reeves had written Mather, suggesting the propriety of their meeting Sibley at Walnut Creek and making necessary corrections in the survey, "but from some cause, I did not receive his answer in time to do so."[91]

Once Sibley was home in Fort Osage, the Commissioners had a hard time fixing upon a place and date for conference. Sibley proposed November 22 at St. Louis. Reeves suggested December 4 in Jefferson City. Illness in his family made it inconvenient for him to go farther away. Net results of their conference, which was held in the new Missouri capitol, are embodied in a letter to the Secretary of War: Delay of the Mexican government in granting permission for survey of the road to Santa Fe had delayed the work of the Commissioners; consequently Reeves and Mather had declined going out to meet Sibley last spring as agreed upon; Sibley had been detained in Mexico until August last; it only remained now for the corrected survey to be marked with mounds from Fort Osage to the boundary. The Commissioners expected to be able to finish their labors within the appropriation.[92] In St. Louis on Jan. 20, 1827, the Commissioners voted to hand over to Sibley all settlement of accounts, to make corrections of the survey as far as the funds would warrant, and then to make the report. Three days thereafter Sibley wrote his brother-in-law, Senator Josiah S. Johnston, that he expected to set out on the resurvey about April 15th. On January 29 he wrote to Edward Bates, offering his lands to the government to satisfy the judgment:

1. 640 acres on Wild Horse Creek
2. 800 arpens on Plattin Creek near Herculaneum
3. 200   ″   near St. Charles
4. 2 lots in St. Louis
5. 640 acres on Sny Ebore Creek in Lafayette County
6. 320   ″   in Jackson County

"All I have," he wrote, "except an unconfirmed claim to the tract on which I live, in Jackson county."[93]

On March 10, Reeves feared that on account of illness of his wife he would not be able to accompany Sibley on correction of the survey, much as he wanted to; but if Mather would not go, he would himself go even at great sacrifice.[94] Sibley in reply suggested:

> If it were possible to provide proper accommodations, I should incline to recommend a journey on our Road to Walnut Creek, but I doubt if a female in delicate health could endure the privations and exposure necessarily attendant on such a journey. Should you think it proper to risk it however, you may assure yourself of my exertions to make our Camp as comfortable as possible and it will afford Mrs. Sibley a pleasure to be able to render her house, &c. agreeable to Mrs. R. while detained in this neighborhood. . . .
>
> Having made my arrangements already to go on this service in May, and knowing the aversion of Col. Mather to make this journey, and the probable impracticability of your going without great inconvenience to your family, not to say pain, on account of Mrs. Reeves's indisposition, I shall with your concurrence proceed as early in May as I can get ready, to complete the 'marking out' of the Road in the best manner I can do it, and with as much dispatch as possible; expecting that there will arise no difficulty whatever with Col. Mather & yourself in recognizing what I do.[95]

A month later he had fixed upon May 15 as the date for his departure. His party would consist of John Walker[96] and Jacob Gregg[97] at $20 a month; Reuben Collins[98] as wagoner at the same wages; Jonathan Cameron,[99] David Overton, and three brothers—Bryan, William, and James Baxter[100] at $16 per month. These with three men that Reeves would send up from Franklin with the Mules—he hoped that

Andrew Carson would be one of the men—and some volunteers who wanted to go along to capture buffalo calves, would be ample men even for a camp guard at night. Walker and Gregg, he pointed out, were both experienced men on the road and peculiarly well qualified for the service, and would afford him very great assistance in other particulars than as common hands.[101]

On May 2, Reeves dispatched Andrew Carson,[102], Jo Hardin,[103] and Kit Richardson[104] with the mules. By Carson he sent also a compass, a ball and socket chain, a spike, and the "light prairie hat," size 22-3/10 which Sibley had requested. In his note Reeves expressed the deep obligation he felt toward Sibley for his undertaking the arduous work of the corrected survey.[105] Sixteen days later, Sibley started off his party— twelve men, fourteen mules, one horse, and one wagon in charge of Andrew Carson—with directions to go on to the upper settlement on the Big Blue. The Commissioner, detained by letter writing and the arrival of Paul Baillio from Taos, was not able to leave until Tuesday, May 22.

The resurvey, though uneventful in the main, had enough annoyances and hardships to be typical of summer travel in the wilderness. In spite of his light prairie hat, Sibley at the start had headaches which plagued him. The hands lost time searching for runaway mules. The game was scarce to the vanishing point. There were storms. The weather was cool. The weather was hot. The mosquitoes were bad; sometimes the flies were a pest. Day by day the party surveyed and threw up mounds of sod to mark the way. Day by day Sibley wrote detailed descriptions of the country he had not been able to observe in his night-time traveling on the former trip.

By June 10, he had reached the fine spring discovered by Ben Jones on the first expedition. "It may be appropriately called, 'The Diamond of the Plains' and so I had it marked on an Elm which grows near & overhangs it."[106] The next day, after a wet morning in camp, he decided to start on his return, making necessary surveys and properly connecting the new way with the old. Farther west, he reasoned, the road as traveled was already well enough marked by the wagons; any mound put up would be soon thrown down by the buffalo and Indians; and moreover he feared he would have to go as far as Walnut Creek for meat. He would make the work more thorough by surveying the route by Blue Springs.

The return journey was miserable enough. The farther east they traveled the more the flies plagued them and the scarcer the meat became. In several days the hunters succeeded in killing only one turkey. Sibley felt that if they exerted themselves more they might do better. One day when they found a little honey, "like children they eat up all at once." The diarist wrote, "I am most heartily tired and wish myself at home an hundred times a day." On July 5 the rain fell pretty steadily nearly all day. Sibley had to get off his horse so often to take the courses that he got wet all through his clothes. "I had my tent pitched, changed my clothes, eat a biscuit, drank a mint sling, and took a nap, after which I felt pretty well again, and spent the rest of the day reading Stern."

The next day was so catastrophic that it ended the survey. During a thunderstorm in the late afternoon, lightning struck one corner of Sibley's tent, splintering the uprights, passed through a leather iron-framed trunk (missing some powder) and all but killed the intrepid Commissioner. "The shock awoke me to the most painful & alarming sensations, for my right side which I lay on, was for a minute bereft of feeling nearly, my foot seemed reduced to jelly, having no feeling, a whirring noise passed thro' my ears continually, & the tent was filled with smoke & strewed with splinters." Of the six men in the other tent, Collins and Carson were shocked most severely. The compass was thoroughly ruined by the lightning flash. "I am obliged to stop the survey here."

Sibley reached Fort Osage on July 8. "Thus ends a most disagreeable trip in which I have effected every object I had in view, & in less time than I expected to have done it."

The rest of the story is soon told. On October 21 he sat down in Eckart's tavern in St. Charles, where Colonel Mather was to meet him, and set to work on the accounts and the report. A week later Colonel Mather arrived, examined, and approved the report. The Commissioners set their names and that of Reeves to it and forwarded it to Washington. On December 7, 1827, Colonel Reeves and Sibley sent on to Washington duplicate copies of the accounts and "two packages of maps, field books, &c.&c." The accounts showed that the Commissioners in surveying and marking "the highway between Nations" had over-run the appropriation by $1504.54. The unbelievable story of how the Commissioners labored for seven years to be reimbursed—how the government lost the first set of vouchers—how Reeves and Sibley went up and down the frontier getting signatures on a second set—how the government lost *them*—and how at last Sibley gritted his teeth, made another set in triplicate, made appearance in Washington to answer questions in person, and eventually lost patience to the point where he called the Highway between Nations "Benton's d--d Santa Fe road"—all of this is governmental ineptitude past all understanding. Only on June 13, 1834, having obtained the signature of Reeves and Mather and affixed his own to the order on the Treasury Warrant, could he write in conclusion, "So that the whole of this business of the Road to New Mexico is at length finally and fully settled."

*T*he Journal of George C. Sibley on
an expedition to survey and mark
a road from the Missouri Frontier to the
Settlements in Mexico. St. Louis, June 22,
to Santa Fe, November 30, 1825.

St. Charles, October 28th, 1827.

Mr. Sibley presents this Journal* (not as any part of the Report of
the Commissioners) in the supposition that it may possibly supply some
facts, not to be found in the field book, that may perchance at some
time be useful—particularly in relation to that part of the Journey from
The Boundary.

Many of the distances here noted have been corrected and shortened
by subsequent surveys.

Journal from St. Louis to Santa Fee, from the notes taken during
the Journey by G. C. Sibley, one of The Commissioners appointed by
The President of The United States to mark out a Road from the
Western Frontier of Missouri to the frontier of New Mexico.

The following is only designed to preserve the notes that were taken
in pencil from day to day.

---

* This manuscript, a book of 104 pages, 12 x 14 inches, is now in the National Archives in Washington, D. C. Lost for over a hundred years, it was
brought to light in 1938 in a Senate Committee room by Mr. Buford
Rowland.

FROM ST. LOUIS TO FORT OSAGE

Wednesday 22nd June

Having completed every necessary arrangement, I started the Baggage Waggons today, seven in number, pretty well laden with Goods for Indian Treaties—coarse Clothing, Provisions, Ammunition &c. Two of them drawn by 4 Horses each, the other 5 each by 2 Horses. Seven Men accompanied the Waggons as drivers, to Wit—Benjamin Jones,[1] James Brotherton,[2] James Wells, Harvey Clark, Benjamin Robinson,[3] Daniel Murphy,[4] and George West. These Men are all engaged as hands for the Trip, or so long as The Commissioners may require their Services. The Waggons, Harnessings &c. are all good and new, the Horses are well Selected, and are in good order for Service.

I gave the whole in charge to Mr. Jones, to whom I furnished Money to defray his traveling expences, and written Instructions for his government, as far as Franklin, where I expect to overtake him.

The Weather is very hot, & the flies bad in the Prairies.

Saturday 25th June.

I left St. Louis today at 9 o'Clk. and reached St. Charles at 1 P. M. The Waggons have but just got out of Town; they have been detained by Rains, breaking down, & repairing, & at the ferry. They went on at 4 o'Clk. this morning, all well.

Monday 27th June.

Altho' quite unwell, with very strong bilious symptoms, I took leave of my Wife & friends and set out on my journey today at 11 o'Clk. Mr. Brown & Mr. Gamble,[5] the Surveyor and Secretary to the Commissioners accompany me. We slept at Mrs. Bailey's[6]—20 Miles from St. Charles. St. Charles is 18 Miles from St. Louis.

Tuesday 28th June.

Started after early Breakfast. Overtook the Waggons at Price's, Camp Branch,[7] late in the evening. They were waiting for night to go through the Loutre Prairie, which is much infested with flies. We waited with them 'till sunset when we all started. We got to Kibby's[8] at about 11 o'Clk. got supper & went to Bed. The Waggons arrived about an Hour after, rested a short time, and then went on through the Prairie to Vanbibber's[9] before daylight. 35 Miles to Mrs. Bayley's. Whole distance from St. Louis 73 Miles.

Wednesday 29th June.

After Breakfast, we Started. We got to Vanbibber's early & found the Waggons. Went on to Fruit's[10] and stopped till Night, then went on to Harrison's[11] & Slept. Distance today 33 Miles. The flies are very bad in all the Prairies above Mrs. Bailey's.

Thursday 30th June.

The Waggons did not get to Harrison's today 'till 10 o'Clk. The flies are so bad in the Grand Prairie that it is impossible to travel through it in the day without very great injury to the Horses. Even at Harrison's we were obliged to keep the Horses Shut up in Stables.

At Sunset we left Harrison's, waggons & all. I got to Regan's[12] at about 12 & went to bed. The Waggons got there a little before daylight, and passed on to the Creek and camped. Distance tonight 18 Miles.

Friday 1st July.

After Breakfast, we left Regan's. Passed the Waggons at the Creek; still in camp. Directed Mr. Jones to go only a few Miles today, & to travel very leisurely—the Horses very much jaded & worried.

I stopped to dine at Sexton's,[13] & then went on & slept at Johnston's.[14] Distance 34 Miles today.

Saturday 2d. July.

Left Johnston's early, and arrived at Franklin[15] to Breakfast at nine o'Clk. 9 Miles.

Find Col. Reeves here, with 20 Men, ready to Start on the Expedition, as soon as Mr. Jones gets up with the Waggons. The weather very hot.

Sunday 3d. July.

The Waggons arrived at Franklin this evening, some repairs and alterations are necessary, which will probably detain tomorrow.

Monday 4th July.

I intended to have left Franklin this morning early for home; but a Committee of arrangements waited on me, & requested that Mr. Brown, Mr. Gamble & myself would join the Citizens of Franklin at a Public Dinner in honour of the day, which polite invitation we were bound to accept.

Had all necessary repairs done to the Waggons, and started them out of Town this evening. In course of the day Col. Reeves & myself drew two Bills of Exchange on the War Dep[artmen]t: one for $10,000 payable to order of Messrs. Tracy & Wahrendorff of St. Louis—the other for $5000 payable to order of Robt. Hood, Merchant of Franklin. We also wrote to The Sec[reta]ry of War, to advise him of our progress; that we expected to reach the boundary line of the U[nited] States early in September; where we hope we may not be detained for want of authority to proceed to N[ew] Mexico.

Tuesday 5th July.

Left Franklin[16] at 11 o'Clk. The day extremely warm. Col. Reeves & the Horsemen overtook us, and we all came up with the Waggons before they reached the ferry, & passed them. We crossed the Missouri at the Arrow Rock, and went on to Reece's[17] and Halted. Nearly All the Horsemen got over the River this evening, but the wind was too violent to cross the Waggons, except two of them.

It is 12 Miles from Franklin to Reece's.

Wednesday 6th July.

Tremendous Storm of Rain and Wind last Night. The Waggons all got safely over this morning, and now our Whole party is assembled ready to move on to the work assigned us. It consists of Col. Reeves & G. C. Sibley, Commissioners—Archibald Gamble, Secretary—J. C. Brown, Surveyor—Stephen Cooper, Sup[erintenden]t of the Hands—and B. Jones, B. Robinson, James Wells, Danl. Murphy, Harvey Clark, Jas. Brotherton, Geo. West, Henley Cooper, Richard Brannin, E. Davis, Jo. Davis, Jas. Davis, G. Patrick, Bradford Barbee, Jo. Reynolds, Bird Pyles, S. Smith, R. Cornelius, L. Cornelius, Neriah Todd, S. Givens,

Wm. Givens, T. Adams, S. Vaughn, D. East, D. Dedmon, A. Broadus—Hired Hands for the expedition.

At Sunset we all started onward; Col. Reeves, Mr. Brown, Mr. Gamble & myself rode on at a good gait 18 Miles to Mrs. McCafferty's[18] & Stopped at Midnight, & went to Bed. I have been sick all day.

Thursday 7th July.

Col. Reeves is indisposed this Morning, and waits 'till the Waggons come along. Mr. B[rown], Mr. G[amble] & I Set off very early & rode 12 Miles to Davis's[19] & got Breakfast. After B[rea]kf[as]t Mr. Gamble & I went on 9 Miles farther to Dustin's[20] & halted, Mr. G. being quite unwell; the day extremely hot. Mr. Brown, who went back from Davis's to McCafferty's for something he forgot there, overtook Mr. G[amble] & I at Dustin's just as Sunset, & we all Spent the Night there. Distance traveled today 21 Miles.

Friday 8th July.

We left Dustin's after Breakfast and rode on to Lexington (20 Miles) where we arrived at 3 P. M. We staid here all Night—spent the evening at Major Findlay's[21] just out of Town.

Saturday 9th July.

Left Lexington after Breakfast and arrived at Fountain Cottage,[22] near Ft. Osage at 2 P. M. Distance from Lexington 22 Miles. Whole distance from St. Louis to Ft. Osage 260 Miles.

Monday 11th July.

In the evening Col. Reeves arrived, accompanied by Col. Thomas Mather of Illinois, who has been appointed to fill the vacancy occasioned by the nonacceptance of Col. Menard as a Commissioner.

Tuesday 12th July.

Today all the Men arrived, with the Waggons &c. and encamped in a Grove near the Prairie. Having many arrangements to make here before we can proceed, such as repairs of some of the Waggons, Shoeing Horses, purchasing some Horses &c., it will be several days before the Party can Start from here. The Green Flies are yet very numerous in the Prairies. The following Men joined us here—Jo. Walker,[23], Jno.

Walker,[24] Jno. S. Davis, A. Long, D. Bohon. Our force now consists of 33 Hired Men, including Capt. Cooper, & our aggregate strength is 38, exclusive of two Servants. We have 57 Horses and Mules, 7 Baggage Waggons, a Good Supply of Provisions, Tools, Ammunition &c. & all in good Spirits.

FROM FORT OSAGE TO THE BOUNDARY OF THE U. S. & MEXICO

The Commissioners have concluded, after a proper examination and enquiry, to Start the survey of the Road from this place. And on

Sunday the 17 July

the expedition Set out from its camp near Ft. Osage and proceeded with the work. The surveyor is instructed to note all the courses very exactly, and to measure as he proceeds. Having some private business to arrange before I can leave home, I did not Start with the Company; but Shall follow on and overtake them as soon as I can finish my business at home. The weather is very warm, & the flies still very troublesome.

Monday 25 July.

I wrote by the Mail today (*unofficially*) to Messrs. Barton, Benton[25] & J. S. Johnston[26] U. S. Senators; & to Jno. Scott Representative in Congress from Missouri, stating to them each, my opinion of the inadequacy of the Sum appropriated, to complete the road, and giving it as my opinion, that about $8000 will be necessary in addition; but recommend an additional appropriation of $12,000, which sum I suppose will be sufficient to complete the work. I accompanied my Letters with Some estimates & calculations.

I meant to have started today, but I am indisposed, & am taking Medicine.

Wednesday 27th July.

This evening Col. Marmaduke[27] arrived at my House with Mr. James Moore, direct from S[an]ta Fee, which place they left about the 1st of June. They came with a large Party, who brought a great number of Mules, Asses, &c. They were met by a Large Band of Osage Indians at the Arkansas, not far from the Mouth of the Little Arkansas, the 14th July, by whom they were robbed of about 120 head of Animals, & some other property, and were otherwise illy Treated.

They met the Road party about 70 Miles from here, going on pretty well, tho' the flies are so bad that they were obliged to travel a great deal in the Night.

Friday 29th July.

I left home today at 3 P. M. with John S. Davis,[28] one of the Hands, and my servant Abram.[29]

I pursued the track of the Road party. Crossed the Little Blue,[30] at a place that may be made pretty good, Eight Miles from Ft. Osage—then thro' a Small Prairie—then through the Woods, passing a Plantation,[31] and a fine Spring, to a Ridge where Joel Walker[32] & Mr. Young[33] are building Houses, at whose camp I Slept all night. Distance from Ft. Osage about 18 Miles.

Saturday 30th July.

Very fine Morning. Started early. Rode about ½ Mile and entered a Prairie—the Waggon Road very plain—then 8 Miles and Crossed Big Blue. Then 7 Miles to a Small Grove of Hycory,[34] where I halted till near Night, & caught 30 or 40 fish. So far today nearly all Prairie—good road—the flies very bad.

I Started again at Sunset, and rode 20 Miles to a Small Clump of Trees on a little Creek, & halted. Very little water to be found, & that little very bad. The Road good, but pretty crooked. Hot day.

Sunday 31st July.

Started very early. Traveled thro' a very long and tedious Prairie about 22 Miles and halted at a Camp lately occupied by our company.[35] The day extremely hot & the flies worse than usual. My Horse quite Stiff and Sick. Water Scarce here. Plenty of Pea Vine. Staid here all Night.

Monday 1st August.

Pleasant Morning. Started at Sun Rise—traveled very Steadily ab[ou]t 14 M[ile]s. to a Creek[36] in the Prairie without any timber. Stopped here an Hour, and then rode on at a good gait ab[ou]t 16 M[ile]s to a Small Creek, and halted for the day at another Camp,[37] ab[ou]t ½ Mile to the Right of the Waggon Road. The day very Hot, & flies still very bad.

Tuesday 2d. August.

Morning sultry. The Horses all left us & Started back; they had got Six Miles before they were caught. We did not start 'till near 10.

We rode a[bou]t 16 M[ile]s & Stopped to rest on a pretty large Creek [Marais des Cygnes] at an old camp; the day excessively Hot. We Started again at Sunset, and rode very steadily about 16 Miles to a Creek [Elm], & camped on its bank, in the Prairie, some time after Dark. This is a pretty, bold running Stream.

Wednesday 3d August.

Started at Sunrise—rode ab[ou]t 4 Miles briskly, and came up with the Party, encamped on a Branch [142 Mile Creek] of the Marais de Cygne, before they were all up. They have been here since the 1st— the Horses are all very much reduced & weakened by the Heat, & flies, & traveling in the Night. This is a considerable fork of The Marais de Cygne, and affords some excellent Land & good Timber. Mr. Gamble[38] is gone, I find, to the Osage Villages, to invite them to meet the Commissioners at some convenient point on the Road farther West. This Camp is 140 Miles from Ft. Osage. Having killed some Elk here, on their arrival, the Gentlemen have called this Creek "*Elk Creek.*"[39]

Thursday 4th August.

We broke up Camp early, & set forward. Traveled seven Miles and halted to graze the Horses & eat Breakfast on a Small Creek [Bluff Creek], in a beautiful young Hycory Grove. In the evening we pursued our journey six Miles farther, which brought us to another Stout Creek [Rock] (a Branch of the Nee Ozho) where we halted in the Prairie after Dark. The flies are now nearly all past. The distance measured today is 13 miles.

Friday 5th August.

Fine morning. Started early. Drove 6 64/80 Miles and arrived to Break-fact at a Main Branch of The Nee Ozho River; and here we find most excellent pasturage, and a Large & beautiful Grove of fine Timber; and we determine to wait here for the Osages, who are expected in two or three days. Our Camp is arranged with the view of receiving our expected Visitors in a suitable manner. Very few flies Here.

The manner that I was obliged to travel from Fort Osage to this place, fighting the flies, if I rode in the day time, without a moment's cessation, or else feeling my way in the dark as I traveled by Night, made it impossible for me to notice the Country as particularly as I wished and intended if I had been able. I may remark generally that the far greater part of the way is Prairie, & that tolerably level & smooth, affording good Road, and with two exceptions, plenty of Water at convenient intervals. As we return, I shall be particular to Note everything worth notice that has been now omitted. The general course from Ft. Osage to this place is South 73¾° West, and the distance as measured upon the Route traveled, 160 Miles.

As we propose to Meet the Osage Chiefs in council Here, to negotiate a Treaty with them for the Road &c. I suggested the propriety of naming the place "Council Grove" which was agreed to, & Capt. Cooper directed to Select a Suitable Tree, & to record this name in Strong and durable characters—which was done.[40]

Saturday & Sunday the 6th & 7 Augt.

Fine Weather. Game is not very plentiful here, but the Hunters kill some Elk and Deer. Issued Rice & Flour to the Men.

Monday 8th August.

Warm day. Mr. Gamble arrived this evening with Fifty of the principal Chiefs and Warriors of the Great and Little Osages, & Wm. S. Williams[41] The Interpreter. The Osages camped near us.

Tuesday 9th August.

Council today with the Osages. The Commissioners explained to them fully & clearly what they desire respecting the Road; and proposed to give them $800 as compensation for the privilege of Marking it through their Land, & the free use of it forever. After a few Minutes conversation among themselves, the chiefs declared their Assent to the proposition, & expressed their Readiness to execute a Treaty to that effect. And they were told that The Commissioners would meet them again tomorrow, prepared to conclude & sign the Treaty as now agreed on. And then the Council Rose, to meet again tomorrow.

Wednesday 10th August.

The Commissioners met the Osages in Council, at 11 o'Clk. The Treaty was prepared for Signature agreeably to the arrangement made yesterday, and in conformity with the Act of Congress, and after it was Read & carefully explained to the Osages by the Interpreter, it was signed in due form by the respective parties, and a Duplicate Copy given to the principal Chief. The Comm[issione]rs then paid them Goods to the value of $300 St. Louis cost, and gave them an order on Mr. Augustus Choteau,[42] a Trader now at their Village, for Ammunition, Knives &c. such as they may choose, to the Value of $500 at fair prices. And this finishes our business with The Osages. I wrote several Letters to Wife & friends, enclosed them to Mr. [Lilburn W.] Boggs[43] at Nee Ozho to be by him forw[arde]d. to Ft. Osage. I gave the Packet in charge Belle Oiseau, who promises to deliver it safely to Mr. Boggs. Latitude here 38°-40'-00''.

Thursday 11th August.

The Weather very fine tho' very Warm after the sun gets up to Meridian. It is sultry this morning. The Osages were stirring very early, and were ready to take leave of us by 6 o'Clk. On bidding me good-bye, they generally expressed to me their entire Satisfaction with the result of their Visit to our Camp. Three or four individuals of but inferior note seemed a little dissatisfied because they had not Shared as largely as they expected in the distribution of the Goods; for this they blamed their chiefs however, under whose direction the Goods were divided.

The Chiefs & principal Men all went away perfectly satisfied, as well they might, for The Commissioners allowed them very liberally, as I think, for the Right of Way through the country claimed by them, as *their* right, is at best a doubtful one, if the Treaty lately Signed by them at St. Louis, with General Clark, is ratified and confirmed by Congress.

We engaged Wm. S. Williams, the Interpreter, to accompany us throughout our whole journey, and to serve as Interpreter, Runner, Hunter &c. His wages is fixed at $33 1/3 per month & a Horse found him. As soon as the Osages left us, Williams Set off to the Kansas Village, to invite the Chiefs and Head Men to meet The Commissioners at some convenient place this side of the Arkansas. The Cotton Wood Grove and the Kansas Spring were named. Williams was instructed however to meet us with the Chiefs as soon as possible. The Kansas Village is probably about 45 Miles from here, upon a course about North 20 West. We should have assembled the Kansas at Council Grove, but our Store of Meat was very nearly exhausted, and from the report of the Hunters, there was some reason to apprehend that a supply cannot be had here, should we stay for the Kansas. We therefore broke up camp early, got Breakfast while the Osages were getting ready to Start, and in half an hour after their departure, our Cavalcade moved onward at ½ past 6 o'Clk. Our Horses and Mules are very much revived, since they have been in this excellent pasture. From our camp, near the great Oak that is Marked, just at the eastern edge of the Grove, to the Crossing of the Nee Ozho the distance is 25 chains [1650 feet]. The Creek is about 30 yards wide, banks & bottom pretty good. We got all the Waggons safely over without difficulty, and entered immediately upon an almost boundless Prairie, which being rough and hilly, obliged us to travel a very crooked way for several Miles, when we got upon a more level plain. The Prairie is very high & is generally Strewed over with Small flakes of Limestone and Flint. The Grass is very short & wiry, except in the low places, where it is rich and good. A smaller branch of the Nee Ozho is upon our left [Elm Creek], nearly parallel with our course running from the So[uth] West, and enters the Large branch a little below our camp. For about 12 Miles on the road, we found Water Scarce. A Large gang of Elk was started, out of which 3 or 4 were killed after a hard chase, which fatigued and injured the Horses engaged in it much more than the whole drove was worth. 2 deers were also killed, & several Goats shot at.

The Prairie becomes more level as we advance westward, but is Still hard and Stoney. The view to the North and South is unbounded. The Road pursues a very high Ridge. We halted on a Small Creek [Otter] where the water is Scarce & bad. The Grazing pretty good and fuel plenty. Mr. Jones discovered a very fine Spring about 300 yards So[uth]. E[ast]. from our camp down the Creek. It is uncommonly large and beautiful, and the Water very pure & cold. I have Seldom seen so fine a Spring anywhere. After so hot a day, this fine Water was a luxury to us all. The distance from Council Grove to Jones' Spring[44] as measured upon our Route is 16 Miles & 32 Chains.

Friday 12th August.

Having Breakfasted, we left Jones' Spring at 7 o'Clk. Our travel today was over a high, dry & pretty level Plain, which is for the most part stoney. Crossed several small branches of pretty good Water, which I should judge to be permanent. Little or no Timber on the Road, tho' several small copses off to the left, at some distance. Saw plenty of Game, but got only one Goat,[45] which was rejected as not fit to eat. Some Elk chased. We stopped, and Camped half a Mile to the left of our course, on a small creek, [Branch of Brook Luta] at a Solitary Cotton Tree, the only one in sight. Water and Grass very good & plenty. Distance measured today 20 Miles & 31 Chains.

Saturday 13th August.

Fine morning. Wind from the South. Started at Sunrise, having no Wood to cook Breakfast with, & in truth no meat to cook. I rode at a good pace, ahead of the Waggons—the country very much the same as that we passed over yesterday, except that it is more broken & cut up with deep Gullies, which obliged the Waggons to travel a good deal out of the course for several Miles. I rode on about 5 Miles, in which was a continual, tho' very gradual ascent, and then came in view of a Small Grove of Trees, the approach to which was by a Slight descent, and off to the left of our general course.

I got to this Grove at ½ past 7, which proves to be what is called the Cotton "Wood Grove" [sic] on the Main Branch of The Nee Ozho. The Waggons arrived at ½ past 9, and here we halted for the day, and pitched our Tents. Distance Measured is 9 M[ile]s & 9 Ch[ain]s. Water plenty on the road this morning. No Game killed, and only one Goat seen at a great distance. The Creek Here affords plenty of good water, & the bottoms, very good Grass. Fuel is also plenty.

Sunday 14th August.

Very fine morning. Wind fresh from the South. We breakfasted, and started onward at half past Six. Crossed the Creek at a good ford. Traveled about 10 Miles over Hilly Prairie soil better than that we Saw yesterday & not near so stoney, face of the country very much like that about Ft. Osage, tho' not near so fertile. About 10 Miles farther, over a more level Prairie, and arrived at a small, brisk running Creek [Running Turkey Creek, east of McPherson], which is the first Water we have seen since we left the Cotton Wood Grove. This is good and plenty & permanent. Not a Tree to be seen except a few at a very great distance down this Creek. The day was very warm and the Horses suffered very much. The Waggons did not get up till near Sundown. No Game seen today except a few goats, none of which were killed. The distance measured today 19 Miles and 63 Chains.

This Creek is a branch of the Little Arkansas. I am inclined to think that a better Route would have been to have turned off more Northward immediately after crossing the Cotton Wood fork, and so to have Struck this Creek higher up some 6 or 10 Miles. I have met with very few Snakes on the road yet. I have observed Yellow Hammers, Night Hawks, Field Larks, Gray Sparrows. There are No Hawks, Buzzards, Ravens, Crows or Wolves—a proof that Game is Scarce hereabouts. The Prairie is of immense extent, and badly watered.

We have no Wood here, & are obliged to use drift Weeds and Buffalo D--g to cook with. A little after night, Williams arrived with two Men of the Kansas. He reports that he left about Fifty more of the Principal Men about 6 Miles back on the Road who will overtake us in the Morning, or some time tomorrow. Sent the two runners back to tell them that we shall wait for them on the first Creek we come to that has any Timber on it. The Cooks contrived to get us a very good supper of Coffee, fried Bacon and Biscuit, all cooked over a fire made of Buffalo D--g.

Monday 15th August.

A very fine Morning, the Wind from the South. We started at 7 after getting Breakfast. I rode on ahead of the Waggons. Followed a plain Road about 12 Miles upon the right course, over a beautiful, rich & level Prairie, passing Timber on the left at 2 or 3 miles distance—but seeing no prospect of getting to any Wood in this direction today, and being too far already for the Waggons, I turned about and retraced my steps about 3 Miles upon the road, and then turned off nearly south to a small Grove of Trees on a little Creek; where I was soon joined by the Waggons and the Kansas and camped under a very large Spreading Oak. This Creek is a Branch of the one we left this morning and is called by the Kansas, *Sora Con:tsa* [a branch of Turkey Creek], in remembrance of one of their People who was killed on it some years ago. It is at present very small affording but little Water, & that very bad. The Musquetoes annoy us very much, and the air is extremely close and oppressive. The Road mentioned above is the one traveled by the large caravan of Merchants and Traders that left Franklin for N[ew] Mexico, in May.[46] We have pursued their course, and traveled frequently in their Track for more than 100 Miles. 10 M[ile]s & 27 Ch[ain]s Meas[ure]d today.

We found water plenty on our route today, but no Game except a few Goats, none of which were killed. A Hunting party of the Kansas have been here recently, (The White Plume's Band) and driven off all the Game. We were all day in view of Buffalo *Sign,* as their Roads tracks &c. [were] in great abundance, but saw none of the animals. Saw a Prairie Wolf, a Blue Crane, a Hawk, field Larks & Buzzards. The timber here is Bur Oak, Elm, Ash, Locust, Hycory, Plum &c. In sight from our Camp is a Range of naked Sand Hills stretching across our course from No[rth] W[est] to So[uth] E[ast]. This range appears to be about 12 Miles off. The Little Arkansas or as the Kansas call it

62

Cheh-tun-ga (Big Lake) runs on this side of those Hills. After we had all got a little settled in camp, we had a council with the Kansas, & having explained to them fully our wishes in relation to the Road, we proposed to them precisely the same terms that we agreed on with the Osages at Council Grove—and these terms they accepted without any hesitation; and agreed to sign a Treaty to the same effect. We told them the Papers would be ready in the Morning, & the Council rose.

Tuesday 16th August.

The Morning fair & pleasant. The Wind from the South West. After breakfast The Commissioners met the Kansas formally in council. The Treaty was exhibited in due form, containing all the stipulations required by the Act of Congress, and the prompt payment of $800 in full compensation for the right of way through the Territory of the Kansas forever—all of which was read and carefully explained, and then the Parties signed and executed the Treaty in due form, a Duplicate copy of which was given to the Head Chief, after which, we delivered them Goods to the value of Three Hundred Dollars, St. Louis Cost; and gave them an Order on Curtis & Eley,[47] Traders near them, for Goods such as they may want to the value of Five Hundred Dollars, at fair cash prices. The chiefs expressed their perfect satisfaction with this arrangement. While they were dividing their Goods, I wrote to Mrs. Sibley, & enclosed my Letter to Mr. [Michael] Eley,[48] to whom I wrote in relation to the order on him in fav[o]r of the Kansas. I put the Letter in the charge of the head chief, who promises to deliver it safely to Mr. Eley. Having now finished all our business with the Kansas, we took leave of them and Set forward again upon our Survey. We are entirely out of Meat and must hasten on without unnecessary delay to the Arkansas, where we hope to find buffalo. We traveled over a very level plain 12 Miles and 43 chains to the Little Arkansas, where we pitched our Tents on the bank of the River. Our Hunters killed several Buffalo today, but they were all very poor, and scarcely fit to eat. No other game killed today. The Little Arkansas is a clear, brisk running Stream, about 25 yards wide, Water Sweet and good. It is now very

Shallow, the bed Sandy, banks high, a few Scattering Cotton Trees along on them. Pretty good pasturage.

Wednesday 17th August.

It rained a little last night, and is cloudy this morning. Musquetoes very troublesome here. Horses done rather poorly.

We set out at 8 o'Clk. after breakfast. Traveled 4¼ Miles over very rough flat ground, much cut up with ridges & holes & slashes, and reached the Sand Hills where we found plenty of good Water, and a great many Plums. After resting here two hours under some very large Spreading Cotton Trees (of which there are many in these Hills) we pursued our course & drove about 1¾ Miles through the Sands, and came to a rough Sandy Prairie, over which we traveled about 1 Mile further to another narrow range of Sand Hills, and then down into the great Arkansas Plain, upon which we rode about 2 Miles and came to a small river upon the bank of which we camped just at Sunset, and just as a heavy rain came on. We have traveled today 9 miles and 21 Chains. The Sand Hills are nothing like what they have been reported to be by travellers; in Extent they are not over two Miles where we crossed them, and of that not over half the distance is very difficult. It is certain however, that if we had pursued the Road that we left on Monday, we might have avoided these Hills entirely; and it is now Still more obvious that the best route of all would have been that mentioned in my Note of the 14th, turning off more Northward at Cotton Wood Grove. The Creek we are now on is called Cold Water Creek [Cow Creek]. It is nearly as large as the Little Arkansas, which it resembles very much. Its water is good and abundant; but there is no timber on it to be seen here. The Grass very good—*some* drift Wood.

Thursday 18th August.

A very heavy rain fell last Night. Still cloudy this morning. Started at six before Breakfast—traveled about 4 Miles, and arrived on the bank of the Arkansas[49]—then kept up the River 2 Miles to a pile of drift wood and Halted to get Breakfast. The Arkansas is here about 500 yards wide from bank to bank, its bed sand, water turbid, current swift, channel full of Sand bars. One of the Men waded across, & found it in no place over four feet deep. Not a Tree to be seen on its banks.

At 3 P. M. we again Started, and continued up on the margin of the River about 4 Miles, and camped for the night on the bank,[50] having measured 10 Miles and 2 Chains today.

The immense plain in which we now are, and through which the Arkansas flows, is almost an uninterrupted level as far as the eye can See to the South and West. The soil is apparently fertile and deep, the Herbage tolerably luxuriant; but there is not a single Tree anywhere to be seen on its banks. Our road this evening lay over some tolerably rough sandy ground, in which Rattle Snakes are very numerous. I observed this Morning as I passed through a Village (as it is called) of Prairie Dogs, several very luxuriant bunches of the common Garden *Pursley*, & some A--e Smart. Saw a Hawk, Prairie Hen & Lark. *Heard* a Partridge. Gofers abundant. Killed a Buffalo in the River. The Grass indifferent here. Horses failing very fast.

Friday 19th August.

Morning fair and cool. After Breakfast we started at 8 o'Clk. Pursued our way up the River by its course pretty nearly, over very much the same kind of ground as yesterday, and after traveling 7 Miles and 51 Chains halted again on the River bank.[51] The Horses very much jaded. Killed several fat Buffaloes today. Saw Deer, Goats, Hares, and Wolves. Buffalo getting very plenty. The River is here 54 yds. wide, no Tree seen yet. One of the Mules bit by a Rattle Snake this evening. These snakes are very numerous & troublesome here.

Saturday 20th August.

Morning fair & pleasant. We remained in camp all this day for the purpose of resting and recruiting the Horses, as the Grass is very good here. I have to Note that the circuitous distance from Ft. Osage to the Arkansas where we Struck it on Thursday the 18th is 262½ Miles as Measured. To this place it is 275 as traveled—213 Miles upon a straight line, on the course So[uth] 74 West. The Latitude here is 38°-11'-29''. Longitude 98°. The River is on the fall. The Weather very fine.

Sunday 21st August.

Morning cool and fair—very heavy dew—the Night quite cool. Nearly opposite our camp, say 300 yds. above, a range of Sand Hills touches the River, some of which are covered with Plum bushes loaded with fruit, and about half a Mile below us on the North side are some other Hills of the same kind. Those on the South side of the River are the first that approach it on that side for about 20 Miles below. Above us in sight are a few Trees on the River. The pasturage in this plain is generally extremely fine. The Grass is soft, short and very nutricious, somewhat resembling the Blue Grass. The Ponds & slashes which are numerous a little back from the River are slightly Saline, & the whole Plain is believed to be so too—and it is from those causes that the Grass is so remarkably nutricious, and so very much relished by Horses, Buffalo, &c. At 8 o'Clk. we struck our Camp, & again proceeded up the River in the Bottom Six Miles & 40 Chains & halted for the day.[52] At 12 the Mercury stood at 84—at 6 P. M. it was 73.

Monday 22d August.

A very pleasant Morning. The Grass being very good here, we Staid in Camp all day for the benefit of the Horses; and it is necessary also to unload & examine the Stores & Provisions, Issue some Blankets and Clothing to the men, and Shoe some of the Horses. Our camp is opposite a small Grove of Cotton Trees. The High ground [is] near the River on the North Side. Some sand Hills still in sight. Mercury 84 at 12—64 at 6 P. M. Mr. Brown says the current of the Arkansas is here about 2¼ Miles per hour.

Tuesday 23d August.

The morning fair and cool. Mercury 66 at 8 o'Clk. in the shade. At half an hour past Eight we started again. The Waggons continued up the River in the bottom. I rode out from the River upon the Hills to view the country. First I went No[rth] E[ast] about a mile, which took me quite out of the River bottom, and upon a high Ridge,[53] from which I had a fine view of the immense level Plain thro' which the Arkansas runs.

I then went on nearly North, about 3 Miles, over high broken Prairie, and got on a high point of a Ridge, from which I Saw off to the Eastward a string of Timber about 5 Miles off, pointing out the course of a Creek, which I know to be the one we left on the 18th called Cold Water [Cow Creek]. This Creek appears to run nearly parallel with the Arkansas, and takes its rise in a High dividing Ridge to the North; which ridge I suppose to be the same that separates the Streams of the Arkansas from those of the Kansas River, and upon which I am of opinion the Road ought to run from the Cotton Wood fork of the Nee Ozho to the Arkansas. I saw many Herds of Buffalo scattered through the Rich meadow grounds over towards the Creek; the Scenery is altogether very beautiful & I enjoyed it the more as the morning was cool and pleasant. I rode on a Mile or two farther towards the North, and then turned more Westward, and fell into a beautiful & very extensive Rich Valley or Meadow, having two small streams running through it, and numerous herds of Buffalo grazing in every direction. The soil in this Valley is very rich. The Grass very thick & Luxuriant of the kind called Buffalo Grass, which never grows tall. I presume the Valley may contain ten thousand acres. It is all beautifully level & thickly set with Buffalo Grass, and looks like an immense field of Blue Grass.

The soil on the High lands is much inferior to this in the Valley. On the declivity of one or two of the Ridges I noticed some Black Rocks; and in the course of my ride among the Hills I saw some very pretty flowers, a Small herd of Goats, a Hare, a Hawk, a Dog Town, several Buzzards, several Wolves, and two bea[u]tiful Water Birds resembling somewhat in shape & manner what we commonly call The Plover, but larger & nearly White. I also saw some Killdeers, and a small species of Hawk that is peculiar to the Dog Towns in which they reside. In one of those Towns I saw several large Rattlesnakes. I spent nearly an Hour in one of them, which is more than a league Square, I think, observing its curious Inhabitants. The Prairie Dog, as it is called from its barking like a Puppy, is about the size & colour of a Rabbit but resembles more the Gray Squirrel in other particulars. It burrows in the ground to a great depth, lives on grass, and in pairs.

They are very wild and difficult to catch or to kill, tho' I made out to shoot one this morning. What is very curious is that the Dogs, Snakes, & Hawks all occupy the same dens—at least I have frequently seen them all run into the same Holes. How they agree together I cannot tell. It is certain that the Dogs are the right proprietors; & the Snakes & Hawks are no doubt intruders, for the purpose I presume of preying on the young Dogs.

I turned in towards the River & got there at 12, where I found the company encamped on the bank,[54] Having drove today 9 Miles. At 12 the Mercury 84, at Sunset 74. The River rising fast.

Wednesday 24th August.

The Morning Cool and Hazy. Wind from the South. Mercury 70 at 7. River falling.

We left camp at 25 Min[utes] past 8. Kept up in the River bottom about 2 Miles, and passed a large Island thickly timbered with Cotton Wood, called the Pit Grove. We passed a few Scattering Trees below this; and above, the River is distinctly marked by those Trees as far as we can see. The Arkansas bottom now becomes much more confined on the No[rth] side, by the great dividing ridge Noticed yesterday; which is here about 3 Miles from the River. We continued onward, and at 12, got to The Walnut Creek, called 6 miles above the Pit Grove.

We crossed the Creek at a good ford, not far from the mouth, and camped on the bank in a Bend, among some Scattering Walnuts and Elms, where we found very excellent pasturage and plenty of fuel. The Creek is about 20 Yards wide. Water clear & good, and plenty. Distance traveled today 8 Miles & 25 Chains—the Road very good all the way.

Thursday 25th August.

The morning fair & pleasant. Busy all day writing and gathering seeds. Buffalo passing all day near camp—several fat ones killed. At a short distance from camp, the men get great quantities of very fine Plums. Horses doing very well here. We intend to stay several days. The day generally cloudy & warm. John Walker lost his Horse, saddle & blankets. He ran off with a gang of Buffalo.

Friday 26th August.

Morning Hazy & Cloudy. Cleared off at 9, & proved a fine day tho' very Warm. Busy Writing all day. Many of the Men out killing Buffalo.

The Latitude of this place ascertained to be 38°-21'-10". The distance as measured from Ft. Osage is 299 Miles. It is South 57 Miles & West 244 Miles from Ft. O[sage]. The direct course from Ft. O[sage] to W[alnut] Creek is South 77° West and the distance on that course air measure is 250 Miles. At 12 o'Clk. today the Mercury stood at 86— at 10 P. M. it was at 76.

Saturday 27th August.

Very fine morning. After early Breakfast Mr. Brown, Mr. Gamble & myself set out on an excursion Northward, over the Ridge, to ascertain the relative position of the Kansas & Arkansas Rivers which are laid down on the Maps as coming close together at this point. Mr. B[rown] took his Instruments with him to get the Latitude. Capt. Cooper and Williams accompanied us. We rode North about 3 Miles, and ascended the Ridge—then over the ridge ab[ou]t 1½ Mile same course, and descended into an extensive low flat Prairie [Cheyenne Bottoms] through which [we] continued about 4 Miles, passing through a marsh half a mile across, & came to a Small Creek running South East, towards a Large Lake which is seen about 2 Miles off in that direction. We continued on the same course, after crossing the Creek, for about a Mile, and came to a large Pond [northern body of marsh], then we turned more westward, and in a short distance came to the Same Creek [Deception Creek] again at a Bend. Coursed the Creek upward in a direction about No[rth] W[est] by W[est] half a Mile, then turned off nearly West ¼ Mile, and came to a Creek [Blood Creek] having some Ash timber on it. These two Creeks lose themselves in the Marsh through which we passed. The Marsh drains itself into the Large Lake, and it is probable (as William asserts) that the Smoky Hill Fork receives a principal supply of Water from this Lake.[55] The Creek we are now on is but small, not over 15 yds. Wide. Its banks are high, and though there is but little Water in it at present, it runs briskly; and from the great piles of Heavy drift Wood seen along its Banks, I should judge it to be a pretty long & at times a considerable Stream. It is very much inferior however to the River laid down on the Maps as the Smoky Hill Fork. I am inclined to believe that there is still another and a Larger stream a few Miles farther North, beyond a High Ridge just by—but the day is so excessively Hot that I Shall decline any further Search at this time. It is certain that the Creek [Blood Creek] we are now on is a branch of the Kansas River,* & the nearest of any other to the Arkansas. Mr. Brown got the Latitude with tolerable precision, which is 38°-30'-29"—so that the distance across from this Creek to the Arkansas is 10¾ Miles

The Mercury was up to 88 at 12. We staid in the shade about 2 Hours, and then set out on our return to camp. We rode up the Creek about 2 Miles—then crossed it and traveled about South West, nearly 2 Miles, thro' a level dry Bottom—then ascended a High Ridge [North of Great Bend], then pursued our course down a very gently inclined Plane, about 4 Miles to the Walnut Creek, which we find rising very fast. We kept down the Creek about 8 Miles, and arrived at Camp just at sunset having traveled today nearly 30 Miles. The Creek was nearly swimming & rising very fast. Current swift, Water muddy, Drift wood passing. As far as I have been able to examine this Creek today, it has a thin growth of Ash, Walnut, Elm, & Box Elder & Cotton Wood Timber all along its banks. A Mr. [Nathaniel Miguel] Pryor[56] arrived at our camp today, with three other Men, on their way to New New Mexico on a Trapping expedition. They came up the Arkansas from Cantonment Gibson.

Sunday 28th August.

There fell a very heavy rain last night accompanied with high wind. We got everything wet in the Tents. The morning fair but very Warm —Mercury 74 at 9. After getting our baggage dried, which was not effected till 12 o'Clock, we struck our Camp at 1 P. M. and moved onward. Traveled over a rough and uneven bottom, near the River 6 Miles & 78 Chains, and halted on the bank [in vicinity of Great Bend]

* "Not so certain as since ascent. It may be the 'Cold Water' Creek." [Sibley's note.]

for the Night. The Timber of Walnut Creek, a southern fork, appears in sight all the way at about 3 Miles distance from the River. The day very Hot. The Mercury 88 at 12.

Monday 29th August.

The morning very clear and Warm. The River pretty full & rising. At 7 the Mercury stood at 72. After breakfast, we started at 45 Min[utes] past 8. Traveled over very rough & uneven ground, through the bottom, very much cut up with wet slashes. The Grass is rough and coarse and very much overrun with Weeds. The Walnut Creek still appears in sight, and is about 5 Miles from the Arkansas. At half past 12 we halted on a small Creek [Ash Creek], near its mouth, having measured today 10 Miles and 46 Chains. The water clear & good in the Creek, but no timber to be seen on it. At 1 P. M. the Mercury was at 88. Buffalo very numerous.

Tuesday 30th August.

The morning clear cool and pleasant, a fine air stir[r]ing. The Creek very high, & still rising, the water very muddy & filthy.

After Breakfast at 30 Min[utes] past 8, we all started. The Waggons and most of the Party kept up the River Bottom. Mr. Gamble and myself rode out upon the high Prairie. We first rode nearly north about a mile to a remarkable Rocky Point [Pawnee Rock] which projects into the Bottom from a High Ridge; these Rocks are very large and of a glossy Black colour; Towards the River, the face is nearly perpendicular. We rode upon the top which is probably 50 feet above the plain below, and from whence there is a charming view of the country in every direction. After we had sufficiently gratified our curiosity here, we proceeded Northward across several Ridges, about two miles farther, and came in full view of an immense level flat. We halted to note the beautiful prospect that here presented itself. The Walnut Creek we Saw distinctly mapped below us. We could see that it forks, and that both principal forks run from the West, the southern one rather from So[uth] W[est] so that the whole appearance of the Creek here is somewhat like a Semicircle. Mr. G[amble] and I went down through

71

the Valley steering a little more West to the Creek which we crossed, and stopped a couple of hours in the Shade of Some Trees, having rode about 10 Miles about No[rth] 45 W[est] from the Camp we started from. We then rode 2 Miles up between the forks; then crossed the Southern one, and steered So[uth] W[est] about 3 Miles then more South 2 Miles and came in sight of a long string of Timber stretching from So[uth] W[est] to No[rth] E[ast], which proves to be the Creek that we left this morning. This we reached about 10 Miles above where we camped last Night, and coursed it down 'till we found the company camped on the North Bank, it being too full to cross the Waggons today. The distance measured today is only 7 M[iles] & 60 Ch[ain]s. The Rocky point is still in plain view about 5 miles to the Eastward. This Creek is extremely Crooked, and well deserves the name we have given it "Crooked Creek" [Ash Creek]. As far as I could see up it, there is Timber—and this is also the case with all the branches of Walnut Creek.

We saw a great many Buffalo today, several Horses, and a variety of other Smaller Game.

Wednesday 31st August.

The morning cool and cloudy and Windy. The principal timber of this & the Walnut Creek, where I saw them yesterday, is Ash, Elm, Box Elder & Cotton. The Creek having run down so that the Waggons can cross, we Set off again after Breakfast at half past 8. Our way was over rather broken Prairie, and at a greater distance from the River than we usually Travel. At half past 10 we reached the Pawnee fork, and camped on the bank, a little below the fording place, at Some large Elm Trees, having measured from the last camp 6 M[ile]s & 56 Ch[ain]s. A heavy rain fell while we were on the road. The Creek appears to be too full now to venture to cross it with the Waggons; besides the banks require some digging at the ford. Here we have a beautiful camping place, & very fine range for the Horses.

Thursday 1t September.

The morning cloudy and cool. Mercury 68 at 8 o'Clock. The Pawnee River is here about 40 yards wide, banks pretty high, bottom sandy,

Water at present Muddy. Timber Elm, Ash, Elder, Cotton Tree, Willow, and Grape Vines. Yesterday I turned off from the direct course and struck the Arkansas at the mouth of this River, and then coursed it up about a Mile to the fording place near which we are now encamped,[57] which is just at the foot of a high rocky Hill. The path leading up from the mouth to the ford passes between the Pawnee and some Cliffs of Soft Rock, upon the smooth faces of which are cut the names of many Persons, who have at different times passed this way to and from New Mexico. Some Indian marks are also to be seen on these Rocks. This ford of Pawnee River is 31 Miles from Walnut Creek, & 330 from Ft. Osage. The direct course from Ft. Osage is South 74 West.

Apprehending more Rain and fearing to be detained here by high water, we set to work cutting down the Banks, and preparing the ford for the Waggons to cross. We got all safe over without any accident or much difficulty by 11 o'Clk. and then proceeded South West through a flat bottom about 6 Miles, and came to a High Ridge. The Waggons passed round the point, still keeping in the bottom about half a mile from the River. I rode upon the Ridge, from the top of which, I could distinctly trace the course of the Pawnee River for a great distance by the fringe of Trees along its banks. Its general course as far as I could see is from So[uth] W[est] to No[rth] E[ast]. It runs nearly parallel with the Arkansas at an average distance of about Six Miles apart, gradually diverging.

The traveling today is pretty good. There is no interruption along the River Bottom, except one little muddy Creek that intervenes about 3 Miles above the crossing of Pawnee Creek [Saw Mill Creek]. The Grass is very good, but Buffalo are scarce, which seems to indicate the recent presence of Indians, tho' we have not discovered any *other* Signs of any. I presume that some of the Pawnees and Recaras may have been in this quarter not long since, this being the usual Summer Resort of those People particularly the Pawnees. But it is more than probable I think, that they have now all returned to their Villages to gather their Corn &c.

We encamped on a Small Creek near its mouth affording plenty of good Water & fine grass. We call it Clear Creek [Big Coon Creek, near Garfield] from the quality of its water. The distance traveled today as measured is 11 Miles.

Friday 2d. September.

It rained nearly all night and continued to rain nearly all this day. We staid in camp, and spent an uncomfortable day—the Mercury about 65 all day. At night the Horses all took fright & ran furiously into camp. The cause could not be ascertained, tho' it was probably a Wolf or a Buffalo.

Saturday 3d September.

A very fine clear cool Morning. The Mercury 62 at 7. After drying our Baggage, we struck our Tents and moved on at 10 Min[utes] past 9. The Waggons still kept along in the bottom. I rode off more Westward upon the high Ridges, from some of which, I again had a good view of the Pawnee fork, which still appears to run from So[uth] W[est] to No[rth] E[ast]. It is here about 10 Miles from the Arkansas. Before I left the River Bottom, I passed over an extensive tract near the foot of the Ridge, a little elevated above the flat bottom, containing perhaps a thousand Acres or more; all over which, I observed piles of coarse gravel and hard stones, some of the latter as large as Hen's Eggs. These were thrown out by the Prairie Dogs and Ants. The surface of this Tract is generally a tolerably Rich sandy loam producing very good grass. I have frequently seen the same appearances in the Bottom before; and the banks of the Arkansas often present the very Same kinds of Gravel & Stones, some 18 or 20 Inches below the Surface. The Highland seen today is *waving* as 'tis called—being a Succession of Ridges, running irregularly, some of which present themselves with abrupt steep points upon the River bottom.

The Arkansas still keeps its width of from 400 to 500 yards, and in other respects is very much as where we first saw it—with the exception of its being better furnished with Timber. Its course can now be traced distinctly for a great distance, by the few scattering Cotton Trees (there are no other) that are Scattered along its Banks & upon its little Islands; and this is the case all the way from about 20 Miles below the Walnut

Creek. Since we crossed the Pawnee fork, the appearance of the country on the south side of the Arkansas is much more rough and hilly, and in general the Hills are closer to the River on both sides. I saw six Wild Horses today on the high Prairie & shot at them, but without effect. Buffalo are scarce; tho' our Hunters manage to kill a sufficiency of fine fat Cows for the company. At 2 P. M. the Mercury was at 80. I then turned in to the River, and found the Party encamped on the Bank. In passing from the Hills to the River through the bottom, I crossed the Clear Creek twice. It is a very pretty, brisk running Creek. Williams who has been hunting today over the River came in just as Sunset with a fat Elk. The distance measured today is 11 Miles & 68 Chains.

Sunday 4th September.

Morning clear & cool and windy—the Wind from the South. Mercury 66 at 7.

Started the Waggons at 10 M[inutes] past 9. Traveled up the River pretty nearly by its course, in the bottom. High Hills and Nobs on the opposite side, some of which are of loose naked Sand. The Hills on the North side are about 3 Miles from the River. The Clear Creek runs down through the bottom about midway between the Hills and the River. I saw and Crossed it frequently during my Zig Zag ride today; it still appears brisk & *flush* and its water clear & good. Its bed gravelly in many places. The Waggons kept along between the Creek and the River—road good. The Bottom is very much the same where we traveled today as usual, as respects soil and Grass &c. The River is also nearly the same in its width, depth and general appearance. Several very fat cows killed today, and an Elk and a Deer also killed, these latter are but rarely seen in these rejions [sic]. Our Men kill daily as much fine beef as would Subsist an army. And yet Buffalo are, comparatively, very scarce where we are now traveling. Halted and encamped on the River bank—distance today 12 M[ile]s 28 Ch[ain]s.

Monday 5th September.

Morning clear, calm & sultry. Mercury 76 at 8. Started at 9. I rode out to the Hills about 3 Miles, and then kept along upon the high

Prairie, nearly parallel with the River about 10 Miles, and returned to the River in the evening. The country not much broken, but very pretty. I saw several Horses and Goats & many Buffalo.

From the High Ridges I could see the Sand Hills on the other side of the River. Some of them are quite large, & some quite naked. These when the sun shone bright on them looked like so many Pillars of fire. Distance measured today 12 Miles and 27 Chains.

Tuesday 6th September.

A severe Storm of Wind and Rain last night—the morning clear & very windy—the Mercury 65 at 7 o'Clk. We started at 9. I again left the company and rode out upon the High Prairie, but saw nothing today worthy of notice, except some chalky looking Rocks. After riding about 5 Miles over the broken Hills, excessively annoyed by the wind, I turned down into the River bottom, and went to the River at a Remarkable Rocky Point or Cliff on the North Side [opposite Ford], close to which the River runs. About 2 Miles above this, I fell in with the Waggons, encamped on the River bank nearly opposite the Mouth of a Creek which enters the Arkansas on the south side, known by the name of Mulberry Creek. The distance measured today is only 4 Miles and 55 Chains.

Wednesday 7th September.

The morning calm and pleasant. Mercury from 50 to 89 between 6 & 12. Staid in camp all day. We are in a small bottom almost encircled by Hills on the North Side—the Pasturage very good & fuel plenty. Our Camp is in the extreme South bend of the River—Latitude 37°-38'-52", Longitude about 99° agreeably to Mr. Brown's calculations and measurement. Distance south 107⅛ Miles. West 300½ from Ft. Osage. The distance as measured & traveled is 383 Miles. General course South 70¼ West, and the distance upon that course 314 Miles from Ft. Osage. Distance lost by circuitous travel 79 Miles.

Thursday 8th September.

Very warm morning—fair and calm. Being so near the boundary line now, where we must wait for further Instructions from our Gov[ernmen]t, we are in no haste to move on very fast, especially as the Weather is very Warm, our Horses tired and poor and Several of them actually given out. As the Grass is Still good here, we will remain at this camp 'till tomorrow. Game is Scarce around here, but we manage to kill sufficient. The River is about 350 yards wide here, very Shallow, & full of very small Islands. The country opposite pretty level.

Mulberry Creek runs from the South West. It is said to be very short, not over 20 Miles, & its head branches interlock with those of the Grand Saline [Branch of Cimarron] which runs parallel with the Arkansas about 30 Miles from it at this point. At least such is the report of two of our Men who have been across there.

Friday 9th September.

The morning cool and pleasant. Raised our camp & started onward at 10 o'Clk. Proceeded up the river 12 Miles and 33 Chains, and halted on the bank at a point where the Hills close in upon the River, just at the mouth of a Ravine or small drain.[58] The River is wider here than just below, & has many small Islands. The Prairie opposite & for several miles below is low and flat. We were obliged to leave one of the Horses this Morning, Lame, tired, poor and Sick.

Saturday 10th September.

The morning cool and fair and very windy. Started at 10 minutes past 10. We proceeded up the Bottom, which still continues to get narrower on the North side—the River full of small islands on some of the largest of which are a few Cotton Trees.

We had rode about 10 Miles, when we came to a large Mass of Gravel Rock of a very remarkable appearance. It presents itself at the termination of a High Ridge and faces the River from which it is about a Mile; a level flat intervening. Its front is rough & broken, & about 200 yards in extent. To judge from appearances, one might suppose that the Arkansas once washed the base of this Rock; but this would involve the supposition that the present bed of the River has been sunk by some convulsion of nature not less than Fifty feet—to justify which, I could discover nothing. The Rock as it is seen at the Bluff is in large

Masses, which are composed of small Gravel Stones and Sand firmly cemented together.[59] These stones when separated generally appear firmly polished, like those found in the beds of Rivers. They are in great varieties as to Colour, Size and Substance. In the mixture there is evidently Lime.

We passed this curious Rock, and then Shaped our course South West over Wet Prairie to the River, and Pitched our Tents on the Bank, just below a high Bluff Bank [3 miles beyond Caches], which is near Some Cotton Trees. The wind very boisterous all day. Distance measured 13 Miles & 13 Chains.

Sunday 11th September.

Morning clear & cool. I left camp early on foot. Walked out to the Bluff about half a Mile, and then coursed it upward about two Miles to where there is a High chalky & gravelly Bluff, the foot of which is washed by the River. The Waggons were obliged to turn out into the High Prairie, and go round a considerable distance to get past this rugged Bluff and several deep Hollows and Ravines; Altogether, I believe this is the worst piece of Road we have had since we left Ft. Osage. It was not very long however, and we soon got round into the River Bottom again, and traveled up through a narrow slashy bottom about 3 Miles and camped on the Bank of the River opposite an Island of 4 or 5 Acres in extent. Distance today 7 Miles & 55 Chains.

We have now arrived at the Point where by Mr. Brown's measurement, and observations, he supposes the 100th degree of West Longitude will Strike the Arkansas—and from which upward, the Arkansas River is the boundary line between The United States and Mexico.[60]

Mr. Brown has no other means of ascertaining the Longitude than with a single Sextant, and by the result of his measurement and survey from Ft. Osage, which place is assumed as being Longitude 93°-51'-5". It is certain however, that there is some inaccuracy in the chaining, and probably some also in the running of the Assistant Surveyor. Mr. Brown attempted to ascertain this matter more exactly by observations, but could not Succeed to his satisfaction, by reason of bad weather, and the obvious uncertainty of succeeding in any such attempt with the

Sextant. The *Uniform* result of all his observations seems to prove that the Survey is somewhat defective; and fixes the 100th degree of Longitude about *Forty* Miles lower down the River than this Point, not far from the extreme south Bend, near which, I believe Major Long fixes it.

We have not yet tresspassed [sic] however upon the Mexican Territory, let the Line be where it may; & we may continue our Survey forty Miles farther up the River, within our own Territory, before we arrive at the usual place of Crossing.

Grass and fuel being good and plentiful here, we determine to remain a few days at any rate. We must in fact wait somewhere in this neighborhood for the additional Instructions that we expect, to authorise us to continue the Road through The Mexican Territory, and this is probably as good a place as we can find.

Monday 12th September.

A fine Morning. Sent out two parties of Hunters, one on each Side of the River, to secure as much Beef as possible from several Herds of Buffalo that are grazing not far off; and which will no doubt be at a great distance soon. It is necessary now to lay in a good supply of meat.

Tuesday 13th September.

Very fine day. Mr. Brown fixes the Latitude of this place at 37°-47'-37". The distance measured from Ft. Osage is 418 Miles—the general Course from that place to this is Southwest and the Straight distance upon that course is [——] Miles. We are now 97½ Miles South and 331½ West from Ft. Osage.

Wednesday 14th September.

There being some contrariety of opinion among the Commissioners, as to the most proper course now to be pursued by them, They met by my Suggestion this morning as a Board for business, Col. Reeves presiding. The first matter decided was that We will not proceed any farther with the Survey 'till we receive further instructions and authority. Upon this point, I differed in opinion with Cols. Reeves & Mather. I thought that we might Safely proceed with the Survey without any violation of our Instructions, or of the Mexican Sovereignty; tho' I did not believe we could properly go on to *Mark* the Road, without further orders from our Government. My opinion was that we Should remain here or in this neighborhood recruiting our Horses and laying in a Sufficient supply of Dried Beef, 'till the 1st of October, unless Instructions reached us sooner—and that on that day, we should proceed, with about twenty Men & four Waggons (The rest to be sent back to Missouri and discharged) to New Mexico, and there remain untill Spring; and that we should survey and measure, and examine, as heretofore we have done from Ft. Osage. I had made estimates and calculations as to expense, and was satisfied that this plan would be the least expensive, and that the whole work would be soonest completed. My colleagues could not agree with me however as to continuing the Survey of the Road; so they decided this question as above stated. Col. Mather agreed with me that we should wait 'till the 1st day of October if necessary. Col. Reeves thought it would be hazardous to wait so long; that if we did the Winter would overtake us before we could either reach the Settlements of Missouri or New Mexico. His opinion was that we should return home after the 15th, tho' he would consent to wait 'till the 20th if necessary. It was decided for the present, that we will wait here 'till the 20th. I was opposed altogether to returning, in any event 'till the Road was completed; and gave notice that I should propose at the next meeting (which was agreed to be on the 17th) that the Commissioners Should go on to S[an]ta Fee with a part of the Men & Waggons and Winter there, sending back to Missouri, to be there discharged, the rest of the Men &c. It was not meant that any survey should be made through the Mexican Territory, upon this new proposition.

Thursday 15th September.

The weather still continues good. The Hunters are not very Successful. Spent the day writing, reading & walking.

Friday 16th September.

Another very fine day, which I spent as I did yesterday. The River here is ab[ou]t 50 yards including Islands which are numerous, on one of which there is excellent pasturage, and our Horses are kept there during the day.

Saturday 17th September.

A very fine morning. At 10 The Commissioners formed a board for business, Col. Reeves presiding. I then moved that we come to the following Resolution to Wit—That we wait here or in this neighbourhood, 'till the 26th Inst. and that if no additional instructions arrive by that time that we will proceed to Santa Fee with a part of the Men and Waggons for Winter quarters; and that the other part be sent back to Missouri; the Men discharged, the Waggons secured, and the Horses provided for, or Sold. This proposition was accompanied with some very minute estimates and calculations that I had prepared with great care and upon good data; all going to Shew that the fund already at our disposal would be sufficient to meet all the expenses and to complete the Work about two Months sooner than if we return home again from this place.

I had prepared a brief written argument upon this point which I read—this I done, because I was perfectly convinced that the Plan I proposed was by far better and every way more proper than the one advocated by Col. Reeves to return home, and having good reason to believe that Col. Mather would vote with Col. Reeves, I deemed it proper that the record should contain not only my proposition, but my reasons for urging it. At the request of Col. Mather, the Question was divided, and then upon his motion, the decision on that part which proposes to wait 'till the 26th was postponed 'till the 20th. And then the other part of my proposition was negatived. At my request, my reasons for urging the plan I proposed were ordered to be entered at large upon the Journal.

Mr. Pryor who has been in company with us since we left Walnut Creek, and has waited here in the expectation that we would proceed to N[ew] Mexico, being apprised of the above resolution, intends to go on tomorrow. Two of our Men (Dedmon and West)[61] having a desire to accompany Mr. Pryor, asked permission to quit our service and they were allowed to do so, paid off and discharged.

I wrote to Mr. Paul Baillio[62] at San Fernando in Taos and enclosed him a letter that Mr. E. Bates put into my hands at St. Louis addressed to *Augustus Storrs,*[63] enclosing as I was informed, a commission &c. as Consul of U. S. at Santa Fee. This Letter I desired Mr. Baillio to convey to Mr. Storrs as soon as possible. I sent Mr. Baillio all the Newspapers that I brought with me from home.

Sunday 18th September.

Another very fine morning. River continues falling a little. Our Horses appear to be recruiting. They have nearly eaten out the Range here, and we intend to move a Mile lower down this evening, to where the Grass is better. Pryor & his Party, Six in all, started this morning upon their journey.

After dinner we broke up our camp, and moved down the River about a Mile, and encamped. Two parties of Hunters have been out today, but none of them killed anything. We are now entirely out of Meat.

Monday 19th September.

It rained nearly all last Night, and is raining this Morning. Several Hunters went out but were all unsuccessful. River still falling. The day was cold and rainy throughout.

Tuesday 20th September.

The morning fair and cool. At 9 the Commissioners met as a Board for business, Col. Reeves presiding. We have waited now 'till the 20th agreeably to the resolution adopted on the 14th and It becomes necessary to decide, whether we will wait any longer (and how long) or proceed immediately homeward. My own opinion was that we ought to wait 'till the 1st of Octo[ber] and Col. Mather appeared to think so too. Col. Reeves thought we had already waited long enough, if not too long; he again expressed his apprehensions, that go which way we would, the winter would catch us out. I was very desirous myself that some plan should be adopted that would be approved by us all; and to that end I proposed the following—That one of The Commissioners should proceed immediately to Santa Fee to Winter, taking with him The Surveyor, Interpreter and nine men, with two of the Waggons, a sufficient number of the Horses & such of the Goods and Stores as may be deemed advisable.

I considered this as a modification of my former propositions, and as it was agreed on all hands that it will be extremely desirable for the Commissioners to know something of the country between this point & the frontier of New Mexico before they can locate properly that portion of the Road already surveyed, I urged again the expediency of the measure, and shewed by fair calculations that we had the pecuniary means. After some considerable discussion (during which it was agreed that the proceedings on the 17th should be entirely annuled, and not put upon the Record) the above proposition was agreed to without objection and adopted. And I was designated by my Colleagues to go to Santa Fee, and to make Selection of nine men, two Waggons & 19 Horses, and such Goods & Stores as I thought proper. It was then decided that Cols. Reeves & Mather Should tomorrow set out on their return to Missouri, with the rest of the Party—and then the Board rose. I should have mentioned, that it was previously arranged, that Cols. Reeves & Mather are to join me at Santa Fee, as early as they can next summer (if the whole road is to be completed) that I am to wait for them 'till the 1st of July, and then if I hear nothing from them or the Gov[ernmen]t. to justify any longer delay, I am to return to Missouri as soon as I can. Having arranged all these matters satisfactorily, I Set about making preparations for my journey. I selected my Men, Waggons & Horses, packed up such of the Goods and Stores as I needed, Selected Some of the Tools, and put up a part of the Rice & flour &c.

Wednesday 21st September.

A very fine day. After dinner, the returning party Struck their Tents, and took leave of me. They intend to go 8 or 10 Miles to the Hunters who were sent out in advance early in the morning. I remained in camp the remainder of the day, arranging the loading for the Waggons, and having some of the Horses Shod &c. Mr. Gamble staid behind also, and intends to remain with Mr. Brown and I tonight, & overtake his company in the Morning. I shall write some Letters tonight to my Wife & others, & put in Mr. G's hands to deliver. I find that my two Waggons are full heavily laden; but I must now go on with them. As the weather is cool & the Horses fresh, I mean to push on pretty briskly, with the view of getting 100 Miles or so on my journey in this Month.

Before I parted from Cols. Reeves & Mather, we drew & signed joint Bills of Ex[change] on The Sec[retar]y of War for $15,000—to say one of $2000, one of $3000, one of $4000 and one of $6000, to be disposed of by Messrs. Reeves & Mather, as may be requisite.

Thursday 22d September.

I sat up very late last Night writing letters home to my Wife and friends. I made up a Packet of Seeds of many different sorts that I had collected in the Prairies, consisting of Flowers chiefly, and sent them by Mr. Gamble to Mrs. S[ibley] together with a number of Letters. A very fine morning. I directed preparation for an early Start, but we could not get ready 'till 9 o'clock. Mr. Gamble took leave of us after Breakfast, and Set out on his return to join his company. My Party consisting of Mr. Brown, Surveyor—Wm. S. Williams, Interpreter and Hunter—Benjamin Jones, Richard Brannin, Bradford Barbee, Benjamin Robinson, Singleton Vaughn, John Walker, Jo. Reynolds, Bird Pyles and John S. Davis, and my Servant Abram, in all 13 persons, with two Waggons and 19 Horses remained in camp. As soon as it was determined that I was to go to Santa Fee, I dispatched Williams on a good Horse, to overtake Pryor and his Party, and let them know that I was coming on, and if they chose to wait till I overtook them, they might have the benefit of traveling in company &c. Williams returned last night, & reported that he had gone about 50 Miles, up the River, to a fording place[64]—that Pryor had crossed there the day before. He went on his track a few Miles farther, but seeing nothing of him, thought best to turn back. He says the Buffalo are numerous above.

At 15 Minutes past 9, everything was in readiness and we set forward, all in good health and fine Spirits. We traveled up in the bottom about two Miles, and then Struck out into the High Prairie, and proceeded upon a general course of No[rth] 75 W[est], over very Smooth and level ground, at an average distance of about a Mile from the Arkansas. The soil is poor, grass very short & wiry, Prickly Pears very abundant and troublesome. Water plenty in Ponds. We saw many large herds of Buffalo today, and the Hunters killed three fat cows in the evening, near the place we halted at to camp, on the Bank of the River.

Grass & fuel good & plenty. Distance traveled today is 15 Miles according to the best estimate we can make, by the Watch & gait of my Horse.[65]

Friday 23d September.

Morning fair and cool. Started at 8 o'clock. Kept up the River bottom 3 Miles, and then turned out to the High Prairie, which we find very much the same as that yesterday, except that it is more uneven and cut up in Gullies, some of which obliged the Waggons to go a good deal out of the course. Buffalo more and more numerous, as we advance. In the evening when we had turned in to the River to find a camping place, We met a large Caravan of our People just from S[an]ta Fee, which place they left about the 1st of Sept[embe]r.[66] There were about 80 persons in this company, & they had about 300 head of Horses, Mules, Asses, &c. & some Beaver Skins. I Bo[ugh]t a Horse from a Mr. Mitchell for $30. Distance today 15 Miles. No[rth] 75 W[est].

Saturday Sept. 24.

Upon the report of the Party we met yesterday that we shall find Buffalo scarce upon our route, I deemed it proper to remain here today and jerk a supply of meat to take along. Some of the men were therefore set to building scaffolds, some slicing up Beef, some bringing Wood, &c. All were busily employed to the best advantage, & at Night I found that we had about 500 lbs. of very Nice fat Beef perfectly well cured, besides two days supply of half cured. The weather has been very fine & favorable since the 22d. Mr. Brown here took some observations tonight for the Latitude, which he fixes for this spot at 37°-54'-9''.[67]

Sunday Sept. 25.

Very fine morning. At ½ past 8 we started, but had scarcely gone 100 yds. before Capt. Brannin one of the Waggoners, broke his Waggon tongue short off. All hands were instantly Set to work to repair this mishap, Some getting Buffalo tugs, some splinters &c. & we succeeded in mending the tongue perfectly strong and secure, & were again under way at 5 M[inutes]. past 10. The River bottom afforded us good enough Road today & we kept in it. At 4 o'Clk. we crossed the Arkansas River,[68] and for the first time entered the Mexican Territory; and then proceeded up the river over a sandy & sterile Plain 2 Miles, and halted on the Bank, near an old Indian camping ground; where we found good grass & fuel. Distance today 16 Miles. Vizt. No. 55 W. 4 M[iles]—No. 80 W. 10 M[iles] to the crossing place of the Arkansas then West 2 Miles up the river to camp.

Monday 26th Sept.

The Morning fair & pleasant tho' rather warm. Started at 45 M[inutes]. past 8. Our route lay over a level sterile plain—soil sandy, intermixed with coarse Hard gravel—grass dry & hard—in some places thickly set with a kind of fragrant herb. Near the River are banks of loose sand, & all along the river is blocked up with small Islands, having on them some Cotton Trees of pretty good growth, & generally good grass. The Plain is more extensively level than where we passed yesterday. At 5 P. M. We arrived with the Waggons at a remarkable point on the River at an Island known as Chouteau's Island,[69] nearly opposite the head of which on the North Side is a high Nob or Mound standing on the declivity of the high ridge, which cannot fail to be readily identified, as it is seen from a great distance, & as there is nothing like it on the river for 200 Miles below. In a Hollow, just below this Mound, same side of the River, is a small clump of green Trees & out in the Plain, South side about 2 Miles from this point, are to be seen 2 Solitary green Trees in the direction nearly South. Our camp is under some large Cotton Trees, opposite the lower point of the Island, and at the upper end of a small grove of Timber (among which are some large Willows) on the South Side of the River, just at the remains of an old log pen or Indian fortification. On a large Cotton Tree where my Tent stood, one of the Men marked *"480 Miles from Ft. Osage."* At this place is most excellent pasturage & fuel. The Latitude as ascertained by a very good observation of Aquilae is 37°-53'-18". Distance today So[uth] 67 W[est] 17 Miles.

Tuesday 27 Sept.

The morning fair & cool & windy. At 35 M[inutes] past 8 we resumed our journey, And as we now take our departure from The Arkansas,

& must find our way thro' the Sand Hills, of which such fearful stories have been told, and then strike over to the Semerone, I shall take every possible pains to take notes for a correct chart of our route. First then, we steered South 5 West, over a sandy and gravelly plain, and at the distance of two Miles came to the Sand Hills, at a Slight hollow about ¼ Mile East of the Easternmost Green Tree. Then we went one Mile South 22 East, to some old standing dead Trees. To get to these dead Trees, the Waggons varied a trifle East of the direct course in order to fall into a Valley which leads to them thro' a large level flat of extremely rich Soil containing about 250 Acres. From the dead Trees, our route lay thro' a sort of winding Valley, upon a general course of South 30 West 1½ Mile, passing a Pond of Water about midway & arriving opposite some green Trees, which stand some 200 yds. to our right. Leaving these green Trees to our right, we pursued the Valley South 10 West 3 Miles farther (passing another Pond of Water) and arrived at the termination of the Sand Hills & found ourselves upon a most extensive level Plain. The winding track through them here, being only 5½ Miles, Our Waggons found no difficulty whatever in getting thro' this pass, as the road is generally hard and level. I observed in this Valley or pass Several spots of good grass, and the Hillocks of Sand are all covered with grass, Weeds, Prickly Pears &c. I saw none entirely naked, nor any very high. I remarked several thrifty bunches of the common Garden Pursley growing in the Valley. So much for *this* Bugbear. We now have to strike across the great Plain before us, for the Semerone.[70] Report has also made a Bugbear of this route. After some consultation with two of our Men who had once crossed over to the Semerone from the Arkansas (passing the Sands lower down) Mr. Brown & I determined to steer due South,[71] and upon that course we set out and traveled 2 Miles, which brought us to a string of deep Ponds of excellent sweet Water. Upon the bank of one we Pitched our Tents for the Night. The day was pleasant. Our courses & distances as follow— So. 5 W. 2 Miles—So. 22 E. 1 Mile—So. 30 W. 1½ Mile—So. 10 W. 3 Miles—South 2 Miles.

Wednesday 28th Sept.

Morning fair, cool, & Windy. Started at 30 M[inutes] past 7, and steered due South. We traveled over a most beautiful plain, so perfectly smo[o]th that the Waggons were as easily drawn over it as they could be over a Bowling green. The Soil is poor however, producing tolerable grass only here and there, it is all thickly set however with short grass. Passed some more Ponds soon after we left camp, and after we had gone 12 Miles came to a small creek [North Fork of Cimarron], the water standing in Pools. Its course when running is to the Eastward & runs into The Semerone. 12 Miles farther, we struck the Semerone just below what is called the lower Spring. We were detained butchering a Buffalo Cow that I shot right on the road, so that the waggons did not get to camp till dark. Here we found the Water & pa[s]turage exceedingly fine. The Creek Water is brackish, & makes a sort of Salt Meadow of a great part of the level flat watered by it.

Thus it turns out, that from the southern extremity of the Sands where we passed them, it is 26 Miles due South to the famous Semerone Spring, over a most excellent road, & that the greatest distance without water is 12 Miles. The day was tolerably cool, but rendered very unpleasant by a strong and unceasing South wind.

Courses & distances today, South 12 Miles to 12 M[ile] Creek, & then South 12 M[iles] to Sem[erone] Spring.[72] Latitude of the Spring 37°-24'-00" as well ascertained by observations of Aquilae.

Thursday 29the Sept.

Morning fair & pleasant. The Horses being much jaded by the last three days travel, we laid by here 'till after dinner that they might profit as much as they could from the very excellent pasturage that is here. At 12 Mr. B[rown]. took an observation of the sun—the result of which confirms the accuracy of that he took of Aquilae last Night; So the Lat[itude] is well fixed here at 37°-24'—. The day excessively hot. The Semerone Spring issues from a Hollow near the So[uth] E[ast] Extremity of the large Valley that it waters. The Valley is in area probably 300 acres, & is for the most part well set with good grass. A part of it is a salt marsh, so that the grazing is peculiarly fine. The

Spring, as I saw it, appeared small, probably because an immense herd of Buffalo had just been treading about it. It no doubt affords an abundant supply of Water when properly opened, as it always is when the Indians camp near it. Its water is cool, sweet and good.

We set out upon our journey up The Semerone at 25 M[inutes] past 3, intending to go only 3 or 4 Miles to some timber, where we expected to find water. We traveled up in the bed of the Creek, which we found quite dry, 2½ Miles to some old dead fallen trees, where were some puddles of putrid Water—continued one Mile farther & halted ¼ Mile to the right of the Creek in a level flat for the Night, made several attempts to obtain Water by digging in the sandy bed of the Creek, but failed to get any. The Horses suffered here for both grass & water. Courses & distances today So. 68 W. 2½ M[iles]—So. 40 W. 1 M[ile]—total dist[ance] 3½ M[iles].

Friday 30th Sept.

We started from this miserable spot at sunrise, the morning very pleasant & fair. Steered So. 47 W. out upon high level Prairie, and at the distance of 3 Miles from camp came to a Pond of pretty good Water, where the grass was also pretty good, here we halted to get Breakfast. At 45 M[inutes] past 10 we cont[inue]d our route over the high level Plain 8 Miles and then turned in to the left So. 10 E. to the Creek which we struck in a large valley, affording plenty of good Grass & running water. Dug in the Sand about 18 Inches deep & got pretty good Water, that which stands or runs on the surface is sulpherous & brackish & strongly *seasoned* with Buffalo Urine. Before we left this place, Mr. B[rown]. took the Latitude by an observation of Rigel and fixes it as 37°-14'-17''. [About 12 miles northeast of Rolla.]

Courses & distances today—So. 47 W. 11 M[iles].—So. 10 E. 1¾ M[iles].

Saturday 1t October.

The morning fair & pleasant—Mercury 70 at 9. We staid later than usual in camp this morning that the Horses may get all they can here. The heat of yesterday and bad fare the night before made them weak. In truth, nearly all the Horses are failing more or less every day, and require all our care to keep them up so as to take us through our journey. We started at 10 M[inutes]. past 9—traveled 2½ Miles over the bottom, which is Sandy & gravelly, So. 85. W. crossing the Creek twice, and ascended to the high Prairie. Then 1½ Mile further upon the same course to the high level Prairie. Then So. 56 W. 1½ Mile further— then So. 50 W. 2 Miles to an elevated Point. Thence So. 45 W. ¾ Mile —thence So. 50 W. 1 Mile—then So. 25 W. 1 Mile, down thro' the Valley to The Semerone; where we found good Water & Grass.

We kept as near the Valley of the Semerone today as we could, & our courses shew pretty nearly the winding of the Valley. We kept it on our left at an average distance of ab[ou]t. a mile & a half. It is probable however that our best route today would have been up thro' the Valley. The Semerone Creek or River exhibits so far but a poor Stream, if that can be called a stream which is only to be seen here & there in Puddles at intervals of from ½ to 1½ Mile, which intervals are of loose dry Sand.

Where we Struck it today however, find a small *rivulet* of clear running, *brackish* Water. The Stones, grass & earth adjacent [are] encrusted with a kind of Saline Substance which to the taste resembles Salts. This Substance is Seen more or less all along this Creek, the soil is strongly impregnated with it and the grass no doubt partakes more or less of the same quality. Our Horses are extremely fond of the Grass & Water both & they thrive well upon them, or no doubt would, if they had time. We generally get pretty good Water for cooking by digging Holes in the Sand. The day was Warm with strong South Wind. Courses & distances So. 85 W. 4 M[iles]—So. 56 W. 1½ M[iles]—So. 50 W. 2 M[iles]—S. 45 W. ¾ M[ile]—So. 50 W. 1 M[ile]—So. 25 W. 1 M[ile]—Total distance 10¼ Miles.

Sunday 2d October.

Early this Morning, Mr. Brown took an imperfect observation of Orionis. He was ab[ou]t 6 Minutes too late. By calculation he was able however to ascertain with tolerable accuracy the Latitude of this Camp, which he fixes at 37°-10'-7". [About 5 miles northwest of Rolla.]

There was a *very* slight shower of rain last night. The Morning was fair, calm & Warm. Mercury 52 at Sunrise. At 50 M[inutes]. past 9 we started. The Waggons went out upon the High Prairie. I traveled up the Valley, for the purpose of noticing more particularly the character of this curious Creek. First I rode So. 74 W. 6½ M[iles] to a high rocky Bluff Point on the No[rth] Side. Then So. 60 W. 3 Miles to the mouth of a brisk running branch, which enters the Creek from the North. I coursed this branch up for ab[ou]t ¾ of a Mile and came to a pretty good Spring,[73] issuing from the high bank on the West Side. This, from the *signs* near it, is a common Camping place of the Indians. I made a signal for the Waggons & party to come to me, & they arrived at the Spring at 50 M[inutes] past 3. The Grass here not very good. The Valley up which I rode today is about ¾ of a Mile wide generally; it is probably an Hundred feet below the common level of the Plain. On the North it is bounded by a range of high ridges & Sand Hills, thinly covered with broom grass & Weeds—on the South, generally by Sand Hills & Nobs. The Semerone meanders thro' this valley from side to side, and is so extremely crooked in its course that in the distance of 6½ Miles, upon a direct line, I crossed it not less than a dozen times; and in that distance the Stream was completely lost in its dry sandy bed for several intervals of nearly a Mile each. It was curious to see sometimes a brisk running stream, and then presently a long space of perfectly dry loose sand, all in the same bed. This bed or channel bears an average width of about 20 feet, the banks are low. The Surface of the Valley is various—sometimes sandy & gravelly with scattering bunches of broom grass, Weeds, &c—sometimes pretty good soil bearing a luxuriant growth of excellent Grasses of several sorts. Today I noticed particularly several flats of fertile sandy soil of several acres each in extent, covered with a *very* luxuriant crop of Bull rushes and Grass; the surface of the ground was literally encrusted over and perfectly white with the same substance noticed yesterday a specimen of which I preserved. The Waggons might have traveled up in the Valley today quite well, & would have saved several Miles if they had done So. A Warm day. At 7 Min[utes] past 7—Mr. B[rown] took the following observation of Aquilae Mer[cury] 61—Altitude 122°-38'-20''—Lati-

91

tude of the Spring Branch 37°-6'-32''. Courses & distances today So. 74 W. 6½ M[iles]—So. 60 W. 3 M[iles]—No. 45 W. ¾ M[ile]—total 10¼ Miles.

Monday 3d October.

The Morning fair & quite cool; but no frost. Mer[cury] 50 at Sunrise; the air was nevertheless sharp. Started at 20 Minutes past 6— traveled on the high bench under the Hill—first So. 60 W. ¾ Mile to a perpendicular rocky Bluff. Then So. 65 W. 2½ Miles—then So. 75 W. 2½ Miles—then So. 45 W. 1 Mile to the Semerone, where find very good Water and Grass. Total distance today 6¾ Miles.

The Horses are evidently drooping and getting tired, and it behooves us to allow them every indulgence that we can for a few days. To this end our daily journies must be shorter for some days, and completed before 12. And we will keep up in the bottom altogether that the Horses may get Water more frequently, the traveling being nearly if not quite as good as it is on the high Prairie.

The Waggons were obliged today to travel somewhat circuitously to avoid some Gullies and Sand Nobs; so that they did not get to camp till 10 oClock. Mercury 86 at 1 p. m.

The Valley not quite so Wide today as yesterday. The meadows better, and Water more frequent in the Creek & better. As we advance up the Semerone, it improves sensibly.

At 3 M[inutes]. past 7—Mr. B[rown]. took an observation of Aquilae Vizt. Mercury 66. Altitude 122°-43'-21''. Latitude 37°-4'-2''.[74]

Tuesday October 4th.

Morning cool and fair. Started at sunrise. Traveled up in the Valley today entirely & found the way very good for the Waggons. We first went West 5¼ Miles. Then So. 70 W. 2½ Miles. Then So. 43 W. ¾ Mile; and halted for the day on the Semerone—having traveled 8½ Miles today. The Valley Continues about ½ Mile Wide, grass very good, and the Creek improving; it is much more *flush,* water purer & less brackish. It is extremely Crooked, winding quite across the Valley in a Zig Zag course.

Wednesday 5th October.

A fine Morning after a boisterous Night—the air raw and piercing. Started a little after Sunrise—continued up the Valley So. 42 W. 3½ Miles, & came in sight of some high Mounds bearing S. 65 W.—then went So. 60 W. 3 Miles and halted for the day on the Semerone. Distance today 11½ Miles—found very good Grass. The Semerone still continues to improve, it is here a pretty, bold running Stream, the banks higher, and the Water perfectly Sweet and good, the bed gravelly, and for about 20 Miles back, the Sands have in no place dried up the Stream. The Weather turned cooler toward night. Heavy Black clouds approaching from the West.

Thursday October 6th.

Ground covered with *Snow* this morning, the air chilly but not Cold. Mercury 38 at 7. Wind from No.W. It continued to Snow a little at intervals 'till 12. Mercury 42. At 1 it cleared off, and at 4 was entirely gone. Altho' this Snow moistened the fuel we have been obliged to use for the last 10 days (Buffalo Dung) and made it unfit for use, we did not suffer for Fire, for we were So very fortunate as to find at nearly a Mile distant a log of Drift Wood, which amply supplied us.

Friday 7th October.

A fair Morning tho' raw. Started at 45 M[inutes]. past 8. Traveled up the Valley So. 81 W. 6 Miles to a Small Grove of Green Cotton Trees, near some high Rocky Bluffs. Here the Semerone looks something like a Mountain Stream—its water cold and clear, bed gravely, current brisk. As far as I could see up it from a high Hill, it is bounded on the No[rth]. by lofty Mountainous rocky Bluffs and precipices, having here & there some scattering clumps of Trees. It flows from the North West. This is the point where we leave this Stream. We directed our March to the left, ascending the high land, upon a course So. 51 W. towards a Clump of Green Trees which are in view, & which we reached after a laborious journey of 5 Miles, over a rather Hilly route. Here we found, Situated amidst huge rocky cliffs *The Upper Semerone Spring*,[75] affording abundance of excellent Water, and the long narrow

Valley that it waters supplied us with plenty of Wood for fuel & pretty good pasturage for our Horses. This is a noted camping place, and is the point from whence we are to take our departure across a sort of Sandy desart [sic] (as report Says) to another Creek to the West.[76] We had Scarcely time to arrange our Camp before a cold rain commenced—distance today 11 Miles.

Saturday October 8th.

It rained, and hailed and stormed all the last Night, and 'till nearly 12 today. In the evening it cleared off finely and again looks like settled good weather. We remained in Camp all day, & employed the Men arranging a part of the Goods & Stores in proper sized Packages preparatory to packing as many of the Horses as we conveniently can, so as to lighten the Waggons & thus relieve the Waggon Horses as much as possible. The Men must all walk from this forward, or at least until we get through the Sandy Country we are just now entering, and into better range for the Horses. Mercury 51 this Morning at 8—48 at 7 P. M.—high Wind at Night.

Sunday October 9th.

A fine cool clear Morning—very Windy. Mr. Brown took an observation this M[ornin]g of *Sirius* at 37 M[inutes] after 5—Mercury at 39. Altitude 73-21-40. Latitude of the *Upper Semerone Spring* 36°-51'-40".

At 9 the Wind having abated, we Set out again, the Horses look chilled, and very badly; fortunately, they are not so heavily loaded. We directed our way, So. 45 W. 1½ Mile, over rocky & rather hilly ground, and ascended to the top of a high ridge, at a pretty abrupt point. From this spot we have a very good view of a great extent of country. Two very conspicuous Mounds called The "Rabbit Ears" (from their *supposed* resemblance to the Ears of a Rabbit) bear S.60 W. & are supposed to be about 40 Miles off. Another larger Mountain[77] bears So. 80 W. This is at present covered with Snow, & looks to me more like a White cloud than a Mountain. Still farther West is seen, tho' much nearer to us, a very lofty and extensive flat; & the Valley of the Semerone is distinctly traced for a great distance, being bounded on the North by a high chain of rugged rocky Hills. Altogether, the Scenery here is extremely beautiful.

The *"Rabbit Ears"* is the first great land mark; and to it, we now shape our course. At first we followed one of our guides directly forward several Miles over a succession of heavy Sand Hills, but finding this too laborious, and seeing no hopes of soon getting thro' these Hills, and no prospect of Water, I turned off from the course & went down to the right into a Valley or bottom, in which found a small Creek, a branch of the Semerone, nearly dry. Pursuing this Creek upward, found a Spring[78] of pretty good Water at a high Cliff of Rocks, and here we halted for the day, having traveled as near as we can estimate it, 8 Miles from the last camp. Some Indians had occupied this spot but a few days ago, else the grass would have been very fine. As it was, the Horses fared pretty well. The day was warm.

Monday October 10th.

A very fine cool frosty Morning. Frost very Slight. Having Breakfasted, we Set out at 8. We turned up the Hill to the right, & got on a broken ridge. Pursuing this about a Mile, came to a Pond of Water under the South side of a Rocky Cliff and stopped to Water all the Horses. There are a few Scruby Trees on the Creek just below this Pond & one or two just above it. The Water is pretty good; & I think permanent. From this Pond we continued up this Creek, across a large Bend, and at the distance of 2 Miles came to a fine large Pool of excellent Water, which is doubtless permanent, as it is supplied by numerous Springs just above it. The country thus far is somewhat rough & sandy, tho' we got along very well.

From this *Pool* we bore off to the right, and ascended a gentle slope, over good smo[o]th hard ground to the top of a ridge, from which we descended over just such another Slope; & at the distance of 2 Miles from the *Pool,* came to the bank of the Creek at a place where the Party[79] camped that went out in June as we suppose. Below this spot a little distance is to be seen a Green Tree, & there is *probably* water there, tho' did not examine—there is none *now* at the old camp. Leaving this place, we continued a mile farther to the top of another ridge, from which we saw a pretty large Valley to the right. We went down into this Valley, and continued in it over very good ground, 2½ Miles, and found (a little off to the left of our route) a small Pond or Puddle of Water, which proved Sweet & good, tho' not permanent, and here we halted for the day, the Grass being very good. Distance today 8½ Miles. Altho' we have deviated since yesterday Morning from our direct course towards the *Rabbit Ears* to find Water & Grass &c. yet we are not now very far if any out of that course; and we have not lost over one Mile in distance if so much. While on the other hand, we have gained much better ground & found Water and Grass plenty. Had we continued strictly upon the Course to the R[abbit] Ears, as has been usual heretofore for travelers to do, we must have laboured over an almost endless succession of Sandy Hills and Ridges & probably found no Water at all for nearly 30 Miles. Such at least was the prospect held out to us by those who had travelled that route.[80]

The best route after leaving the Semerone Spring is to get into the Valley, or rather keep in it, and keep up it as near the left hand Hills as practicable to the Spring [Mire Spring] that we camped at on the Night of the 9th and so on, by the route just described. This district of country is generally very sandy & sterile producing Scarcely anything but Weeds & broom Grass except in the little Creek bottoms, where we occasionally find very good rich Grass. Here & there on the high Prairie are spots of pretty good Soil bearing a thick crop of Short Buffalo Grass. Yesterday I remarked several *patches,* of an acre or so in extent, of Coarse hard Gravel & Stones; these are found occasionally all over the Sandy Hills. Game is getting Scarce as we advance. We continue however to get ample supplies of fat Beef.

Our poor Horses are daily growing more & more weak. Nearly every one of those that draw the Waggons have occasionally given out & refused to draw, tho' they are all excellent Horses—so that it requires our best management to get along *safely* at the rate of about 8 Miles a day. My riding Horse Stands it extremely well. Mercury 69 at 2—45 at 10 P. M. Weather very fine.

Tuesday 11th October.

Observation of Sirius 33 M[inutes] past 5—Mercury at 44—Altitude 73°-34'-50''. Latitude of The Puddle 36°-45'-04''. A very fine Morning—no frost. Started at 8. The Horses are much refreshed here. (Mr. B[rown] Says that the direct course from The Upper Semerone Spring to this Puddle is So. 62 W.—16 Miles Straight). From this place we steered, first So. 75 W. 1¼ M[iles] to the top of a Ridge from which we have a good view of the Country before us. The Rabbit Ears bear So.56 W. as thus

No. 2 are The Rabbit Ears—No. 4 The White top Mountain—No. 3 the Mound seen from this ridge for the first time, not very plain; and to which we are now to steer. Proceeding 4¼ Miles, came to a Hill, from which we see very distinctly all the above, and some other prominent Landmarks. 6½ Miles farther, and arrived at a Creek, in the bed of which found a large Pond of good Water at some distance below 2 green Trees, and camped for the day, having traveled 12 Miles. Here we found very good Grass and plenty of Drift Wood. This Creek [Corrumpa] somewhat resembles the Semerone; it is in a deep Valley, & is frequently lost in Sand. Saw no Trees on it except the 2 noted above, tho' from the great piles of Drift Wood seen, it must be well timbered above, & from the Water marks I should Judge it to be a formidable Creek at some seasons. Its general Course is from No.W. to South E. It forks just above our Camp.

A considerable party of People left this place this Morning, & to judge from appearances, left in some haste. We suppose they are Hunters from the nearest Spanish Settlements; and I think it probable have been hunting on the Semerone. They may have taken alarm at our Party, & are hastening home in the supposition that they are pursued by Indians. This is all conjecture however. Upon some fragments of old

Clothing which some of our People picked up, there were some *body Lice* found; which circumstance confirmed us all in the belief that the camp had been occupied by Spaniards. We took the precaution to Pitch our Tents at a respectful distance from the old Camp. The Creek having no name, we now gave it the name of *Louse Camp Creek*. [McNee's to Wislizenus; now called Corrumpa.]

At 34 Min[utes] past 6, Mr. Brown took an observation of *Aquilae*. Mer[cury] at 38—Altitude 123°-31'-10"—Latitude 36°-40'-37". The day was very fine, and the Horses traveled very well.

Wednesday October 12th.

A fine Morning. Mercury 58 at 7. Wind from the South. Left camp at 45 Min[utes] past 8. First steered So. 65 West out from the Creek, rising a ridge at a little distance from Camp, & then continuing over uneven but hard ground to the top of a high ridge, which is 1¾ Mile from the Creek. Here we fell into a plain Waggon way. We now went on 1¼ Mile farther over the ridge to a Point from which [we] have a pretty good view of many of the great Landmarks before us—these now appear nearly thus

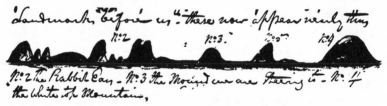

No. 2 the Rabbit Ears. No. 3 the Mound we are steering to. No. 4 the White top Mountain [Sierra Grande]. The Snow has now nearly all disappeared, having probably only a small deposit from the late Snow Storm noticed. We now Steer So. 68 W. towards the Mound No. 3, and continued upon that course, varying a little sometimes to avoid Hollows & Sand Nobs, 7½ Miles & struck a Creek [Alamos] running in a very deep hollow, among great ledges & Cliffs of Rocks. The approach to this Creek, particularly with the Waggons, was a little troublesome on account of the numerous ridges & hollows that interpose. We got down very well however, and halted[81]

at a small grove of Cotton Trees opposite a high Cliff of Rocks, where we found very excellent Water, Grass and Wood. The Water is in Pools. This Creek [Alamos] is a principal branch of the *Rabbit Ear Creek* [Cienguilla] & enters it about 1½ Mile below us. It has Scattering Cotton Trees & Willows all along up it as far as we could see. We call it *Turkey Creek*. Distance today 10½ Miles. Our route was a good part of it over heavy Sandy & Hilly ground today, & the weather pretty Warm, so that the Horses are very much jaded.

Observations of Aquilae at 31 M[inutes] past 6—Mercury at 68. Altitude 123°-38'-00"—Latitude 36°-36'-41".

Thursday 13th October.

A very fine day. The Horses requiring rest again, We lay by today. The Hunters killed some Turkies this Morning, which are the first we have seen since we left the Waters of the Osage River. These are different in their Plumage from the Wild Turkies of the Missouri, having more white about them, & resembling somewhat our Tame Turkies. One of the Hunters says he Saw one nearly white this Morning.

We have plenty of fat Buff[al]o Beef now, fresh, & Jerked—& altho' Game is comparatively Scarce, we still find means to kill plenty for our Subsistence.

Friday 14th October.

Very fine Morning—a *Slight* frost. The Horses seem to be quite refreshed. We started at sunrise. Kept up the Creek ab[ou]t ½ Mile to a Crossing place; then ascended to a high ridge by a gently sloping plain. Distance to the top of this ridge *direct* from Camp, No[rth] 89 W[est] 1 Mile. From this ridge [82] we now see all our Landmarks again, & again shape our course towards the Mound No. 3. 2½ Miles farther to another ridge from which [we] have a view of the Valley of the Rabbit Ear Creek and Several other Mounds not noticed before. One of them shaped as it now appears like a Sugar loaf (No. 5) bears So. 75 W. & we now steer toward it—1½ Mile farther, So. 75 W. reach a small creek having good Water in Several deep holes among great Rocks; & here we halted to get Breakfast, & let the Horses graze.

The way thus far today has been pretty good, with the exception of two or three ridges that the Waggons were obliged to cross, which however were by no means bad.

At 12 Mr. Brown took an observation of the Sun for the Latitude & for the time—Mercury at 72.

Altitude, Lower Limb, 89°-46'-10'' Latitude ———. My Watch is precisely right, & proves an excellent time piece. The Rabbit Ears are from this Spot 2½ Miles So. 32 E. They are in Latitude 36°-33'— and are 43 Miles from the Point we first saw them from.

We resumed our journey again at 2 P. M. and continuing as nearly as was practicable, in the course to the Mound No. 5, [Mount Clayton?] struck the Rabbit Ear Creek in 3½ Miles travel. I then meandered the Creek for the distance of 2½ Miles up it, and halted at a rich grassy point opposite which is a very high and extensive steep Rocky Bluff. Here we find excellent Water, Wood & grass, & abundance of them and a very beautiful spot to camp on. Distance today 11 Miles.

Our journey today has been over good firm ground, and tho' a little rocky & Hilly in some places, the Waggons got along with great ease & perfect safety. They were obliged however to deviate frequently from the general direct course to avoid several deep ravines, & some abrupt Nobs & Hills. Our course today May be Set down thus—No. 89 W. 1 Mile—So. 68 W. 2½ M[ile]—So. 75 W. 1½ M[iles]—So. 75 W. 3½ M[iles]—So. 75 W. 2½ M[iles].

It is proper to remark, that tho' these are the courses that would have led us directly to the Mound No. 5 [Mt. Clayton?], which we are steering to, yet from the broken nature of the country, we could not possibly avoid very frequent variations from them. Our camp tonight is probably a little North of the true course, Say 15 degrees—or from the Creek We Breakfasted on, due West, instead of So. 75 W.

The Rabbit Ear Creek is larger even here than any We have seen since we left the Arkansas. It is still however only a small stream. Where I first struck it, the bed is deep and Rocky & perfectly dry. Here and there I found holes of Water in the channel as I ascended it, & sometimes found it running over the Rocks. It resembles the Semerone in this respect, except that its Waters are lost in the rocks instead of Sands. The Water is very good. On its banks are occasional clumps of Cotton Trees, Willows, Grape Vines, Dwarf Roses, and several kinds of good Grasses, and on the cliffs are some scattering Cedars. On the Southwest side, this Creek is bounded for many Miles, about 20, by an almost inaccessible rocky Bluff, which frequently has an elevation of 100 to 150 feet above the level of the creek. The rocks which form this great Bluff are Black and Hard & glossy generally. I went over to the top of this Cliff, & found the country an extensive & beautifully level Plain.

Saturday 15th October.

The morning fair and cool. Started after an early Breakfast. Continued up the Creek upon a course nearly West, 4 Miles, & halted to Graze & Water the Horses. Just before We Stopped, passed a Mule Pen, which has been occupied about 4 or 5 days Since, found hung up in the Bushes near it several Pack saddles, whips, &s., the whole appearance indicating a party of Spaniards, & that some of them had lost their Mules.[83]

We staid here about 3 Hours, and then Started again. The Creek bears now more to the South; So we here leave it & direct our course more westward. The Mound No. 3 [Mt. Dora] is about 2 Miles from this bend, on the So[uth] Side of the Creek, & rather above it. We proceeded over some ridges & Hollows, (without difficulty) 2 Miles & ascended a Rocky Hill upon a hard smooth level plain; where we found the road very plainly marked, & the Mound No. 5 [Mt. Clayton?] in full view. Continued over this beautiful Plain 5 ½ Miles to the foot of the Mound No. 5—(from which the large Mound [Sierra Grande] bears No. 50 W. & is not less than 10 Miles off). We then Went on 4½ Miles farther upon the same course nearly, & halted after dark at a Spring in a Hollow among Rocks. The grass very bad here, & the Horses tired. Distance today 16 Miles.

It is proper to Note that after leaving the Rabbit Ear Creek just above or at the Mule Pen, there is good Water in 5 Miles, & again off to the right 2 Miles farther, or nearly opposite Mound No. 5. Then it is 5 Miles to the Spring we are now at. The grass is good at the two first named places, and very poor indeed at the last.

Sunday October 16th.

Started very early and moved on to a small creek 1 Mile & halted to let the Horses graze; & to get Breakfast. The grass good. Water in Holes very bad. Severe frost this Morning. Ice on the small Pond where we camped. This is the first Ice & the first *Severe* frost we have had. The weather very fine. After the Horses had filled themselves, we continued our journey. For the first 4 Miles our route was rather circuitous. 5½ Miles from the Creek passed a pretty large Pond of Water on our left —3 Miles farther came to a small Creek, having plenty of good Water & pretty good Grass. The route so far is over good Ground, but is generally Hilly. There are several ridges to pass over, tho' none of them are very steep or difficult. Some part of the distance, nearly half, is pretty near level. We continued over two long high ridges 1½ Mile, & then got upon a high level Plain. 1½ Mile over this plain, came to a Creek[84] (or rather two of them, just above their junction) and halted for the day upon a beautiful level where the Grass & Water are plentiful and good & fuel Plenty. Distance today 12½ Miles. Fine cool day. Horses a good deal jaded. Since we passed the Mound No. 5 we have been shaping our course, direct, towards another large Mound [West of Malpai] which is about West from the other [which is east of Malpai in forks of Carrizo Creek]. The mountain scenery around us today is extremely romantic and pretty. Saw at a very great distance part of the great range of Mexican Mountains. They appear like white clouds. At 24 M[inutes] past 9 Mr. B[rown] took an observation of Fomalhaut—Alt[itude] 46°-5'-10". Mer[cury] 36. Latitude 36°-27'-20".

Monday October 17th.

Observation of Procyon at 2 Min[utes] past 6. Altitude 118°-27'-20". Mer[cury] 50. Latitude 36°-26'-49". This being a very good observation, Mr. Brown relies more on it than on the one taken last night. A very fine morning. No frost. Staid in camp all day to give the Horses an opportunity of recruiting a little. The Hunters killed 2 Deers today. From the Hill just west of our camp the scenery is pretty nearly thus in front

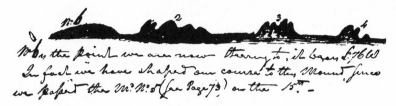

[handwritten caption below image 1:] No. 6, the point we are now steering to, it bears So. 76 W. In fact we have shaped our course to this Mound, since we passed the No. No. 5 (see Page 73) on the 15th. —

No. 6 is the point we are now steering to. It bears So. 76 W. In fact we have shaped our course to this Mound, since we passed the Mound No. 5 on the 15th.

A little below our camp, southwardly, and in sight, there is a Grove of small Cotton Trees, and not far below that, another—where the Creek is much larger, having received several Branches, and from whence it bears the name of *Rio Don Carlos* [Carrizo], from a great victory achieved there over the Comanche Indians, many years ago, by a detatchment [sic] of Spanish Troops & Militia commanded by an officer named *Don Carlos*.

Tuesday October 18th.

A delightful frosty Morning. We started after early Breakfast—directed our course to the mound No. 6 [Point of Rocks] to its southern extremity, So. 76 West—passing over three Ridges, and through two Vallies, the distance of 2½ Miles, arrived upon a High commanding Ridge, from whence the view in front is something like this

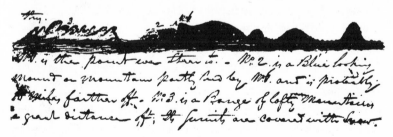

[handwritten caption below image 2:] No. 6 is the point we steer to. — No. 2 is a Blue looking Mound or mountain partly hid by No. 6 and is probably 15 miles farther off. No. 3 is a Range of lofty Mountains a great distance off; Its summits are covered with Snow.

No. 6 is the point we steer to. No. 2 is a Blue looking Mound or Mountain, partly hid by No. 6 and is probably 15 Miles farther off. No. 3 is a Range of lofty Mountains, a great distance off; Its summits are covered with Snow.

We traveled 3 Miles farther, and halted to dine & rest the Horses on a Rocky Creek [Ute Creek] in the bed of which we found a Pool of pretty good Water. While the Men were eating and the Horses grazing, Mr. Brown and I took our rifles and walked on to the P[oin]t of Mound No. 6 at *A* which we reached after a Walk of ab[ou]t 1½ Mile, over level stony Prairie. We ascended to the Top of the Mound, which is probably ab[ou]t 500 feet above the level of the Plain, and staid there an hour, climbing about over the Rocks, of which it seems to be chiefly composed.

From the top of this height we had a very full view of the great Range of Mountains before us. It appeared to be only a few Miles off, tho' in fact it was near 40. Many of the highest points are covered with snow. This view is truly sublime. At the foot of this Mound, or Mountain, are several very large Springs of excellent water. The Lat[itude] of P[oin]t No. 6 is ascertained by observation of the sun, to be 36-25-42. At this point,[85] we fell into a very plain Trace, which leads directly to the Pass of the Mountain, by which Mules usually enter the Valley of Taos. Pursuing this Trace 4¼ Miles over very good level ground, thro' a kind of Valley, we came to a narrow deep Valley, or Hollow among Hills & Nobs, which we kept down for the distance of 1¾ Mile, and entered an open level plain of great extent and beauty; then we traveled 2½ Miles over this plain, and came to a Creek, in the bed of which found some good Water in a Hole after some search & halted for the Night, having traveled today 15 Miles. The grass very poor here. After passing the P[oin]t No. 6, we have a Range of high rocky Ridges on our right, which seem to extend from that point a little north of our route quite to the great Range of Mountains.

Wednesday 19th October.

A very fine Morning—slight frost. After Breakfast we started. We first rode ¾ of a Mile So. W. and came to a kind of Pass or Gap between ridges on the right and a long Mound on the left. Then So. 75 W. on the Trace down a Valley to a Creek, with good Water & Grass ¾ of Mile—then up the Slope of the Valley (passing another small dry Creek) to the top of a high Ridge 1¼ Mile. From this Ridge, the view of the Mountains in front is extremely beautiful. The course from the P[oin]t No. 6 to this Ridge on the Trace is So. 85 W. But to get here it is somewhat circuitous, following Vallies & avoiding Hills &c. There is a very plain Trace all the way, and the ground is hard & Smooth, tho' a little Hilly. The Waggons got along with great ease. From this Ridge, we can see the entrance to the *Taos Gap,* as it is called, which bears from here So.82 W. We continued on the Trace over the Ridge down a gentle Slope 1¾ Mile to a Small Creek [Rio del Plano] with good Water & good Grass—then 1 Mile up a gentle Slope to the top of another Ridge; then 3¾ Miles down a very gentle slope to a large, beautiful and brisk running Creek, upon the bank of which we camped for the Night.

This Creek is about the size of the Little Blue, and is probably one of the principal head branches of the Canadian fork of the Arkansas. It bears the name of *Rio Colorado* [Canadian River] from the mistaken notion that it is a head branch of The Red River. Its banks and Margins afforded excellent pasturage for our Horses, but we found fuel Scarce. The Water excellent. Today we have traveled 9¼ Miles.

Having determined to enter the settlements at the Valley of Taos, and to get my Baggage Waggons over the Mountains if possible— I wrote after Night to Mr. Baillio at San Fernando, desiring him to send me 10 good packing Mules and two Packers to take my Baggage & stores over the Mountain by the nearest route. And to send me a Guide to conduct my Waggons over, if any can be had. I put this Letter into the Hands of John Walker & S. Vaughn, & directed them to set out with it by daylight tomorrow morning; and to Meet me with the Mules &c. at the foot of the Mountain, by Sunday or Monday, if possible.

If I had attempted to reach S[an]ta fee, by way [of] *San Miguel,* my Horses must nearly all have failed, and many of them been lost. If I attempt to haul the Waggons over the Mountains loaded as they are, the Horses must necessarily fail. If I leave the Waggons & Pack the Horses, still the Horses must fail, & probably the Waggons be lost entirely. If I hire Mules to pack my Baggage &c. over to *Taos,* I believe I shall be able to get the empty Waggons over the Mountains, and thus at a small expense save all my Horses and Waggons, & *prove* the existence of a Waggon route over the Mountains into the Valley of Taos; And I determined, upon all these considerations, to adopt the latter plan.

Thursday 20th October.

A very fine pleasant morning. Walker & Vaughn Started for Taos at daylight, on two of the best Horses.

After early Breakfast, we moved onward. Having dug out a Road in the Creek bank, got all safely over without any difficulty. The bottom is gravel, the going in very good, & the going out on the West side easily made so. Soon after we left the Creek, two Men came to us from below. They were on Horseback, and proved to be frenchmen, and belonged to a Small party of Trappers from Taos. Having satisfied their curiosity, they returned at full speed towards their camp, a few Miles below where we lay last Night. Our course, upon the Trace, is So.82 W. this Morning; upon which we traveled 4¾ Miles, over *tolerably* good ground, and came to another handsome Stream [Cimarron Creek], on which there are some Scattering Willows and Balm Trees. We traveled up this Creek 3¼ Miles to a very good Rocky ford and halted for the day under C[otton] Balm Trees. Here is plenty of very good grass, and fuel. This Creek is called *Rio Pone* [Cimarron Creek now of which Rio Ponil is a northern branch]. Distance today 8 Miles.

Friday October 21t.

The morning cool and a little cloudy. Heavy clouds hanging over the Mountains. At 30 Min[utes] past 8 we started, having got Breakfast. We crossed the Creek at the ford, and followed the Trace 5 Miles and came to another Branch [Rayado] of the same Creek, which we crossed at a good ford, and then kept up it 6 Miles, and halted on its bank at the first small grove of Balm Trees. Here we found good pasturage, and plenty of fuel. We are now about 5 Miles up in a sort of Cove or Valley, and about 5 Miles from the foot of the Mountain. We traveled 11 Miles today, the greater part of which is over good road. Frequent showers of rain during our journey today; and the air was quite Sharp & piercing.

Saturday 22d October.

It rained and stormed last Night, and a little this Morning; The Mountains in front of us are white with snow. It cleared off about 12, and continued fair & pleasant all the rest of the day. We lay by all day. The Hunters brought in plenty of fine fat Venison.

Sunday 23d October.

A very fine pleasant morning. After Breakfast, moved 2 Miles nearer the Mountain, for the Sake of better grass. I rode up to the Gap, following the Trace, which is about 2½ Miles farther, from our new camp. The whole way, up to the very ascent of the Mountain, is sufficiently smooth and level for the Waggons. But the Gap is very rough and Steep at its very entrance.

On my return to camp, I gathered some mountain cherries to preserve for seed. The Hunters continue to supply us with abundance of fat Venison. The Latitude of this Gap is 36°-18′. And the distance from Ft. Osage is according to the best estimate I can make 710 Miles. From the foot of the Mountain to San Fernando in Taos, by the nearest route, is said to be 30 Miles—so that it is 740 Miles from Ft. Osage to San Fernando—830 from Franklin—and I will say, a round 1000 from St. Louis.

Monday 24th October.

The morning rainy and Warm. At noon it cleared off. At 3 P. M. Walker & Vaughn returned from Taos, bringing with them the Mules, Packers &c. Mr. Baillio also came over with them, and he was accompanied by an old Comanche Indian, who has undertaken to point out a route for the Waggons over the Mountains, through a pass south of the usual Mule route. Previous to the arrival of Mr. Ballio &c. I had arranged all the stores & Baggage in a proper manner for Packing; and issued to the Men what clothing they Wanted.

Tuesday 25th October.

The Morning cold and Windy—very black and heavy clouds in the Mountains; and every indication of a great Storm from the North West. These threatening appearances delayed our preparations 'till near

10 o'Clock, when it cleared off finely, and tho' pretty cold, turned out a pleasant day.

At 12, the Mules started with the Baggage, &c. in charge of Vaughn and Davis, who are to make the best of their way over the Mountains, by the nearest route, to San Fernando. As soon as the Mules had got fairly off, I set out with the rest of the Party and the Waggons, nearly empty, to find a pass farther South; conducted by Francisco the Guide,[86] & accompanied by Mr. Baillio, who kindly volunteered to go round with me, and to serve as Interpreter. The Guide speaks Spanish very well, but no English.

Our first course was nearly South for about 8 Miles, passing over one high, steep & Rocky Ridge. At the end of this 8 Miles, we came to a pretty large Pond[87] & halted just at dark. The Water in this Pond is so strongly impregnated with Salts that it was impossible to use it, and we must have suffered if some of the Men had not found some sweet Water during the Night more than a Mile off.

Wednesday 26th October.

Morning cloudy and Cold, very severe frost last Night. We started after pretty early Breakfast. The Horses evidently weakened by the too free use of the Pond Water, of which they were all very fond, and drank of it freely during the Night. We continued our journey southward about 4 Miles to a point or projection of the Mountain on the right; then turned about West into a large and Handsome Valley, thro' which runs a Cold Creek [Sweetwater].

We traveled up this Creek, crossing it once, about 8 Miles, and halted just at sunset on its bank at what may be called the entrance of the Gap. So far we have got along very well—except that three of the Horses were obliged to be left. One of them very Sick—one tired out, & the other stifled—all unable to go any farther. Traveled 12 Miles today.

Thursday 27th October.

The Morning fair and cold—the Mercury at daylight stood at 24. This is the very first Winter morning that we have felt, and it is only so from our being surrounded by Mountains.

The Latitude of *this* Gap is fixed at 36°-10'-20''.

At 9, the wind abated, the sun shone out clearly and it became warm and pleasant; and we then started forward. We kept up the Valley upon a course generally about No.W. six Miles, which brought us to the foot of a mountain, which the Guide gave me to understand, we must ascend & pass over. It looked pretty formidable, upon the first view of it; but by winding along in a Zig Zag kind of way, and resting often, our poor jaded Horses made out to drag the Waggons to the Top; which I suppose may be about a thousand feet [3 contours of 325 feet] above the level of the Plain. I am well enough satisfied that a good road may be made up *this* side of the Mountain for loaded Waggons at a small expense. The distance from bottom to top, by the winding way we were obliged to ascend, is about 1¾ Mile. The view from the top of this Mountain is very fine. The Point No. 6 [Point of Rocks] bears from here No. 78 E.

Having got fairly up this Hill, & rested the Horses a little, we pursued our way nearly Westward, over pretty good, open & level ground 3 Miles and camped just at dark, on a little rill—having traveled today 10¾ Miles. The day was quite Warm and pleasant; but at sunset, it turned colder. The Mercury stood at 16 at 9 P. M. This is the effect of Mountain air.

Friday 28th October.

The Morning fair & cold. The Mercury 14 at daylight. At 9 it moderated, and became quite mild and pleasant; & we then proceeded. We traveled 2 Miles over good ground, and arrived at the descent of the mountain. It is say 5 miles across the level summit of this Mountain, which whole distance is an open plain except perhaps about half a Mile, in all, that we had to pass through some beautiful groves of Balm and Aspin Trees, which we got through with very little cutting. The soil on the top of this Mountain is exceedingly rich, and the grass fine, and plenty of most excellent Water. We found the descent much easier than the ascent, of course—tho' we had more *trouble* to effect it, as the timber is thicker and we had a good deal of clearing to do to get the Waggons along. It is not as steep as the other side, and not over 1¾ from top to bottom. The whole distance over this Mountain from base to base, by the nearest & best route that may be had for Waggons cannot exceed 8 Miles. After we had got fairly over this Mountain, we fell into an extensive and fertile Valley, watered by a beautiful Creek [Coyote]. We kept up this Valley & Creek 5 Miles; and then entered an open Pine forest, through which we traveled 2 Miles over excellent Road, and arrived at the foot of another Mountain, and encamped for the Night on a small Creek. The Distance traveled today is 10¾ Miles. Very fine day.

Saturday 29th October.

Fair cool Morning. Mercury 16 at daylight. Started very early, and immediately commenced the ascent of the Mountain. Here it was necessary to cut away a great many Shrubs and Trees. The Axemen were able to keep ahead of the Waggons very easily, for the Horses were so weak and tired that the Waggoners were obliged to double teams and take one Waggon up at a time. In this manner they effected the ascent of this Mountain with more ease than the other. This is in fact, by far the least difficult of the two. It is about 1 Mile from the bottom to the top, the way we ascended it; but I ascertained that a much better route may be had by following up a Hollow to the left hand of our route. This would cost some Labour, and perhaps lengthen the distance half a Mile; but it will afford a road that may be traveled very conveniently with Loaded Waggons & good Horses.

The descent was easy, and effected without the least difficulty or delay. After we reached the top, we traveled about 1½ Mile over hard level Prairie, & then about 1 Mile down into a Valley; then 3 Miles down that Valley, and fell into the great Mule Trace leading to Taos from the Gap we left on the 25th. The Mountain just crossed is part of the great dividing ridge between the Waters of the Arkansas &c. & the Rio Grande del Norte.

We are now fairly and, as I hope, safely over the Mountains, in effecting which, we have encountered much less difficulty than I had anticipated.

After resting a Short time, we proceeded on our way. Our Course is now more to the West. The Trace leads down a deep Narrow Valley, thro' which flows a most lovely Creek [San Fernando], which we frequently cross. We continued our journey 5 Miles down this Valley without any material detention or difficulty; and halted on the bank of the Creek for the Night—having traveled today 11½ Miles.

Francisco the Guide here left us and went home, considering us now no longer in need of his aid. He has discharged his duty faithfully and very much to my Satisfaction, & so I told him.

Sunday 30th October.

Another very fine Morning. At daylight the Mercury stood at 17. We started after Breakfast, at 9. We kept down the Valley and Creek 8 Miles, in which we found no obstruction or difficulty; and at 12, arrived at the Village of San Fernando.[88] Our Poor Horses seemed to pluck up fresh Spirits, on sight of fields and Houses; they entered the Village merrily at a good Trot as if they meant to enjoy their *full* Share of the honour of bringing the First Waggons over the Mountains into the Valley of Taos. The whole distance from the foot of the first mountain that we crossed (on the 27th) I mean the eastern side, to the Village of San Fernando, is 35 Miles by the route that we traveled, of which 25 Miles, at least, is over good level ground, well watered, and affording good Grass.

The mountain *sides* are thinly clothed with Pines of several sorts, the far greater part of which is rather short and Scrubby; It is only here and there that a handsome tall, straight Tree is to be Seen. The summits of both Mountains are open level Prairie, and all the Vallies are also open Prairie; so that about 28 Miles of the whole distance is open Prairie; Some of the Vallies are very extensive, and the soil is generally good. Some of it very fertile. Game is generally plenty in the Mountains and Vallies; it consists of Elk, Common & Black Tail Deer; Goats, Bear of 2 or 3 kinds—Turkies, Pheasants &c. Upon the whole, I feel authorized to say that this route is a good one, and that the expense of making a Road over it, fit for loaded Waggons to pass quite easily would be very trifling. Twenty men with proper implements, say Axes, Mattocks & Crow bars, might do the work in 20 days, I am sure.

I have Said, that the distance from Ft. Osage to Taos is 740 Miles. I think it probable that we shall be able to Straighten the Road in several places as we return, and that it will be thus Shortened about Forty or Fifty Miles; so that the actual distance between the two places will, as I suppose, be fixed at 700 Miles. Of this 700 Miles, at least 680 is open Prairie. Indeed, I doubt if there be more than 15 Miles of Woodland altogether, upon the whole route, as the Road goes.

On my arrival at San Fernando, I found that a small Party of Traders had got there the day before from Franklin. They had passed along upon the Mule Trace through the Mountains, while I was going round with the Waggons. This party left Ft. Osage about the 14th of September. They met Cols. Reeves & Mather on the 29th of that month at Walnut Creek, & on the same night the Party that I met on the 23d Sept. got to Walnut Creek also. I have received a Letter from Cols. Reeves & Mather, saying that they were going on very well, & enclosing a Letter from the War Dep[artmen]t that they received, dated the 6th of August, in answer to that which Col. Reeves & myself addressed to Mr. Secretary Barbour from Franklin on the 4th of July. We are advised in this Letter that Mr. Poinsett has been instructed to obtain as speedily as possible the consent of The Mexican Gov[ernmen]t to the marking of the Road &c., and that such consent, if obtained, will be communicated to The Commissioners thro' the local Authorities in New Mexico. I am extremely disappointed in not receiving a single letter from home. No doubt my family and friends were ignorant of the opportunity, or they would have availed themselves of it to have written and sent me some News Papers.

As I shall remain at this Village or somewhere in the neighbourhood, at least 'till my Horses are a little recruited, and probably all winter, I made enquiry immediately after my arrival, for a suitable House to rent, and was Shewn two, a little out of the Village, which I concluded to take; and gave directions to have them cleaned out immediately, so that we may move into them tomorrow. These Houses are situated about a Mile from San Fernando on a very pretty little creek. They are about 300 yds. apart, one has two rooms and a kitchen; the other 3 Rooms & a Kitchen, and a large Gallery or Shed. The first will answer for Mr.

Brown & myself; the other for the Men, and the Shed will afford excellent Shelter for the Horses.

It was near night when I returned to the Village, where I found the Alcalde & the Curate waiting for me—who it seems had called on me officially to enquire my business &c. Altho' I suspected that these Men were acting a little arrogantly, yet I deemed it proper to treat them with proper civility. I therefore gave them to understand, as briefly as I could, why I had come here and told them that I should explain myself more fully to the Governour of the Territory, as soon as I conveniently could. After some consultation between themselves, they took leave of me very civilly, without asking any more questions. A very fine day.

Monday October 31t.

After Breakfast, we Moved into our new quarters, which are, compared with the Buildings of the country, quite neat and comfortable.

I made arrangements for procuring a good Supply of Provisions for the Men, and corn for the Horses; and I have no doubt now, but we shall all do very well, and at a moderate expense. Grain is at present cheap and plenty here; that is, cheap considering the usual prices they sell for. Corn & Wheat can be purchased now at $1 a Bushell. I am told that the prices will advance in a short time, & that before Spring they will be up to 3 or 4 dollars a Bushell. I have ordered 500 Bushels to be bought immediately. If the whole of it should not be wanted, the surplus can be readily Sold in the spring for much more than it cost. Beef and Mutton are to be had on moderate terms, and of good quality. All these things are much dearer down at Santa fee; and I am now perfectly satisfied that I came here instead of going round to Santa fee; and am determined at all events to quarter the Men and keep the Horses here through the winter. Mr. Brown and I will go down to S[an]ta fee, & take up our residence there, as soon as I can properly arrange matters here. The weather continues uncommonly mild and pleasant.

Tuesday November 8th.

Today I wrote to Govr. Narbona[89] to inform him of my arrival &c. and to enquire if he has received any instructions in relation to the Road.

I should have written sooner to the Govr. but have been waiting for the arrival here of the Collector, who has been expected every day for a Week past; from whom I expected to obtain some information, & whose return to S[an]ta. fee would afford a safe conveyance for my Letter.

Williams, the Interpreter,[90] having expressed a wish to employ himself Trapping Beaver 'till June, I permitted him to do so; and he is now making preparation to start. His Wages ceases from the 6th Inst. & until he joins the party again in the spring.

Saturday 12th November.

The Collector Senor Behil [Vigil] has at length arrived as I am informed. His business is, I believe, to collect some duties from Messrs. Pratt, Robidoux and others, who have recently brought Merchandise into the country. He is in haste to return to S[an]ta fee, to send off the Mail to Mexico (he being Postmaster) which is to start on the 18th. I wrote today to Mr. Poinsett, the Minister of The U[nited] States at Mexico, enquiring of him what measure the Mexican Gov[ernmen]t has taken or intends to take, in relation to the Road from Missouri. I requested Mr. P. to write me on the Subject immediately, so that I might communicate the information to my Colleagues in Missouri by a Party that will leave here in February for that country. I enclosed this Letter to the Governour, and requested him to forward it by the next Mail. A small party of three Men (two Brothers by the name of Smith & another Man named Cook) are to leave San Fernando on Monday Morning, for Missouri. They say they will go to St. Louis by way of Ft. Osage, if the Weather should be good when they reach the Arkansas. But if the weather is bad, they will travel down the Arkansas to Ft. Gibson and then take water & go home to Tennessee. They offer to take charge of any Letters I may have to send, and to deliver them either at Ft. Osage or Ft. Gibson. I shall avail myself of this opportunity to forward Letters to Missouri. And I immediately set about preparing them.

Sunday 13th Novr.

Busily engaged all the day, & 'till after midnight, writing Letters. I put up a large Packet of Letters, &c., sealed and secured very well, directed to The Post Master [at] Ft. Osage; I wrote a Note to the officer commanding at Ft. Gibson, requesting him to forward the Packet Speedily to Ft. Osage by way of Union and Harmony Missions in the event of Mr. Smith being obliged to abandon his intention of going to Ft. Osage.

Among the Letters put up are two to Cols. Reeves and Mather,[91] giving them an account of my safe arrival here; enclosing each of them a Map of my Route,[92] & suggesting to them some matters of policy & economy in relation to our proceedings in the Spring with the Road. I wrote all these Letters in such haste that I did not preserve any copy of any of them.

Monday 14th November.

Mr. Smith and party set out on their journey at about 10 o'clock today. The weather is very fine and appears settled, and I am in hopes they may have a quick and pleasant journey.

Having determined to remove to S[an]ta. Fee as soon as I can conveniently, I dispatched Capt. Brannin[93] to that place today, to provide a House for my accommodation, and to hire Mules to take down my Stores & Baggage.

Wednesday 16th Novr.

Today I sold the greater part of the surplus Indian Goods and clothing to Mr. Baillio, at an average advance of 50% on the cost. The sale amounts to $666 37/100. Br. Baillio has undertaken to furnish me the Wheat and Corn that I want; & as it is in his power to furnish those things quicker and on better terms than any one in this part of the country, I consider the Sale and arrangement to be a very fortunate one.[94]

Thursday 24th November.

Capt. Brannin returned from S[an]ta fee. He brought with him a sufficient number of Mules to convey my Baggage down & a Packer to manage them; and reports that he has procured a House, which is to be in readiness by the time I can get there. Govr. Narbona writes me that he has not received any instructions yet from His Gov[ernmen]t in relation to the Road, or any information what the Government at Mexico intends to do in the matter.

I cannot suppose for a moment that the subject has been overlooked, or that the Mexican Govt. has refused its assent to the measure; and yet it appears very strange to me that some Official Order has not been given to the Governor respecting it.

Mr. Brown has taken lately a number of Observations for the Latitude and Longitude, from which the Latitude of San Fernando is well fixed at 36°-24′ and the Longitude only tolerably at 105°-31′.

Saturday 26th Novr.

Sent off my Baggage &c. to S[an]ta fee today, in charge of Pyles and Barbee; Mr. Brown and I intend to start tomorrow. Having ascertained pretty nearly the expense of Subsisting the Men here, I thought it best every way to give them each $5 pr. Month in lieu of Subsistence, and let them purchase their own provisions. This they all agree to, and the arrangement is to take effect & commence on the 1st of December. I drew up some Instructions for the Gov[ernmen]t of the Men, Management of the Horses &c. which I gave to Capt. Brannin in whose charge I leave the party. Davis is to employ himself at his Trade of a Tailor pretty Steadily, and it is understood that a *part* of what he makes by his work is to go towards the payments of his monthly Wages. Ben. Robinson goes out Trapping with Mr. E. Young[95] for a Month or two, he starts tomorrow, & his Wages is to cease during his absence. The Men I leave here are Richd. Brannin—Benjamin Jones—John S. Davis—John Walker—Bird Pyles—Joseph Reynolds—Singleton Vaughn and Bradford Barbee.

They have in charge Sixteen Horses, two Waggons, and the Harnessing for eight Horses; besides some Tools and Camp equipage, Tents &c. I leave them in good Quarters, quite comfortably fixed, Plenty of provisions for themselves, and plenty of Grain for the Horses.

Sunday 27th November.

After making some necessary arrangements with Capt. Brannin, which detained me ’till 11 o’Clk. Mr. Brown and I started upon our journey to S[an]ta Fee, accompanied only by my negro servant Abram. We traveled down the Creek in the Valley about 3 Miles to a Small Village —then we went on 12 Miles farther down the Valley on pretty good level Road—then 4 Miles over broken and Hilly ground to the foot of a Mountain—then 2½ Miles up to the top of the Mountain, which is steep and high—then 2 miles on the level summit over good road—then about 3 Miles down to the southern base of the Mountain, and came to a House where we halted for the Night. Distance today 26½ M.

Monday 28th November.

The morning clear and cold. We started at sunrise—rode 1 Mile & passed a small Village—then we traveled ab[ou]t 5 Miles over broken Hilly ground, and fell into a large and beautiful Valley watered by the Rio Grande del Norte. We continued down this Valley upon an excellent road which passes near the River, & which leads thro' several Villages and Settlements, 9 Miles, and halted to get Breakfast at Signior Juan Andre's, a very neat & comfortable House. After Breakfast we pursued our journey down the Valley, bearing quite off from the River, ab[ou]t 10 Miles, on good Road to the Village of Santa Cruz. We passed through this Village and entered a Broken country, through which we continued 6 Miles to another Village, a very small one, where we halted for the Night. Distance today 31 Miles.

Tuesday 29th November.

Started very early. It had snowed a little last night, & continued to snow when we started. We found the road pretty rough. After we had traveled about 3 Miles, [we] overtook the Men with the Mules & Baggage; and then we kept with them all the balance of the way to Santa fee, say 12 Miles, which is generally broken, and covered as it was with snow, was as I thought very bad road. We got to S[an]ta Fee at 12 o'Clk. Distance today 15 Miles.

According to the best estimate I can now make of the distances from San Fernando to Santa Fee; which by the by I was unable to do with my usual accuracy, the whole distance appears to be 72½ Miles. I set it at 70—probably it is less. The general course is ab[ou]t So. 25 W. About 30 Miles of this distance is *very* good road—About 20 perhaps, tolerably good, and 20 very rough & bad.

It would be impracticable I think to get a Waggon from Taos to S[an]ta Fee by the route I came down. I am informed tho' that there is another & a better route a little more Eastward,[96] by which Heavy *Ox Carts* have been brought down; and I have no doubt but a way may easily be found, & made practicable for loaded carriages to pass easily between the two places at a very Small expense; if ever it should be thought necessary.[97]

Wednesday 30th November.

I waited on Governour Narbona at 11 o'Clk. this morning accompanied by Mr. Brown & Mr. Storrs the U. S. Consul, who acted as our Interpreter. The Gov[ernou]r received us with great cordiality, and expressed the most friendly sentiments towards the Gov[ernmen]t & citizens of The United States; said he hoped the two Governments would agree perfectly in relation to the Trade between the two countries, & that the Road proposed to be marked out by our Government would be completely and promptly finished.

Govr. N[arbona] has only been in office here a little over two months. He is a Gentleman of pretty good talents, quite a man of business, and having been recently appointed to his present Station by the Gen[era]l Government by whom he is well known, I have no doubt heeds their views pretty well & has their confidence.

The following Table exhibits the Latitudes (and some of the Longitudes) of the principal Points between Fort Osage & Santa Fee as ascertained by actual observations on our Way out. The Latitudes may be relied on as correct; the Longitudes are probably nearly so. They could not be ascertained with sufficient accuracy for want of the proper Instruments. I expect that we shall be able on our return to fix the Longitudes correctly.

Names of Places	Latitude	Longitude	Distance From Place to Place	Whole
Fort Osage	39°-10'-19"	93°-51'-05"		
Western boundary of Missouri	38°-54'-28"	94°-17'-22"	31	31
Council Grove, Neeozho	38°-40'-00"	96°-12'-22"	129	160

Walnut Creek-No. Bend Arks.	38°-21'-10"		139	299
South Bend Arkansas	37°-38'-52"		84	383
U. S. & Mex. Boundary Line	37°-47'-37"	100°-00'-00"	33	416
Chouteau's Island, Arks.	37°-53'-18"		63	479
Lower Semaron Spring	37°-24'-00"		34	513
Upper Semaron Spring	36°-51'-40"		72	585
Rabbit Ears (two Mounds)	36°-33'-00"		43	628
Rocky Pt. on Mound No. 6	36°-25'-42"		51	679
Taos Gap (Mule route)	36°-18'-00"		42	721
Taus Gap (Waggon route)	36°-10'-20"			
San Fernando Village	36°-24'-00"	105°-31'-00"	35	
Santa Fee City	35°-41'-00"	106°-10'-00"	70	

*D*iary of George C. Sibley from the Arkansas to Santa Fe, October 12 to December 31, 1825.

Wednesday 12th October 1825.

A fine M[ornin]g. Mer[cury] 58 at 7. Wind from South. Started at 45 M[inutes] past 8. First Steered So. 65 W. out from the Creek [North Fork of Canadian][98] Rising a Ridge at a little distance & continuing over Rather uneven but hard ground 1¾ Miles (from the Cr[eek]) got on a Still higher Ridge & fell into a Road; then 1¼ M[iles] further over the Ridge to a P[oin]t from whence is a tolerable view of the great Landmarks upon our Route. The Creek forks—one of the forks Seems to Come from the West, the other from the Southw[est]. Some Small Scattering Trees Seen off to the No.W. The Landmarks appear thus

No. 2 are the Rabbit Ears. No. 3 the M[ountai]n we Steer to [Mt. Dora]. No. 4 the White Top M[ountai]n we Saw 30 Miles back [Sierra Grande]. The Snow has now disappeared however, being only a Small deposit probably from the late Snow Storm noticed. We now Steer So. 68 W. towards the Mo[untain] No. 3 [Mt. Dora] and cont[inue]d upon that course (varying a little Sometimes to avoid Nobs & Hollows) 7½ Miles, and Struck a pretty Large Creek [Alamos][99] having excellent Water in Pools, where we halted for the day opposite a high Cliff of

Rocks at a Small grove of Cotton Trees. Here we find excellent Grass for the Horses. Distance today 10½ Miles, which the Waggons did not effect till 4 P. M. The Route was a good part of it very Hilly and Sandy; and no Water to be found. The day was pleasant. Killed a fine fat Cow & Saw plenty of Game. Observation of Aquilae 31 Minutes past 6: Thermometer at 68. Altitude 123°-38′-00″. Latitude 36°-36′-41″.

To get down to this Creek, which We call Turkey Creek, it is rather bad traveling for Waggons, as the Ridges are very numerous and abrupt. The Waggon Road we followed today for Several Miles Crosses this Creek Some distance above. This is a Branch of a larger Cr[eek] [Rabbit Ear to Sibley; Cienquilla now] a few Miles West—it falls in just below here. The Main one Runs near the Rabbit Ears & is a Branch of the Canadian. The Creek we left yesterday morning is *not* a Br[anch] of Canadian as I Supposed. I Shall call it Louse Creek [Corrumpa].

Thursday 13th October.

Fine day. We lay by here today to Rest and Recruit the Horses. The Hunters killed 3 Turkies this M[ornin]g—the first we have Seen Since we left the Waters of Osage River.

There is here & there Clumps of Trees along this Creek, and all along it Willow thickets.

Friday 14 October.

Fine Morning. Slight frost last Night. The Horses appear to be much Refreshed. A little after Sunrise we Started. Kept up the Creek ab[ou]t. ½ Mile to a Crossing place, then ascended to a high Ridge by a Sloping plain. Distance to the Ridge, direct from Camp No[rth] 89 W[est] 1 Mile. From this place we again See our Landmarks & again Shape our Course to the No. 3 [Mt. Dora] & travel towards its most Northern extremity S. 68 W. 2½ Miles to another Ridge from Which we have a view of the Valley of the Rabbit Ear Creek and Several other Mounds & high Nobs in a Range between No. 3 [Mt. Dora] & 4 [Sierra Grande], one of which Resembling a Sugar Loaf [Mt. Clayton]. We now Steer to upon a course of So. 75 W. Going upon that course 1½

Miles we came to a Small Creek having water in Several deep holes among Rocks, & here we Stopped to get Breakfast & let the Horses graze. The way thus far today has been pretty good, with the exception of two or three Ridges that we were obliged to cross with the Waggons.

At 12 Mr. Brown took an observation of the Sun for the Latitude & for the time. Altitude 89°-46'-10"—Mer[cury] 72—Latitude —————— . My watch is precisely Right. The Rabbit Ears are ab[ou]t 2½ Miles So.32 East from us. They are in Latitude [36°-33'] and are [43] Miles from the point we first Saw them from. After Resting about 4 Hours during which time the Horses fared well, we Set out again. Cont[inue]d the course So. West 3½ Miles and Struck the Rabbit Ear Creek just below a Bluff Rocky point. I then meandered the Cr[eek] upw[ar]d for the distance direct of 2½ Miles & halted on the Right Side, ascending at a Rich grassy bottom opposite which is a very high & Steep Rocky Bluff. Here we find excellent Water, Wood & Grass, and very beautiful ground.

Our journey today has been over good firm ground & altho' a little hilly in Some places, the Waggons got along with ease. They were obliged however to deviate considerably & frequently from the general course in order to escape Several deep Ravines & Some abrupt Nobs & Hills—but the general Courses as traveled today are as follows—No. 89 W. 1 Mile—So. 68 W. 2½ Miles—So. 75 W. 1½ Miles to Breakfast and took Latitude—So. 75 W. 3½ Miles to Creek—So. 75 2½ to Camp.

It is proper to Remark that altho' the above are the courses which would have led us direct to our Landmark which we are Steering to, yet from the broken nature of the Country we could not possibly avoid frequently deviating from those courses. Our Camp tonight is probably a little North of the true course, Say 15 degrees, or from the Br[ea]k-f[as]t Cr[eek] due West instead of So. 75 W.

The Rabbit Ear C[reek] is larger even here than any that we have Seen West of Arkansas. It is Still however but a Small Cr[eek]. Where I first Struck it, the bed was deep & Rocky & perfectly dry; here and there I found water holes as I ascended & Sometimes found it Running over the Rocks. Its Water Seems to be Subject to lose itself like that of the Semerone, but with this difference among Rocks instead of Sands.

The Water is very good. On its banks are here & there a few Cotton Trees, Some Willow thickets, Grape Vines, Dwarf Roses, & various kinds of Grasses. On the Rocky Cliffs are Some Scattering Ceders. 11 Miles today—day Rather too Warm but Still pleasant.

Saturday 15th Octo.

M[ornin]g fair cool & Windy. Wind from North. Started after early Breakfast. Traveled up the Creek upon a course generally West, 4 Miles, and halted to graze. The Creek Still of the Same Character as yesterday, Water in Pools, and generally good grass. Plenty of good Grasses. At this place we leave the Creek, which bears more Southward. Our course is Still towards the Sugar Loaf Mound [Mt. Clayton?]. We started again a little after 12.

Left the Cr[eek] & Steered West 1 M[ile] to the top of a Hill, having a deep hollow on the So[uth] Side which runs into the Cr[eek] Valley a little below Mo[und] No. 3—which is on the left Side of the Cr[eek].[100] From the Hill, we have a view of the White Mo[und] [Mt. Clayton]—the one we Steer to and 2 other irregular ones to the left of it [Mt. Tripod & Don Carlos Hills] and 3 others [Palo Blanco, Loughlin & Antelope] to the Right. Ab[ou]t one mile farther crossing a Valley, & ascended a Rocky Hill upon a beautiful level Plain upon which we travel with great ease. From the Cr[eek] to this Plain is 2 Miles, then it is 5½ Miles to Mo[und] No. 5. Big Mountain (No. 4) [Sierra Grande] bears No. 50 W. from No. 5. We then went 4½ Miles farther to a Spring & camped after Night, having made 16 Miles today.

Sunday 16th October.

Started Early & went 1 Mile to a Small Creek where [we] found muddy Water in holes & halted to let the Horses graze (having little or nothing last Night) and to cook Breakfast. Grass good. Severe frost last Night. Ice on the Pond—this is the first Ice we have Seen & the first Severe frost—the air very Sharp this M[ornin]g. Weather very fine. It is to be noted that after leaving the R[abbit] Ear Creek, just above a Mule pen, there is Water in 5 Miles—& again off to the Right 2 Miles farther. There it is 5 Miles to the Spring we camped at last Night and 1 Mile farther to this Creek. At the first, Water and grass is good & at the 2nd pretty good also—at the Spring it is very bad—at this Cr[eek] very good. The Road is good all the whole distance, & is very distinctly marked from the Rocky Hill where we enter the level plain.

The Horses having well filled themselves, we Set out again at 15 Min[utes] past 11. Our Route for the first 4 miles was rather circuitous. 5½ Miles from the Creek passed a Pond of Water on our left— 3 Miles farther came to a Small Creek—having plenty of pretty good Water & pretty good Grass. The Route So far is over good ground, but is a good deal hilly. There are Several Ridges to pass over, though none of them are very Steep or difficult. Some part of the distance, Say half, is nearly level. The Mountain Scenery around us today is extremely Romantic and beautiful. Just before Reaching the last named Creek, had a view of a part of the great Range of Mexican Mount[ain]s at an immense distance.

1½ Mile from this Cr[eek] over two very high Ridges, & came upon a high level Plain. 1½ Mile over this Plain, and came to a Creek [Carrizo] in a deep Valley, & halted at Sun Set. Whole distance traveled today 12½ Miles. Observation of Fomalhaut at 24 M[inutes] past 9—Alt[itude] 46°-5'-10" Mer[cury] 36. Latitude 36°-27'-20".

Monday 17th. October.

Observation of Procyon at 2 Min[utes] after 6. Mer[cury] 50. Altitude 118°-27'-20". Latitude 36°-26'-49". This being a good place & the Horses needing Rest, lay by this day. The last observation was a very good one, and the Result of it, 36°-26'-49", is Relied on in preference to the other.

From the Hill just west of our Camp, the Scenery is pretty nearly thus—facing the West—

No. 1 [the Round Mound?] is the point we are now Steering to. It bears So.76 W. We have in fact Steered to this mound from the No. 5 passed on the 15th.

Tuesday 18th. October.

A delightful frosty Morning. Started after Br[ea]kf[as]t. Directed our course to Mo[und] No. 1 to its Southern extremity—So. 76 W. Passing over 3 Ridges & thro' a Valley or two, arrived at the distance of 2½ Miles upon a high Ridge from whence the view is Something like this

No. 1 is the p[oin]t we Steer to. No. 2 is a Blue M[ountai]n partly hid by No. 1 and is probably 15 Miles off. No. 3 is a Range of lofty Snow Cov[ere]d Mountains at a great distance. The Nobs to the Right of No. 1 & No. 1 are only 4 or 5 Miles off. See Nos. 2, 3 & 4 other Side. We passed two Small dry branches of the Creek we left—3 Miles further to a Creek & halted to Graze. 1½ M[iles] to the P[oin]t of No. 1. Went up on it & Saw the whole Range of Shining M[oun]-t[ain]s [Sangre de Cristo][101] in front of us. This Nob is 500 feet above the level Plain. From the P[oin]t of M[oun]d No. 1, pursuing a plain Trace, Rode 4¼ Miles over good ground thro' a kind of Valley, to the head of a deep, narrow valley or Hollow, then 1¾ Mile down that Hollow to an open level Plain—then 2½ Miles over that Plain to a Creek, in the bed of which found a Hole of Water. The Grass only indifferent. 15 Miles today. Observation of the Sun today at the Point of M[oun]d No. 1 fixes the Latitude at 36°-25'-35". After passing

P[oin]t No. 1, we have a Range of Bluff Rocky Ridges on the Right for 6 or 8 Miles.

Wednesday 19th October.

Very fine Morning. Slight frost. After Br[ea]kf[as]t We Started again at 30 M[inutes] past 8. S. W. ¾ Mile to a kind of Pass or Gap between Ridges on the Right & along M[oun]d on the left; Then So. 75 W. on the Trace down a Valley to a Creek with Water & Grass ¾ Mile—then So. 75 W. up the Slope of the Valley (passing another Small dry Creek) to the top of a high Ridge 1¼ Mile. From this Ridge, the view of the Mountains is Sublime. Many of the highest Peaks are of a brilliant Snowy White. There is Some Reason however, to doubt whether or not this White Shining appearance is produced by Snow. The course from P[oin]t No. 1 to this Ridge in the Road is So. 85 W. but to get here the Route is Somewhat circuitous, following Vallies & avoiding Nobs &c. There is a very plain Trace all the way, & the ground hard & good tho' a little hilly.

From the top of the Ridge to the Taus Gap the Course is ab[ou]t So. 82 W. We cont[inue]d on the Trace over the Ridge & down a gentle Slope 1¾ M[iles] to a Small Creek with water & good grass— then 1 Mile *up* a gentle Slope to top of a Ridge, then 3¾ M[iles] down a very gentle Slope to the Creek called Rio Colorado [Canadian]. It is a brisk, clear Stream about as large as the Little Blue, & is probably the main head Branch of the Canadian Fork of Arkansas. We halted on it for the day and found good Grass & very good Water but very little wood for fuel. Distance today 9½ Miles.

After Night, I wrote to Mr. Baillio of St. Fernandez desiring him to Send me over 10 Packing Mules, Saddles &c. & a Sufficient number of Packers and a Person to Pilot the Waggons over the Mountain &c. and directed Jno. Walker & S. Vaughn to Set out early tomorrow with the Letter, to assist in procuring the Mules & Pilot & conduct them over to our Camp by Sunday if Possible.

Thursday 20th October.

Very fine pleasant Morning. Walker & Vaughn Started at daylight.

After Breakfast, we moved onward. Having dug out a Road in the

Creek Bank, got over without difficulty. The bottom is gravel, going is very good, the West bank Steep but easily cut down. This is by far the largest Creek we have passed Since we left the Pawnee Fork of Arkansas. 4¾ Miles on the Same Course we traveled Yesterday, So. 82 W. Came to the Rio Pawnee[102] on which there is Some Scattering Willows & Balm Trees & plenty of Drift wood. Then traveled up the Creek 3¼ Miles to the ford at 6 Balm Trees, & halted for the day. 8 Miles today.

Friday October 21t.

M[ornin]g cool & a little cloudy. Heavy clouds hanging over the Mountain. Started after Breakfast at 30 M[inutes] past 8. Crossed the creek at a very good gravelly ford, proceeded up the Creek on the Trace Same course as yesterday 5 Miles & Crossed a Creek [Rayada], then continued 6 Miles further & halted on the Creek at Some Balm Trees, the first wood we came to, nearly up to the foot of the Mountain, in a Hollow. The Route very good all the way. A little Showery & the wind cool. Clouds constantly hanging over the Mountain. Observation of Fomalhaut at 3 Min[utes] past 9 P. M. Mer[cury] 43. Altitude 46°-14'-50". Latitude 36°-17'-51".

Saturday October 22d.

It Rained & Stormed a little last night, & early this Morning. The Mountains which are about 5 M[iles] off are white with Snow.

It cleared off ab[ou]t 12 and continued fair & pleasant all the day after. We lay by all day. The Hunters brought in a very fine fat Buck, & Shot 2 others.

Sunday 23d October.

Very fine pleasant Morning. After Breakfast, moved our Camp 2 Miles nearer the Mountain for the Sake of better grass.

I Rode up to the gap, following the Trace, which is about 2½ Miles. Mr. Brown ascended to the top of the first Ridge, & Reports that the Waggons may be got up there with Some Labour.

On my Return, I gathered Some Mountain Cherries to preserve for Seed. The Hunters Supply us with plenty of Venison.

Monday 24th October.

Rainy Morning—quite Warm. Cleared off at noon. At 3 P. M. the
2 Men Returned from Taus, bringing the Mules, Pilot & Packers &c.
Mr. Baillio came over with them. The Pilot Says he can conduct the
Waggons Safely over the Mountain thro' a pass South of this place.
Arranged Some of the Stores today for Packing and issued Some
Clothing to the Men.

Tuesday 25th October.

Very heavy Black Clouds in the Mountain with every appearance of
a Snow Storm there. Wind from the No. West & getting quite cool.
Set the Men early to work preparing to pass the mountains.

At 9 it cleared off, & tho' cool proved a fine day. At 12, having
packed the Mules, Started them off in charge of Vaughn & Davis by the
nearest Route to San Fernando & we immediately Set off with the
Waggons nearly empty to find the pass farther South. We went about
8 Miles down South, passing over one high Rocky Ridge & camped on
a pond of very bad Water. It is So Strongly impregnated with Salts
that it cannot be used at all—& we Sh[oul]d have had to do without
Water if Some had not been brought from nearly a Mile off.

Wednesday 26 October.

Severe frost last night. Cloudy, cold morning. Started at 9. Contin[ue]d
our journey Southward ab[ou]t 4 Miles farther, and then turned
ab[ou]t West into a handsome valley, thro' which Runs a bold Creek
[Sweetwater], which we crossed and then soon fell into an old Trace
leading up into the mountains. This Trace we pursued, passing over
one Steep Rocky P[oin]t which we got easily over, & at an hour by
Sun halted on the Creek—having traveled not less than 12 Miles today.
We are now at what may be called the entrance of the gap. So far it
is quite good & easy traveling. Left 3 Horses today on the Creek—1
Sick—1 tired out & one lame—all unable to go any farther.

Thursday 27th October.

Morning fair and *cold*. Mercury 25 at daylight. This is the very first *winter Morning* we have felt, & is only So from our being in the mountain.

At 9 the wind abated, and the Sun Shone out clearly & it became very pleasant, & we Started. Traveled up the Valley No. W. 6 Miles & ascended a high Hill with Some difficulty & loss of time. To the top of this Hill, it is probably 1½ Mile from the foot, by the winding way we were obliged to pursue, & altho' our poor jaded Horses were a long time dragging the Waggons up it, I have no doubt that it can be made passable for loaded Waggons at a Small expence. The M[oun]d No. 1 [Point of Rocks] bears from this mountain So. 78 E. or about that. Having got fairly on the mountain we pursued our way nearly Westward over pretty good open ground 3 Miles & camped on a little Rill. The Horses very much tired today.

Mr. Brown took an observation this M[ornin]g of Procyon. Mercury 24°. Alt[itude] [————] Lat[itude] [36°-10'-20''] of the entrance of this pass.

The elevation of this M[ountai]n above the level plain is probably 1000 feet. The day was quite mild & pleasant, but at Sun Set it turned cool. The Mer[cury] Stood at 16° at 9 P. M. This is the effect of Mountain air.

Friday 28th October.

The M[ornin]g fair & cold. Mer[cury] 14° at daylight. Mr. B[rown] took an observation of Procyon. Altitude [————] Latitude [————]. It moderated Soon after 9 & became pleasant. We proceeded ab[ou]t 2 Miles to the descent of the Mountain which we found much easier than the ascent, that is[,] less Steep & not So long. It is however 1½ Mile from the top to the very bottom. Had Some little clearing out of Trees &c. to do. Having got down, proceeded ab[ou]t 5 Miles thro' a Valley, then 2 Miles to the foot of another M[ountai]n. & camped. Fine day.

Saturday 29th October.

Fair Cool M[ornin]g. Mer[cury] 16° at daylight. Latitude [————]. Started early, & immediately commenced the ascent of a Mountain. Here a good deal of Cutting was necessary, & we were obliged to put

6 Horses to a Waggon & take them up one at a time. In this way we effected the ascent with less difficulty than we did the one day before yesterday. It is ab[out] a Mile to the top of this M[ountai]n, over which a very good way may be had with but little expense. The descent was easy & Soon effected—& then we fell into a large Valley which led us into the Mule Trace from Taus to the Gap we first Struck. It is 2½ Miles over this M[ountai]n & ab[ou]t 3 Miles to the Trace. We now turn our course more Westward, pursuing the Trace down a deep Valley thro' which Runs a beautiful Creek [San Fernandez]. We traveled down the Trace 5 Miles & halted for the Night. We found Some very ugly places, but managed to get along them pretty well, with very little Labour.

The M[ountai]n we crossed today is a Spur of the great dividing Range that Separates the waters of the Miss[issipp]i from those of Rio del Norte &c. Very fine day. Another Horse lost last Night, carelessness of one of the hands.

Monday [Sunday] 30th October.

Another very fine M[ornin]g. Mer[cury] 17° at daylight. Latitude here [————].

Started at 9. Kept down the Valley & Creek ab[ou]t 8 Miles and arrived at 12 at the Village of San Fernando,[103] have had very little difficulty. We have thus completed our long Journey within the time expected & with as little loss & difficulty as anyone could have anticipated. I found on my arrival a letter from my colleagues enclosing copy of one from the War Dep[artmen]t. This L[ette]r came by a party that arr[ive]d yesterday & which left Missouri on the [14th] day of September. They met our party at Walnut Creek on the [29th] day of Sept[ember] going on well.

In the evening I walked out ab[ou]t a Mile from the Village to look at Some Houses to Rent. On my Return found the Principal Alcalde & his Son the Curate waiting for me. The had waited on me officially to enquire my business, &c. which I very briefly explained to him & informed him that I intended Soon to inform the Governor that I had arr[ive]d & the object of my visit & they then departed.

Tomorrow, I intend to move out into the Houses I examined, lay in a Stock of Flour &c. & live in our own way, for I am Sure I cannot easily Reconcile myself to the living of the poor inhabitants here.

Monday October 31t.

After late Br[ea]kf[as]t Moved out to the Houses Rented. They are Situated very pleasantly on a beautiful Stream, & are compared with the Houses of the Country, tolerably comfortable. The two are ab[ou]t 300 y[ar]ds apart; one has 3 Rooms & a Kitchen, the other 2 rooms & a kitchen. The first the Men will occupy, & Mr. B[rown] & I the other.

Novr. 8th.

Wrote to Govr. Narbona. See copy on file.

Sat[urday] & Sun[day] 12th & 13th Novr.

Busy writing Letters &c to Send in to Missouri by a party about to Start tomorrow. Wrote to Col. Benton, Col. Reeves, Col. Mather, Mr. Gamble, Genl. Clark, & a L[etter] to Mrs. Sibley to whom Sent a Bundle of Seeds & enclosed a Map to Col. Benton & one to Cols. Reeves & Mather. I also wrote to Mr. Poinsett, U. S. Minister at Mexico, to enquire what the Mexican Gov[ernmen]t means to do in Relation to the Road; this L[ette]r was dated the 12th & is enclosed to Govr. Narbona at S[an]ta Fee with the Request to for[war]d it by the Mail which is to leave S[an]ta Fee for Mexico on the 18th or 20th.

Monday 14th Novr.

Mr. Smith[104] & his party Started this Morning for Missouri. He took my packet of Letters & promises to deliver it Safely to the Post Master at F[ort] O[sage] or if he Sh[ou]ld not go that way, he is to put it into the hands of the Officer commanding Ft. Gibson, & Request him to forw[ar]d it to Ft. Osage via Union & Harmony, Missouri. I dispatched Capt. Brannin[105] to S[an]ta Fee today to engage & prepare a House for the accommodation of Mr. Brown & myself & to bring up Mules to pack our Baggage &c. down. I have determined to take up my Quarters at S[an]ta fee, & to leave the Men here with the Horses.

Wm. S. Williams[106] having a desire to go Trapping, I consented to his doing So. His Wages is to cease from the 6th Inst. 'till he joins again, which he Supposes will not be till in June.

He Started today down the Rio del Norte.

Friday 25th Novr.

Capt. Brannin Ret[urne]d from S[an]ta fee last Night. He brought 7 Mules & a Packer, & has engaged a House, Wood &c. I Rec[eive]d a L[ette]r from Govr. Narbona, in which he Says he has not yet Rec[eive]d any instructions or official information from his Gov[ernmen]t in Relation to the Road.

Sat[urday]. 26th [November].

Started the Mules with my Baggage & Stores & Sent Barbee & Pyles along to Assist &c.

The Weather has been uniformly fine Since the day I arrived at San Fernando. Latitude of San Fernando 36°-24'. Longitude 105°-31'. I have made an arrangement with Mr. P. Baillio to whom I Sold Goods to the Am[oun]t of $66.37½ to purchase from 4 to 500 Bus[he]ls of Corn & Wheat for the Horses at the prices those Articles are now Selling at here ($1 a Bag) and I have agreed to pay the Men $5 each per Month in lieu of Subsistence from the 1t of Decem[be]r.

Gave Capt. Brannin written Instructions for the government of himself & the Men, in Relation to the Horses &c. Davis is to Work at his Trade Steadily, & acc[oun]t for what work he does to me in the Spring, when a fair & just Settlement will be made with him.

Sunday 27th Novr.

Ben. Robinson Starts this Morning on a Trapping expedition. His wages ceases of course 'till he joins again which he expects to do Some time in February. I Slept last Night at San Fernando—left there early this M[ornin]g. Mr. Baillio Sick. At 11, Mr. Brown & I left the Men's Quarters, & proceeded on the Journey to Santa fee.

The Weather getting bad. We traveled down the Valley about 3 Miles to a Small Village [Ranchos de Taos] where we found Mr. Anderson[107] from whom we got Some directions.

We then Rode 12 Miles further down the Valley on good Road, then ab[ou]t 4 Miles over broken Hilly country to the foot of a Mountain. We ascended this M[ountai]n ab[ou]t 2½ Miles, & found it Steep & high. Then we Rode ab[ou]t 2 Miles on good level ground, then Night caught us & we had to descend ab[ou]t 2 Miles in the dark to the foot of the M[ountai]n. Having got fairly over & into a Sort of narrow Valley, we found a Habitation with Some difficulty at which we Staid all Night. A Storm overtook us before we found this House, & the darkness was So great that we were for an Hour or more completely bewildered.

Monday 28th Novr.

M[ornin]g cold and clear. Started at Sun Rise. Rode 1 Mile & passed a Village with a church in it. Then we Rode over Some pretty Rough places for about 5 Miles among Hills & Nobs—& entered a Most beautiful Valley thro' which runs the Rio del Norte.

Traveled up this Valley passing Several Villages, 9 Miles and arr[ive]d at an Juan Andre's where we Stopped 2 Hours to B[rea]kf[as]t &c.

After which, we cont[inue]d down the Valley 10 Miles to the Village of Santa Cruz, where Mr. Anderson directed us to Stay all Night. But as it was early we thought it best to get on farther, & did not Stop in this Village.

The beautiful Valley here terminates. Southward, it is about 20 Miles from where we entered it to Santa Cruz—thickly Settled, well watered & pretty good Soil. We Rode 6 Miles farther over a broken country & got to a Small mean Village after dark, & put up at a very poor House for the Night.

Tuesday 29th Novr.

Snowing when we Started—the Road covered with Snow & otherwise pretty Rough. Overtook the Mules & Packers after we had traveled ab[ou]t 3 Miles, & kept with them till we arr[ive]d at S[an]ta fee. The Road pretty Rough & hilly all the way (ab[ou]t 15 Miles from where

I Slept) to S[an]ta fee, where we arrived all Safe at 12. The Snow ceased & the weather moderated.

Sent the Baggage &c. to my House which I took possession of, tho' not yet properly Repaired. Dined with Mr. Storrs. Engaged boarding at Juan Bacas.

The gov[erno]r called after dark to offer his assistance &c.

Nov. 30th Wednesday.

Called on the Gov[erno]r and Sat with him half an hour in his office.

Tuesday 6th Decr.

Dined with a Select party in celebration of the approaching wedding of two young People which is to take place this evening after candlelight; at which I am invited to be present.

Wednesday 7th.

I was at the Wedding & Ball last Night till after 12.

Sunday 18th Decr.

Dined today with Gov[erno]r Narbona's. Fine day.

Monday 19th.

Kept as a Religious and Political festival—the People all very merry and Noisy. Bonfires &c. &c.

Wednesday 21t.

The Priest gave a Fandango,[108] to which I went & Staid till 12.

Saturday 24.

Fandango all night—the People danced and Prayed all night.

Sunday 25.

The day kept by the People pretty much as with us. Fine day.

Monday 26 Decr.

Kept Same as yesterday.

Tuesday 27th.

The Mail arrived today & brought the news of the fall of the Fortress of S[an] Juan d Ulluo[109] the last hold of the Royalists. A Salute was fired just before Sun Set—& Bonfires lighted throughout the City—and a Fandango given all in honor of this event.

Wednesday 28.
Fandango at M[anuel] Sena's.

Thursday 29.
Fandango at Gov[erno]r Narbona's. Fine day. The measles getting common here.

Friday 30 Decr.
Fine day. Nothing occurred worth notice.

Saturday 31 Decr.
Another Fandango at Governor Narbona's—there is to be another Tomorrow Night, & another on Monday Night. All these Balls are intended to do honour to the event mentioned on Tuesday. Besides these, there Seems to be Something like Rejoicing every day, & at Nightfall Bonfires are lighted up around the Public Square.

The Weather has been Remarkably mild and pleasant throughout this month. There is a little Snow on the Mountains, but very little. In the Valley none.

MATERIAL ON FLY-LEAVES

Ft. Osage	39°-10'-19"
Council Grove	38°-59'-28"
Walnut Cr[eek]	38°-21'-10"
South Bend	37°-38'-52"
U. S. Line	37°-47'-37"
Chouteau's Island	37°-53'-18"
Lower Semerone Sp[ring]	37°-24'-0 "
Upper Semerone Sp[ring]	36°-51'-40"
Rabbit Ears	36°-33'-0 "
Mo[und] No. 1 [Point of Rocks]	36°-25'-42"
Taus Gap	38°-18'-0 "
San Fernando	36°-24'-0 "
S[an]ta Fee	35°-41'-0 "

Saturday 26th Novr.

Having packed up all the baggage &c. & put it on the Mules, the party Started at ½ past 11—consisting of a Spanish Soldier—Barbee & Pyles with 5 Mules Packed & 2 Mules & a Horse to Ride. They will go but a few Miles today. P[ai]d Baillio $24 Davis $3; Men for Subsistance 50$. Slept at St. Fernando at Luna's.

List of parcels also, what went to Santa Fe, what remained with the Men at Taus, what was marked for return to the States.

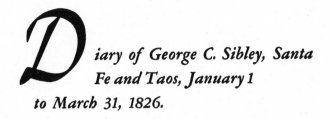

Diary of George C. Sibley, Santa Fe and Taos, January 1 to March 31, 1826.

Sunday January 1t. 1826.

Very fine day. Fandango at Governor Narbona's in honour of the conquest of St. Juan D. Uluo. It is Reported that 9 Deaths have occurred in Town since yesterday Morning.

Monday 2d.

Another very fine day. The Americans gave a fandango tonight, at the Gov[erno]r's House, in compliment to the Recent victory &c.

Tuesday 3d.

Another fine day.

Wednesday 4th.

Another fine day. Capt. Brannin arr[ive]d from Taus. Went to the Church at candlelight, to witness the Baptism of an Infant Child of Manuel Sena's.

Thursday 5th January.

Wrote to Gov[erno]r Narbona & Sent him a Map &c. See file,—also Sent him $21 to pay for the hire of his Mules &c. Fine day.

Friday 6th.

Another fine day. The Mail went off at Sunset.

Saturday 7th.

M[ornin]g cool and cloudy—turned out a fine day. The Measles has been in Town for the last 10 days, & many are down with it.

Mr. Ward & Mr. Floyd arr[ive]d from the Passo.

Sunday 8th.

M[ornin]g warm & cloudy—fine day.

Monday 9th.

Fine day. Wrote to P. Baillio, & Jno. S. Davis. Great Stir in town catching Thieves and Housebreakers.

Tuesday 10th January.

M[ornin]g Warm. Rained & Snowed a little. Capt. Brannin Returned to Taus. I gave him directions about getting Mules &c. The day turned out Rather a pleasant one.

Wednesday 11th.

M[ornin]g Warm and cloudy—the day warm and pleasant.

Thursday 12th.

M[ornin]g Warm & cloudy—day Warm. A Snow Storm in the Mountains. No Snow fell in the Valley.

Friday 13th.

A most delightful day. The Mail arr[ive]d at 1 P. M. No news of importance.

Saturday 14th.

Another very pleasant day. Nothing occured worth Notice.

Sunday 15th January.

Another very fine day; nothing occured worth notice.

Monday 16th.

Still another very fine day. A funeral of a Child in afternoon. The Measles very bad in town.

Tuesday 17th.

It Snowed a very little, late last night—the ground just covered. The morning fair and pleasant—and the day proved a very fine one. Two burials today—one of a grown person—the other of an Infant—born prematurely, in consequence of its mother (Senora Baca) having the Measles.

Wednesday 18th.

Morning cloudy & Snowing. Bargained with a Mr. Dempsey[110] of Missouri for 3 Mules to be delivered immediately at Taus to Capt. Brannin, for which I agree to give him an order for one of the 5 Waggons & Gears, now in Missouri, or if the Waggons are Sold, to pay him $30 a piece for the Mules.

The Mules to be good ones or not to be Received. Walker & Reynolds come down from Taus this Morning. Pleasant day.

Thursday 19th January.

The Morning cloudy & Warm. It began to Snow ab[ou]t 12, & con[tinue]d about 2 Hours. Snow 4 Inches deep. The day moderately cool.

Friday 20th January.

A fine pleasant day, tho' much colder than usual.

The People continue to die with Measles & fevers &c.

Saturday 21t. January.

Very fine pleasant morning. Bo[ugh]t 2 Mules for $70. But the Man *Rued* & took one back. He left the best, & took $30 for it. The day was fair & pleasant.

Sunday 22d.

The Morning cloudy & Snowing—ab[ou]t 2 Inches of Snow has fallen Since midnight. There were two burials today; One in the Morning of a Grandson of Governor Baca's[111] 6 or 7 years of age & one in the evening of a Poor Lad. The day cold & fine.

It is Said that many persons are ill in Town, & this evil is augmented by a Quack Doctor who has Recently located himself here from Kentucky.

Monday 23d January.

A Mr. [Ewing] Young[112] with whom Benjamin Robinson[113] (one of my Men) went out Trapping in Nov[embe]r arrived here Yesterday and Reports that Robinson died of Sickness before they had got out of the Settlements.

I am Resolved to Send Six of the Men in to Missouri, and to Start them about the 10th or 15th February—and I am providing Mules for them to Ride & Pack (two for each). There are abundant Reasons, and good ones, for this Step.[114] It will Save considerable expense for one thing and afford better means of proceeding in the Spring with our Work. Engaged today writing Letters &c. M[ornin]g *cold* and fair. The day cont[inue]d fair & cold.

Tuesday 24th January.

This is my dear Wife's[115] birthday. God bless & preserve her & may She live to enjoy many more happy years.

The morning *cold* and fair. Walker & Reynolds Started back to Taus; they took one Mule with them that I bo[ugh]t from Mr. [John] Switzler.[116] Mr. Young took another for me, a White one that Mr. [Elisha] Stanley[117] bo[ugh]t for me on Saturday for $30.

Very fine day, but pretty cold.

Wednesday 25th.

The Morning fair & pleasant; the day a very fine one. Funeral of an Indian child. Busy writing all day, and till after midnight.

Thursday 26th January.

Morning fair and pleasant—another very pleasant day. Nothing occured worth notice.

Friday 27th.

A very fine morning. Funeral of Juan Baca's[118] oldest child, a Daughter, at 10 o'Clock. The child died Night before last of Dysentery after the Measles—the family very much afflicted. The Corpse was very richly dressed and carried above the heads of the People Standing upright. The procession was a very long one chiefly composed of the most Respectable Inhabitants, many of whom marched in front of the Body, carrying lighted Tapers and wreaths of Flowers. The Priest was dressed in his Richest Robes and the whole moved with a Solemn pace. Several Voices Singing and Several Violins playing. The day was fair & pleasant.

Saturday 28th January.

A very light Snow last Night. Morning cold and cloudy. The day Raw & unpleasant. Two funerals today.

I was indisposed all day. The Mail arr[ive]d in the evening.

Sunday 29th.

The Morning fair and cold—turned out a pleasant day.

Monday 30th.

Another very fine day. I engaged 120 yds. coarse woollen Stuff a[t] 25¢, 50 lb. Yarn a[t] 37½¢ and 1000 lb. clean Wool at 12¢ a pound— the Yarn & Stuff to be del[ivere]d immediately, and the Wool in May next.

Tuesday 31t January.

The Morning warm & rather cloudy. The day a very fine one. I had headache all day.

Wednesday 1t. February 1826.

A delightful morning. I had the headache very bad nearly all night, & Still have it Slightly this morning. Mr. Baillio arrived from Taus just at night, & with him Jno. Thorp. It is Said that 5 deaths have occured in Town in the last Twenty four Hours. A very pleasant day.

Thursday 2d.

Morning cool and fair. A Slight Snow fell last night. This is a festival,[119] nearly all the People were idle, and frequently assembled at the churches. One burial, of a Child, today.

The day fair & pleasant, tho' pretty cool.

Friday 3d. February.

Another very fine morning—and another very fine day.

Saturday 4th.

Pleasant morning—fine day.

Sunday 5th.

Another fine day.

Monday 6th.

Still another fine day.

Tuesday 7th.

Mr. Baillio Ret[urne]d to Taus this evening. Very fine day. Busy writing Letters.

Wednesday 8th.

Fine day. Busy writing all day.

Thursday 9th.

A little Snow last Night. The day Rather pleasant.

Friday 10th Feb[ruar]y.

I have written the following Letters dated the 7th.

1t. One to Cols. Reeves & Mather to advise them of my two D[ra]fts of this date, one in fav[o]r of E. Stanley at ten days for $1500, the other for $200 fav[o]r John Switzler at 10 days. And another on Tracey & Wahrendorff for $200 fav[o]ur Mrs. Sibley at Sight. In this L[ette]r I Request them to put those Gentlemen in Cash to meet my D[ra]fts and direct their payment.

The D[ra]ft for $1500 is chiefly for my expenses here—that for $100 to pay for 3 Mules bought from Switzler for Public Service. The one for $200 is for my private Acc[oun]t. The whole of them am[ountin]g to $1800, I charge to my Account and will acc[oun]t for that Sum.

2d. Two Letters to the Same, advising them of my having Sold three of our Waggons now in Missouri to T[homas] H. Boggs & J[ame]s Dempsey, including the Harness belonging to them, for Nine Mules that I have Rec[eive]d from them. In case the Waggons are Sold before these orders are presented Boggs is to be p[ai]d $210 and Dempsey $90

142

in full for their Mules, in Cash. These Letters are del[ivere]d open; one to Boggs & the other to Dempsey.

3d. One Letter to the Same principally on the Same Subject, and advising them to Retain the two Waggons Nos. 4 & 6—and to bring them out with them in Spring. That Boggs & Dempsey are to Receive the Waggons as they find them without any allowance for common Wear and Tear.

4th. Another L[ette]r to the Same in Relation [to] our official aff[ai]rs generally.[120] Advise them not to bring out any other Men than the Six I Send in— (Brannin—Pyles—Barbee—Walker—Vaughn and Reynolds). Give my opinion that the $30,000 will be enough, if we use proper economy. That Men enough may be hired here in the Spring on good terms—that the Horses now in Missouri Should all be Sold, & that Mules only Sh[oul]d be brought out in Spring. That I have promised the Men who go in that they Shall be Retained in Service till the Road is finished if they desire it. In this Letter I enclose List of Articles to be brought out to Am[oun]t of $400.

5th. 2 Letters to Cols. Reeves & Mather, one to each, on the Subject chiefly of our Road.

These two are private—all the others are official.

6th. Letter to R[ober]t Hood of Franklin to advise him of my two Bills on him in fav[o]r of E. Stanly for $1500, & Jno. Switzler for $100 and that I have written on the subject to Cols. Reeves & Mather.

7th. a L[ette]r to Tracy & Wahrendorff to Say that I have drawn on them for $200 fav[o]r Mrs. Sibley &c. and to enclose them Samples of wool of which I ask their opinion &c.

And I have also written the following—Vizt.—

1 to Col. T. H. Benton.

2 to J. S. Skinner[121] enclosing him Some Wheat & onion Seeds.

1 to W[ilson] P[rice] Hunt, enclosing Some Wheat for Several Persons in & near St. Louis.

1 to Col. [Pryor] Quarles[122] with Onion Seed.

1 to Genl. [Thomas A.] Smith,[123] with Wheat.

1 to Majr. [Jonathan Smith] Findlay[124] with Several Parcels of Wheat.

1 to Same with Onion Seed.

1 to Col. [John] Thornton[125] with Wheat.

2 to Dr. [Robert]Simpson[126] with Wheat & Onion Seed.

1 to W. P. Hunt on many Subjects.

1 to Archd. Gamble on various Subjects.

2 to Rev. N[athaniel B.] Dodge[127] of Harmony, with Wheat & onion Seeds.

1 to J. Kingsley with a bundle of Wheat to be distributed.

1 to Same concerning Wheat.

1 to Same concerning Onions & Grape Cuttings &c.

1 to Same about matters & things in general.

1 to Col. Reeves with Wheat.

1 to Com[mandin]g Officer Ft. Atkinson with Some Wheat.

Packed the following for home

No. 1 Bale—

    41 lbs. Woollen Yarn.

    2 Indian Bowls, Onions &c.

    1 bundle Wheat heads.

    1 Do. Grape Cuttings for [John] Hardeman[128]

    6 yds. Herga for Wrapper.

       canvas & rope.

No. 2 Bale—

    1 p[ie]ce 52¾ yds. Herga.

    1   ″   18¼ ″ Do.

        4 yds for Wrapper.

       ———

      75 yds in all

      canvas & Rope

No. 3 4 Bales—

    1 p[ie]ce Herga[129] 19 yds.

    1   ″   ″   11½ yds.

    Wrapping ″   9½ yds.

        ———

      [Total] 40 yds.

1 Spanish coverlid.

1 Do. Bl[an]k[e]t.

1 Box Grape Cuttings &
1 Box Onions
1 Box Grape Cuttings.
1 Bundle G. Cuttings.
8 Bundles of Letters Seeds &c.

Saturday 11th Feb[ruar]y.

Fine M[ornin]g. Started at 11 O'Clk. for Taus. Rode about 35 Miles & halted for the Night at a House near the Rio del Norte.

Sunday 12th.

Arrived at Taus at Sunset. Find the Men nearly Ready. Very fine day.

Monday 13th.

Fine Morning. Finished my private Journal up to & including this day; the last page is 75. This J[ourna]l and another of 100 pages from the Notes of my Journey from St. Louis to S[an]ta Fee, from 22d June to 30th Novr.[130] I enclosed to Mrs. Sibley.

Tuesday 14th. Feb[ruar]y.

Busily engaged all day and all night writing Letters, and packing up &c. In addition to the Letters already noted; I have today written 1 to Cols. Reeves & Mather, to Say that I have Sent them 12 Mules and 2 Horses & List of which, with the Saddles, Bridle, Ropes, bags &c. I enclosed them—also a Statement of the Acc[oun]ts of the Men who go in. I also advised them that I Shall *not* Sell the Waggon No. 1 but Retain it & that I have told Mr. Baillio that if either of the Waggons, No. 4 or No. 6 Sh[oul]d be Sold in Missouri, he Shall have the Refusal of it at a fair price if not otherwise previously engaged.

    1 L[ette]r to J. Kingsley on many Subjects.

    1 L[ette]r to W. P. Hunt about Some Seeds enclosed him.

    1 to Gen. [Thomas A.] Smith [on] Same.

I packed the following—

        1 Box con[tainin]g 3 kinds of Grape Cutt[ing]s & 2 Parcels of Wheat.

        1 Box con[tainin]g 4 Large White Onions.

1 Box cuttings for Mr. [Joseph] Charless[131]
1 Bundle Do. for Mr. [John] Hardeman.

For the better convenience of Packing the Mules, I divided one of my Bales in two: So that I have 4 Bales to Send instead of 2. I have also packed 3 Iron bound Kegs full of *Penones* [piñon nuts] Say ab[ou]t 16 Gal[lon]s. On two of the kegs are two Hair Ropes Secured under the Wrappers.

Wednesday 15th.

A violent Snow Storm which lasted 'till near Night. At 2 P. M. Capt. Brannin & his Party Started, the Storm Still Raging. They let one of the Mules get away last night, so that they Started with 11 only. Mr. [Thomas H.] Boggs applied for one of the Small Waggon Horses in exchange for a Mule. I let him take the Horse, on condition that he either furnishes Capt. Brannin a first rate Packing Mule, or to pay Col. Reeves $40 for the Horse, which is the price I gave for him at St. Louis.

After Night I wrote again to Col. Reeves to let him know the arrangement with Boggs—that I had p[ai]d Capt. Brannin $8½ on Acc[oun]t Since my Statement was enclosed to him, & that the Mule got away &c. Very cold day.

The following is a List of the Mules & Other Public Property taken by Capt. Brannin &c.

No. 1—Yellow Horse Mule ⎱ a match.
  " 2—Yellow Horse Mule ⎰
  " 3—Sorrel Mare M[ule] White mane & tail.
  " 4—D[ar]k Bay or Br[own] Mare M[ule] ⎫ a match.
  " 5—D[ar]k Bay or Br[own] Mare M[ule] ⎭
       these 5 are all branded with the Letter ꟽ on the left Side of the neck
  " 6—D[ar]k Sorrel Mare Mule
       these Six bo[ugh]t from Mr. T. H. Boggs.
  " 7—D[ar]k Brown Horse Mule. ⎫
  " 8—Mouse col[ore]d Stud M[ule]. ⎬ Bo[ugh]t from Jas. Dempsey
  " 9—Sorrel Horse M[ule]. ⎭

" 10—Bl[ac]k Mare Mule.
" 11—L[igh]t Gray Horse M[ule].   ⎫
" 12—D[ar]k Br[own] Horse M[ule]. ⎬ [John] Switzler
                                    ⎭
     This Mule got away & is left:
" 13—L[igh]t Roan Horse.
" 14—L[igh]t Dun Mare.
" 15—Sorrel Horse for Boggs.
  5 Spanish Riding Saddles.
  1 Common Do.   Do.
  8 Pack Saddles.
  6 Common Bridles.
 14 Trail Ropes or Halters.
  8 Lash Ropes.
 10 Sheep Skins.
  1 Chopping Axe.
  4 Twill Bags
  6 Woollen Bags.
  Sundry Cooking Utensils.

Capt. Brannin has particular instructions to deliver all the above to Col. Reeves, except two of the Mules that Jno. Walker has charge of, Saddles &c. belonging to them, which Walker is to keep at home near Ft. Osage if he will agree to do it on fair & Reasonable terms. The following is a List of Private Property, belonging to G. C. S. Sent home by this Party. Vizt.

Bales Nos. 1, 2, 3, & 4.

Kegs Nos. 8, 9, & 10.

1 Brown Mare Mule—$50

1 Yellowish White Mare Mule—$30.

2 Pack Saddles—2 Lash Ropes.

2 Hair Rope Halters.

1 Bearskin M[ar]k[e]d "Sibley."

The Bales contain

41 lb. Woollen Yarn @ 37½	....	15.37½
120 yds. Herga......20	....	24.00
2 Indian Bowls	....	$ 1.75

1 Spanish Blanket	6.60
1 Do. Coverlid	10.00
1 Box Grape Slips &c.	12.50
1 Do. Onions	75

& the following Packages of Letters, Seeds, &c. Vizt. 1 for Mrs. Sibley con[tainin]g Letters, Seeds, & 2 p[airs] Buffo. Gloves.

1 for W. P. Hunt con[tainin]g Letters for Col. [Thomas H.] Benton —Col. [Pryor] Quarles—Gen. [William] Clark—Dr. [Robert] Simpson—Major [Richard] Graham[132]—Jno. C. Sullivan[133]—W. C. Carr[134]—& others enclosing Wheat & Onion Seed.

1 to Gen. [Thomas A.] Smith of Franklin con[tainin]g Wheat— Onions—Onion Seed &c.

1 to Col. B. H. Reeves con[tainin]g Sundry official communications, & Some papers of Seeds.

1 to Robt. Hood con[tainin]g Sundry Letters to himself & others, from myself Mr. [Elisha] Stanley and others.

1 to Maj. [Jonathan Smith] Findley con[tainin]g Sundry Small Packages of Seeds.

1 to Ch[arles] Wahrendorff con[tainin]g a Box of Grape Cuttings for Mr. [Joseph] Charless.

2 For Jno. Hardeman cont[ainin]g Some Grape Cuttings of 3 kinds.

1 to Jno. [K.] Walker St. Louis from Mr. Brown.[135]

1 to J. Kingsley con[tainin]g Sundry Letters con[tainin]g Wheat & Seeds &c. to many persons, & to himself.

1 Paper con[tainin]g Some Heads of Wheat.

2 Packets for Baltimore cont[ainin]g 4 Papers of Wheat[136] & 4 Papers of Onion Seed, & 2 Letters ab[ou]t them to Jno. S. Skinner.

Also 3 Kegs cont[ainin]g 16 Gals Penones & 2 long Hair Ropes. *These 3 Kegs* their Contents Wrappers &c. cost me .... $17.50 and all the contents of the 4 Bales, the Mules & their equipment &c. Cash $152.50

The Whole Cost of What I have Sent home when there delivered may be Set down at $165 or very nearly. I think they are fairly worth as follows Vizt.

41 lb. Yarn @ 75¢	$30.75
120 yds Herga @ 50¢	60.00
2 Blankets	16.00
2 Indian Bowls	1.75
2 Mules & their equipment	100.00
	208.50

3 Kegs Penones—Box Slips—Onions &c. are worth $20 at least.

Thursday 16th Feb[ruar]y.

Fine day. This M[ornin]g I wrote to Cols. Reeves & Mather by Mr. Baillio, to advise them that I have this day drawn on Tracy & Wahrendorff for $128 for P. Baillio: $70 on acc[oun]t of Jno. S. Davis & $58 on acc[oun]t Wm. S. William's Wages, [and] that I had arranged with Mr. Baillio to take one of the Waggons, No. 4 or No. 6, at a fair Price to be Settled here with him, as in Pay[men]t for Wheat &c. Next Summer. I Wrote also to Tracy & Wahrendorff advising them of my D[raf]t &c. and informing them that I have entered into a copartnership with Baillio to carry on the Wool Trade, & that he, Baillio, Starts today for St. Louis to procure necessary goods, which he may apply to them for, & they may furnish if they choose, upon my credit, understanding clearly the Situation of my Affairs &c. Mr. Baillio & I Signed a Memo[randum] cont[ainin]g the terms of the New Copartnership, which is to be Styled "Sibley & Baillio"—& P[a]id Baillio $55 on acc[oun]t in Cash. At 11 Mr. B. Started to overtake the party pretty well equipped for the Journey.

In the evening, a Spaniard [Tonorio] found & brought back the Runaway Mule, & I immediately Started Thorp off to overtake the Party & deliver the Mule to Capt. Brannin. Thorp Returned ab[ou]t Midnight & Reported that he overtook the party ab[ou]t 15 Miles on the Road encamped. I directed him to tell Capt. Brannin to deliver the Mule to Col. Reeves, with the others & to explain to him ab[ou]t it running off & being found &c.

Thorp Says Mr. Baillio Requested him to bring him a Vial of Laudanum that he forgot, & which he may Suffer much for the want of.

Friday 17th.

Thorp Started early this M[ornin]g to take the Laudanum to Mr. Baillio. He Returned ab[ou]t 11 o'Clk. P. M. & Says that he overtook them ab[ou]t 25 Miles from the Village going on Pretty well, tho' the Snow is pretty deep & has a hard crust on it, but not quite hard enough to bear the Mules.

He Says that Mr. Boggs has got the Sorrell Horse; but has no Mule to give for him that Capt. Brannin will Receive; & that in consequence, he expects to pay $40 to Col. R[eeves] at Franklin for the Horse.

On his Return Thorp met 3 or 4 Men on their way to overtake the party—which will be about 22 Men Strong when they all get together. I count upon their getting to Ft. Osage, about the 25th of March. I have paid away the following Sums Since I left S[an]ta Fee—

Traveling Exp[ense]s Self & Thorp . . . . $	2.25
5 Riding Saddles av[erage]d @ $4.70	23.50
8 Pack Saddles $3.12½	25.00
8 Lash Ropes complete	8.00
14 Trail Ropes	14.00
10 Sheep Skins	2.50
pd. for an Axe	3.00
pd. Tonorio part of his comp[ensatio]n for Services	3.00
pd. Do. for catching Mule	1.00
pd. for Bread	1.00
Baillio on Acct	55.00
On Subsistence Acct. of the 8 Men for Feb[ruar]y & M[ar]ch	80.00
Luno on Acct. House Rent	25.00
Jno. S. Davis on Acct.	70.00
Wm. S. Williams order on Acct.	58.00
Mr. [Sylvester] Pratt on my own Acct.	23.09
	394.34
Recd. from Mr. [Elisha] Stanley at Sta. Fee	100.00
Recd. from Pratt order on Stanley	200.00

Recd. from Capt. Brannin	24.12½
Recd. from Jno. S. Davis	22.00
Draft. Tracy & Wahrendorff favor P. Baillio	128.00
Recd. from Mr. T. H. Boggs, as Cash, &c.	35.00
" from Stanley by Jno Walker	8.00
" from Stanley by Mr. Brown	100.00
Am[oun]t p[ai]d out Bro[ugh]t down	394.34
Pd. for a Coverlid	10.00
Pd. Mr. Brown	135.00
Pd. for a Mule	100.00

Tuesday 21t. Feb[ruar]y.

Today I bought a Saddle Mule from Senor Kirstana for $100 Cash. The price is high, but the Mule is very good. I want it to Ride on my Journey down the country, on which I am to Start in a day or two.

Wednesday 22d.

Settled today with Davis in full up to the 1t. of April. His work Since 1t Nov[embe]r Am[oun]ts to about $176. He has been uncom-monly industrious, & has worked early & late, & is as I think fairly entitled to all he has made, deducting out of it his Wages Since 31t. Octo[be]r. He has attended to his two Horses, & done other Services about the quarters &c. equivalent to the Am[oun]t of his Subsistence, which has been paid him up to the 1t of April.

Davis is now disch[arge]d from the Service of the Comm[ission]ers & is p[ai]d up in full, & owes them about $40—which I am to Settle for him. I have promised him that if he Sh[oul]d wish to Return to Missouri with us in July, that he may join the Party then as a hand if he chooses.

I have also exchanged my Yager, Powder Horn &c. with Davis for a certain Bay Horse colt that he left at my House (the Same that he got from Rothwell) on condition that I *get* the Colt on my Return home. It is also understood that if I want the Yager again when I am Starting home, I am to have it, & then the bargain is annulled.

If I get the Colt, I am to have a New Snaffle Bridle with him that Davis left at my House, in the care of Betty [Easton], as he Says.

The Weather is now Mild & pleasant, & I am in hopes Capt. Brannin & his party are getting on well.

Thursday 23d Feb[ruar]y 1826.

Fine pleasant day. I walked over to the Village to meet 2 Men who were Sent to me from the Alcalde to Say that he is Ready to Settle a Judg[men]t Rendered by his predecessor ag[ains]t a Man who Stole Some Axes, &c., the detention of which pay[men]t by this present Alcalde I had complained of. I Settled it with the Men that the Alcalde is to pay the Judg[men]t $29, the day after tomorrow to Mr. Brown—in default of which I will complain to the Gov[erno]r.

I Sent word to the Alcalde that I expect him to investigate the facts in relation to a Man who Stole corn Some Time Since, & that Remuneration will be looked for &c.

Friday 24th Feb[ruar]y. 1826.

At ½ past 9 A. M. Started to S[an]ta Fee, & on my journey to Sonora & Chihuahua. On the Top of the Mountain Met Williams just Returning from his Trapping expedition. He Says he has had good Success. An hour after dark got to Senor *Diego Cisnero's* & Staid all night. Fine day.

Saturday 25th.

Started after Breakfast, pretty early. Arrived at S[an]ta Fee 2 Hours before Night very much fatigued & quite unwell. Went to bed early. Fine day.

Sunday 26th.

Got up this morning with a pain in my breast. The Gov[erno]r Sent me over a Letter that had been enclosed to him from Mexico. It is from Mr. Poinsett, dated the 3rd Dec[embe]r. It acknowleges Rec[eip]t of my L[ette]r to him of 12th Nov[embe]r, and informs me that he has "hitherto failed to induce the President of these States to take any part in the Survey of the proposed Road, until after we Shall have concluded our Treaty of limits. "As there has been lately a change in the Administration, I have again Renewed the Negociation, and will inform you of the Result by the earliest opportunity. Your account of the Route is highly Satisfactory, and will I hope aid me to bring this affair to a favourable conclusion."[137]

I was quite unwell all day, and did not call on the Governor, as I intended.

Monday 27th.

I waited on the Gov[erno]r this Morning with Mr. Beard[138] for Interpreter, to enquire if he had Received any official intelligence from his Gov[ernmen]t in Relation to the Road. He assured me that he had not heard a word, & appeared Surprised when I told what Mr. Poinsett had written to me.

The Gov[erno]r expressed an opinion that we Sh[oul]d hear Something more favorable on the Subject when he got answers to his communications forwarded on the 6th of Jan[uar]y, in which he enclosed mine to him, Map & all, of the fifth, &c.

The Party Started for the Lower Country today at Noon, to Wit —Mr. Douglass[139] with two Waggons for Chihuahua & Mr. Floyd with one Waggon for the Passo. George West went with Douglass. Unless I Receive certain information from Mr. Poinsett by tomorrow's Mail, of the Assent of the Mexican Gov[ernmen]t to the completion of the Road I Shall be obliged to decline my trip down the country. Quite unwell today.

Tuesday 28th Feb[ruar]y.

Fine day. Unwell Still. I hear Nothing by the Mail; So I give up my journey below, & Shall Return to Taus to Stay as Soon as I arrange my affairs here, and get well enough to Ride. At present the pain in my breast would make it impossible for me to travel without great injury.

Wednesday March 1t. 1826.

A most delightful Spring Morning. I am much better today—engaged writing all day. Find out that my Servant Abram has been carrying on a pretty extensive game of thieving & Roguery here. Thorp has got on the track of Some of his Thefts &c. and the more he enquires and examines the more he discovers; to get to the end of them Seems to be hopeless, & to Recover anything equally So. All that is left for it is to punish the Villain as he deserves. Fine day.

Thursday 2d.

The day not very pleasant. Sent Robinson's[140] Map to The Gov[erno]r as a present, having no further use for it, & it being not worth taking home. If offered for Sale it w[oul]d not bring a Dollar here.

Friday March 3d.

Sold a Black Horse to Mr. [John] Ward for $45. The weather Still fine.

Saturday 4th.

Very busy all day writing and arranging my Papers & Acc[oun]ts &c. I am Still unwell.

Sunday 5th.

Fine day. I wrote to Mr. Poinsett today in answer to his L[ette]r to me of 3rd. Dec[embe]r. See file. Sent this L[ette]r[141] to the Gov[erno]r & Requested him to forw[ar]d it to Mexico by the Mail which departs tomorrow, which the Gov[erno]r Sent me word he will do. I am more unwell today than I have been before Since I came here. I had a pretty high fever last Night, & am by no means clear of it today. The pain in my breast is also very troublesome Still. Very fine day.

Monday 6th M[ar]ch

I feel much better this M[ornin]g and am determined to Set out today for Taus & to Start all my baggage &c.

Having packed up all my baggage, I put it in charge of Sen[o]r Vigil,[142] who has engaged to Transport it up to Taus; and at ½ past Ten I mounted my Mule, and Set out for Taus, accompanied by Thorp. We Reached the Village of S[an]ta Cruz (25 Miles) just at Sun Set, & Stopped at the Priest's who Received me with much politeness & kindness, & treated me with the utmost hospitality.

Tuesday 7th M[ar]ch.

I indulged myself in bed 'till it was pretty late this M[ornin]g. When I arose, found a Servant with Water, Napkin &c. & after I had finished Washing, was Served with a Cup of very fine, Rich chocolate —& in half an hour Breakfast was Ready.

I left the hospitable Priest's at ½ past 9, and felt every way the better. The pain in my breast was only Slight, and I had no fever. I Rode Slowly but Steadily about 20 Miles to Sen[o]r Lusaro's and halted for the day at 2 O'Cl[oc]k. I felt very unwell, & lay down on a Mattress & went to Sleep for an Hour. When I got up felt worse. Directed Thorp to make me Some Coffee of which I drank a little, & felt better. Went early to bed.

Very fine day, as was yesterday.

Wednesday 8th M[ar]ch.

Arose early, having Slept very well, & find myself much Refreshed. Thorp made me Some chocolate, & afterwards I ate Some Breakfast.

Started at 8 O'Clock, the day very fine. Arrived at Taus at about 2 O'Clock. Feel somewhat fatigued & feverish.

Thursday 9th M[ar]ch.

I Slept well last night, & am this morning quite free from the pain in my breast & of fever.

I find that Williams has employed himself Gambling Since his Return from his Hunt, & has not yet joined the Service.[143]

The Horses are doing pretty well, but the Corn goes very Rapidly. Very fine weather.

Friday 10th.

Fine day. In the evening Sen[o]r Vigil arrived with my baggage all Safe from S[an]ta Fee.

Saturday 11th.

Wrote to Mr. [Elisha] Stanley by *Vigil* who Set out on his Return to Santa Fee this morning.

A War party of the Pawnees Said to be ab[ou]t 300 Strong has been Recently here. A Small detachment of it, about 30 Men entered the Valley & drove off in the Night a number of Mules & horses. The Pueblos pursued them next day, & found them in the Mountain & killed two & wounded many others, & Recovered all the Mules & Horses. Another very fine day.

Sunday 12th.

Fine day. A Spaniard Returned from the other Side of the Mountains, where he had gone with a Small party of Buffalo Hunters, and Reports that he fell in with about 100 Pawnees who Stripped him & his whole Party of their Mules, Horses, Meat, Clothes, Arms, &c. & were Seriously inclined to kill them all. He Says that he knew Several of the Principal Men of the Party, having Seen them at Ft. Atkinson once. They knew him also, & Returned him *his* Gun, but kept everything else. He understood that another party of about 100 Men were gone down South towards the Settlements of Moro & San Miguel, with the view of driving off Stock &c. This Man did not know of the Pueblo's having killed any of the Pawnees the other day, & he Supposes that the band he Met must have been ignorant of that affair too, otherwise they would Surely have killed him & all his Party. He means to Start to S[an]ta Fee tomorrow I understand, to See The Gov[erno]r about this affair.

Sen[o]r Luno from whom I Rent the house I am in, informs me that he Shall want it very Soon, & that I may occupy his House in the Village. As this will be extremely inconvenient I Sent Thorp yesterday to find another House, & he Reports that a Sen[o]r Romaro who lives at The Rancho offers to Rent me a large House &c. Situated about a Mile & half lower down the Creek.

I walked down to look at the Tenement offered, & find that it will answer extremely well, & determine to move to it as Soon as I can.

I wrote to Mr. Stanley on the 11th to Say that I wished him to direct Mr. *Floyd* to purchase for me 20 breeding Jennets, & a Horse at the Passo, & to Sent [sic] them up to me here, by the middle of May.

Monday 13th March.

Another fine day. Busy preparing to Move.

Tuesday 14th.

Busy preparing to move. Fine day. Had the corn thrashed out.

Wednesday 15th.

Moved today into the Houses Rented from Sen[o]r Romaro.

In the evening Mr. Samuel Chambers[144] called, & I took occasion
to have the bargain between me & Romaro well explained. It is in
Substance as follows—I am to have the use of the buildings, Horse
Pen, & Pasture ground belonging to the establishment, *uninterrupted*
as long as I wish it at the Rate of $10 p[er] Month.

Friday 17th March.

A Very Windy & Stormy day. Sen[o]r Romaro called, & Requested
me to Ride to The Ranch tomorrow morning to arrange Something
formal Respecting the Rent &c. Having no interpreter at hand I could
but imperfectly understand his meaning. I promised however, to See
him at the Rancho early tomorrow.

Saturday 18th.

After early Breakfast I Rode to the Ranch, ab[ou]t 4 Miles, accompanied by Thorp. I found Sen[o]r Romaro at the Alcalde's, & he gave
me to understand that his object was to have our bargain explained
& put in form before the Alcalde. I Sent for a Mr. Gordon, who lives
in this Village, and who Speaks the Spanish Language pretty well,
& employed him to interpret for me. After he had conversed Some
time with Romaro & the Alcalde he informed me that it was proposed
to have a written contract drawn up by the Alcalde which would probably cost me about $2. I immediately discovered that the plan was
to get a fee out of me for the Alcalde; and I told them at once that
I would Submit to no Such imposition, that I wanted no written instru-
ment from Romaro, having already had the bargain fully explained by
Mr. Chambers & that I Should Sign no paper but of my own writing.
That there needed no writing at all about the matter, but I was willing
to give Mr. Romaro my obligation to pay him $10 p[er] Month for
the Rent of his Place as Long as I occupied it without interruption—

& to pay at the end of every Month. I wrote & Signed an Article to that effect, gave it to Romaro, & went home.

Romaro is a Simple well meaning fellow, I think. But the Alcalde is as thoro' going a Scoundrel, I believe, as I ever came across.[145] The day was cold & windy.

Sunday 19th March.
A raw disagreeable day. Snow Storm in the Mountains.

Monday 20th.
Day cold and unpleasant.

Tuesday 21t.
Another cold Stormy day. In the evening it Snowed.

Wednesday 22d.
Ground covered with Snow but the weather much moderated. Snow nearly all gone before Night.

Thursday 23d.
Fine day.

Friday 24th.
Another very fine day.

Saturday 25th.
Fine day. Rode to the Mountain ab[ou]t 4 Miles.

Sunday March 26th. 1826.
A fine day. Since my Return from S[an]ta Fee, I have got entirely well again, and am now in as good health as I ever was.

In the Supposition that Capt. Brannin & his Party have by this time Reached Ft. Osage, I am today indulging myself with tho[ugh]ts of home. To be Sure my tho[ugh]ts are daily there, but now they are attended with the idea of my Wife & friends being employed Reading my Letters &c. & they are consequently more than usually agreeable.

The Spring is Rapidly advancing. The People Seem to be busily engaged preparing to Pitch their little Crops in all directions. I observe them plowing & clearing off their little Patches. Some have already put in their Wheat. They Plow with Oxen & Wooden Plows, & Seem to Succeed pretty well.

Monday 27th M[ar]ch.

The Morning cloudy & Rainy. We had April Weather today—Showers and Sunshine. It Rained as I Suppose a great deal in the Mountains. They were often entirely obscured by dark heavy clouds. Some Thunder.

Tuesday 28th.

M[ornin]g Cloudy & quite cool—ground covered with Snow, & it contin[ue]d to Snow lightly 'till 10 o'Clock, when it cleared off & became windy. The Snow lay but a few Hours in the Valley; but the Mountains are all White.

Wednesday 29th March

The Morning fair & pleasant. Employed the Men lying Corn for Hominy. We are obliged to make Ashes of the Corn Cobs there being no other material convenient, & not half enough of that.

This is a fine warm day, and makes the grass grow very fast. The Horses are very evidently improving already, altho' the Grass is but just beginning to look green.

Busy all day arranging my Accounts &c.

Thursday 30th March.

A very delightful morning. Heavy White frost last night. The day turned out a very pleasant one. [John S.] Davis came down this evening to See us and to Settle Some Acc[oun]ts &c.

Mr. Brown went up this evening to See Senor Luno ab[ou]t Rent, Horse Troughs, &c. and to effect a final and complete Settlement with him—which he did after Some little difficulty. Luno charges me $16 for 3 or 4 Troughs and Some forage. This is to be Sure a very high charge indeed, but is less by about $5 than he demanded at first. The $16 was finally allowed him, which with $16.50 for Rent of his Houses makes $32.50 that I have paid him altogether—and Mr. Brown Says he expressed himself entirely content and Satisfied.

I occupied his Houses Five Months and a half. So that the Rent including Troughs &c. may be Set at $5.91 per Month.

The troughs were very materially injured by the Horses & in fact Rendered unfit for the uses they were originally intended for. Two of them I had Removed to my new quarters, where they are wanted to feed the Horses in. Upon the whole, I have got off better than I expected with Senor Luno.

Friday 31t. March.

A very pleasant day.

I arranged and Settled up all my Accounts today and find that my Whole Expenses Since I arrived here on 30th October last amount to $1468.20 Vizt.

For Subsistence	$492.27½
House Rent	61.12½
Grain & forage for Horses	541.30
Fitting out Party to Missouri	83.25
Expense getting over to Taus	38.50
Ex[pense] moving to & from S[an]ta fee	100.12½
Fire wood S[an]ta fee	23.75
Furniture	68.12½
Contingencies	60.75
Including Goods paid away	18.87½

Herga & Yarn value	23.00
Gloves	1.50
Bl[an]k[e]ts & Coverlid	20.62½
Casimere Pantaloons	10.62½
2 pr. Nankeen Do.	
2 Sheets & 3 P[illow] Cases	18.00
Sund[rie]s	5.00
Nuts	5.00

Baskets		1.75
Grape Cuttings, Onion &c. Seeds		13.75
		‾‾‾‾‾
		99.25
Ropes		2.00
		‾‾‾‾‾
		101.25
2 Mules & Saddles	$88.00	
Herga &c.	12.37	
	‾‾‾‾‾	
	100.37	100.37
		‾‾‾‾‾
		201.62

*D*iary of Joseph Davis, on return from the Mexican boundary, September 30 to October 25, 1825.

As was named in the latter end of the first volume We descended the river on the 30th September to our old encampment[147] of the 23 August which we made in ascending the river. From which I was to commence the correction of the original survey;[148] and at which we expected to leave the Arkansas River finally.

Accordingly on the 1st October, though the last day of the week, after calculating the course to a given point [Cottonwood Grove] at which we wished to intersect the original Survey, we set out steering N 81 E, and traveled near 14 miles, when coming to Badger Creek [Little Cow] we encamped for the night.

In the Sabbath and 2nd of October after crossing the creek we pursued the course of the 1st N 81 E, and after travelling about 15 miles we came to a small creek which we supposed to be the little Arkansaw and encamped for the night. Saw a great many Buffaloes but all Bulls. None having been killed since we left walnut creek: that is that were good meat. We feel as if we have been favoured, it now being the 2nd as above named, and not a single frost that was hard enough to kill the most tender plant of the valleys or plains has fallen this season. The weather for some days has been beautiful; but it is now threatning: but cleared off without a deviation from beauty.

On the morning of Monday 3rd we breakfasted early and set out on the same course which we had been travelling on the preceding days. Proceeded about 6 miles, and unfortunately it took us to the steep ground on the head of the Caw, or *Kansas* River. But thinking that we could avoid it after one or two miles travelling through it, we did not alter our course: but continued to travel five miles farther, and then coming to a branch of beautiful timber, we considered it advisable to encamp by running off two miles to the south at right angles, As the country was too broken to soot the future waggoner. On this day saw an immensity of bulls, but only one gang of cows of which we got none. This day was disagreeably warm, but clear.

On Tuesday the 4th set out on the parallel line at the distance of 2 miles from the original line [N 81 E], and travelled 16 miles over very level ground at which distance we came to the heads of the Caw waters again; encamped on a small branch of the same, where there was as beautiful water as heart could wish. On this evening it clouded up and threatened rain, likewise it rained and the wind blew after night, but the storm was lighter than usual.

On the morning of Wednesday the 5th we set out after breakfast, and after travelling 3 miles we found that the country was too steep to pursue the course of N 81 E, consequently we directed it S 55 E. On which course after travelling a fiew miles we came to the original survey 9 miles from our place of destination (to wit) the cotton wood grove [on Cottonwood Branch of Neosho]. But there to our great disappointment, stuck a paper upon a tree with intelligence of Capt. Becknell[149] having been there on that morning with some papers from Government which we supposed to be instructions, but here must remain on suspense untill he returns as he informs us he will return in a fiew days. But to the relief of our suspense, and the disappointment of our expectations about 10 o'clock we heard a gun just across the creek from the encampment, at which moment every man sprung to his gun to make ready for action. The night was very dark: but directly he made himself known who proved to be the Capt, but no additional instructions; notwithstanding there were papers communicated to Colo[ne]l Reeves; but we think relative to the intirnal government of our own State.[150] At the cottonwood grove we intended lying at camp one day for the refreshment of our horses and mules, which we did accordingly. This Creek which was spoken of in our first number Capt. Becknell informs us, is the stream called Verdigris;[151] but we were before informed that none of the tributary streams of that river came from a source as far northward as our road, and that cottonwood and other creeks near it were all streams that empty into the Neozho, however these facts will be ascertained in a future day, to the satisfaction us us [sic] all.

As above named we lay by on Thursday the 6th, on which day it rained considerably.

On the morning of Friday the 7th we set out after breakfast and travelled until in the night before coming to wood and water sufficiently to encamp at. On this day saw but three bulls and expected they were the last we would see on our way home. Of course there was some anxiety displayed at that time, to see who would kill one but amongst us all only one was killed, they running a different course to that which we were travelling we did not pursue them far.

On Saturday the 8th in consequence of bad weather we did not move from our late encampment. Severe rains fell on this day, and night following.

On the morning of Sunday the 9th we set out after early breakfast, and travelled very rapidly. On this day passed the good spring [Diamond Spring] of which we spoke in the first Book: the encampment of 11th Augt: as going out. On this day we came to the council grove; but tired several horses in the afternoon. The weather has now faired up and it was as beautiful weather as we could be blessed with: but no frost; however on the night of this day there came the largest frost that we had seen on this fall.

On monday the 10th we we [sic] lay at council grove for the refreshment of the horses; likewise to try to get some venison and honey, accordingly we killed some deer and found one beehive; but it was worthless. On this day some conversation took place relative to sending after more horses, to take the waggons into the settlements. The question was whether will we send some man or men with Capt. Becknell or not. (he not having left us yet).

On Tuesday the 11th it was agreed that Col. Mather should go into the settlements with Capt. Becknell and one or two more men for the purpose of sending horses back to us. This day lay at the above camp for more recreation. The weather now most delightful, clear and warm to an exception for the lateness of the season.

Accordingly on the morning of Wednesday the 12th, Col. Mather, Capt. Becknell and Henly Cooper set out for Fort Osage to get horses and the two latter to bring them back to us. On this day likewise we set out and travelled about 6 miles then encamped for the night. The vegetation here is very dry, notwithstanding the warmth of the weather and the seasonable rains which we have had during this fall. On this day no game discovered at all. We lay at our encampment of the 4th August at a creek [Hickory, now Rock Creek] opposite a cliff. Some small groves of timber are here, consisting of black walnut, Elm etc. The soil here in the bottom is very rich but ridges poor and broken. Settlements no how justifiable to an American farmer; in fact there are no watercourses on this road between the Blues and the boundary line which would justify a farmers settlement with the exception of the Neozho: which was spoken of, and the situation of which is described in our first Book under head 5th August.

On the morning of Thursday the 13th we set out after breakfast and proceeded 12 miles and encamped on the creek [142 Mile Creek] where we killed the first elk as we went out. It was the encampment of the 1st August at which Major Sibley overtook us. At this creek there are nice little groves of timber sufficient for the future traveller to find himself plentifully supplied with fire-wood. This day cloudy, but no rain.

On the morning of Friday the 14th we set off and travelled exceedingly well, passed the encampment of the 30 and 29 July at which we encamped on it being on a fine creek [Wagon, a branch of Soldier Creek], but very little timber, though in the evening we found a bee tree of good quality on it.

On the morning of Saturday the 15th after gathering the horses two of which the boys had found on the preceding day which were supposed to have been lost by the stock merchants a fiew days before who were in advance of us. We proceeded to our encampment of the 28 July it being a beautiful place; not so with the creek [110 Mile]; it is an ugly stream and can only be crossed at chance places with waggons, which is the case with almost the whole of these creeks that are tributary streams of the Osage River. At this creek there is a fine little grove of timber; the best of any between the Blues and the Council Grove; here we found 4 bee-trees, though indifferent ones.

On the morning of the 16th and Sunday, we proceeded early with the expectation of proceeding to our encampment of the 25th July; but did not get so far, it being 21 miles. At this time no meat was our lot, with the exception of a little dry buffaloe meat which was too full of green mold to be eaten: But we had plenty of sugar and Coffee, Rice and Tallow; which we fared sumptuously on. We lay on a small branch of the Osage river on that night.

And on the morning of Monday the 17th we set out a little after sunrise and travelled to the encampment of the 25th July above named, and on the same day killed a fine deer and found a bee-tree; consequently all scarcity was forgotten, and we now lived in pomp and splendor.

On the morning of Tuesday the 18th the conclusion was to tarry at the above encampment, and hunt bees, with the exception of 4 men who were appointed to go forward to our encampment of the 24th July [15 miles east] for the purpose of hunting bees. On this day we found 3 bee-trees which were very good ones; but killed no deer. Here we could see the Prairie on fire in different directions which we suppose to have been done by the Indians of the adjacent country.

On the morning of Wednesday the 19th (after leaving one horse which was disabled by lying in the mire all night) we set out for our encampment of the 24th which was about 15 miles. After travelling about 10 miles we came to some Indians in the prairie who said they were from the Caw nation. They made signs of their being encamped at a small distance from the road on a branch of the Kansas river, and their sign in this part of the country manifested the same to us. They likewise insisted on our going by and eating with them but we did not accept the offer. In the evening when we arrived at the encampment our hunters had killed 4 deer, one elk and found two bee-trees but these trees were indifferent.

On this day we travelled on the dividing ridge between the Osage and Kansas rivers. The heads of the latter rendered the country very broken; but the heads of the former descended gradually, and through Prairie of good quality. On this day likewise we saw more groves of timber than we had on any day since our returning. The groves are very small but alternately on each side of the ridge.

Thursday the 20th we set off with expectations of meeting Capt. Becknell and his accompanyants with horses to our relief. But we travelled all the day without seeing any persons but some Indians, or rather one Indian who came to the waggons and pretended that our party had put a cheat on him in the exchange of a mare for his mule in our travel out to the line. He showed simptoms likewise of wanting his mule back again, said that he had shot the mare, and that the white man who swapped with him "was a big liar."

After passing ours of the 23rd July we proceeded about 6 miles and encamped on a branch of the Osage river. At this place there was a great deal of Indian sign which looked as if it was made on the preceding day.

On the morning of the 21st to wit Friday in consequence of the reduced state of our horses Col. Reeves concluded we had better lie at camp and await Capt. Becknell's arrival, who had not come yet. Accordingly we did so, and some of the boys who went out on a hunt found one of our horses about a mile and a half below us on the creek hoppled with an Indian's rope and alone hid in the brush. It was immediately brought back of course and turned with the others. On this day about 10 o'clock to our agreeable surprise Capt. Becknell arrived with his accompanyants, three ewks of oxen, and 4 horses were brought to our relief. Likewise Mr. Joel Walker come with them and assisted them in bringing one of our beeves which ran away from us on the 27th July which was spoken of in our first book. On this evening we moved about one mile and encamped on another fork of the same; but saw no more sign of Indians at this place.

On Saturday the 22nd we set off and travelled rapidly (our teams being refreshed) for probably 18 miles. Through rain at different times on this day, and encamped on a branch of the Kansas. On this day nothing killed: but nothing was required as beef was plenty. On this day passed ours of the 22 July.

On Sunday the 23rd we set out early, passed ours of the 21st and and [sic] 20; after which we encamped on the big Blue. The weather now very clear and warm, and we can say with thanks that we have not had a single frost yet hard enough to kill the young sedge grass which has sprung up in the late burns of last summer. On this day got plenty of honey and found one horse and one mule, which we supposed were lost by our United States merchants, in consequence of our red neighbors showing symptoms of hostility to them about that place. But we hope that this is only report, occasioned by the pusillanimous spirit of those who devised it.

On Monday the 24th we pursued our travel again, crossed big Blue and with some less difficulty than we expected got up the bluff. We then proceeded past ours of the 18th July [near Independence] and encamped in the timber of little blue, at the house of one Mr. [Henry Burris], at which place we got some pumpkins for our horses. It is surprising to relate the number of families that have come into these parts since we passed here on our way out. It is unnecessary to recapitulate the richness and beauty of this country; it is sufficient to say that it shows to much better advantage than it did in the summer season.

On Tuesday the 25th we set out and after crossing little Blue arrived at Fort Osage where we commenced our survey of the road on the 17th of July 1825.

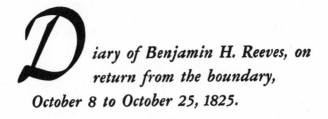

iary of Benjamin H. Reeves, on return from the boundary, October 8 to October 25, 1825.

Saturday 8th. Octr. 1825.

This day raind hard & very cool, we remaind Stationary. Our Horses appear as if they must fail before we get in. This little Creek [probably Camp Creek] upon which we are encampd, may be called a wet weather stream, not running water, but a sufficiency standing in holes, to supply the traveler. The banks of the Stream lin[e]d with a thin skirt of (principally) Elm timber. Soil good. This night, stormy.

Sunday 9th.

Set out ½ past 8 in the Morning. The storm ceased—a beautiful day with a clear sunshine. Traveld 5 miles (haveing passd two or three wet weather streams with standing water with some timber[)] & came to a most beautiful limistone spring [Diamond Spring] large & Cold. Soil very good, timber scarce; thin skirt of timber down the branch, principally Elm. At this spring we threw up a *mound* or pile of limistone rock & markd 176 miles to Ft. Osage—At this spring a good settlement can be made by ditching for fencing. Firewood may be had—Rock or Brick for building—many little groves or *patches* of timber in sight but of too low & scrubly a nature for any other purpose than fuel. Passed the spring, five or six miles, & crossed another wet weather creek with water in holes, thinly timberd. Frequently today we pass over limistone rock & passd the head of a small creek [Elm] which ran nearly east & empties into the Neeozho Just below "Council Grove." This creek appears to be thicker timberd than those we crossd. We arrived at Council Grove about sunset. Several of our Horses gave out this afternoon. We intend resting here a day or too to recruit our Horses.

Monday 10th Octr. 1825.

We Rest today to recruit our Horses & to repair one of our waggons haveing two or 3 days ago lost the tire of one wheel. We repaird it by putting on a *tire* of raw *buffaloe* hide. We have a most pleasant day of warm sunshine. This creek Neeosho on which we are encampd empties into the Arkansas River one or two miles below the mouth of the "Verdegris," as we are informd by Captains Cooper & Becknal.

Tuesday 11th.

Rested our Horses.

Wednesday 12th Octr.

Col. Mather Cap Becknal & H. Cooper left us & went into the Settlements to procure & send fresh horses to meet the waggons with which I stay. 20 minutes past 10 in the morning I started with the waggons. In two miles past [passed] a small creek [Big John Creek] with running water—thinly timberd, principally with Black Walnut & ash. Passed on to another & a larger creek [Rock] with running water & thinly timberd. Bur oake, Hickory, walnut & elm. This creek is about 15 feet wide. Soil good, prairies high, fertile & rolling. Distance 6 & ¾ miles. Just at the moment of setting out this morning we ascertain that one of our Mules was sick. We was compeld to leave it.

Thursday 13th Octr.

Set out this morning ½ past 8. Cloudy & very much like rain. In going about one mile from the creek on which we was encamped over a level & fertile valley, we arose a *high* & rocky eminence from which we had an extensive view of the country as far as the eye could reach. Many little groves of timber in sight, the prairies high & rolling, in places coverd with flakes of limestone rock. Came to another creek [Bluff Creek] of running water of a few feet wide thinly coverd with oak, Hickory & Walnut timber. This is the last branch of the Neeozho, & consequently of the Arkansas waters which we have to cross. We crossed the divide between Arkansas & Osage waters & came on to the "Elk" fork [142 Mile Creek] of the Osage & encampd. Distance 13 miles. On this fork of the Osage settlements may be formd. Timber does not abound but is of a tolerable good quality, principally of bur oak & some walnut. This fork is from 10 to 20 feet wide.

Friday 14th.

Morning cloudy & misting rain. Set out at 9 in the morning, traveld over high & rolling prairies 2¾ miles & came to a creek of Osage [Elk Creek, a branch of Marais des Cygnes] about 20 feet wide, clear running water, thinly timberd, principally of Elm & walnut, with some Sycamore & oak. Soil good 2d rate. Passed on over high prairies 10 miles & came to another fork of the Osage [branch of Dragoon Creek] 15 or 20 feet wide; in places high rocky banks, bold running currant, good ford, thinly timberd, oak, elm, walnut &c. Came 2 miles further to another fork of Osage about the same sise, currant bold, good rocky ford [Wagon Creek, a branch of Soldier Creek]. Growth some large walnut & sycamore oak &c. Encampd distance 15¼ miles.

Saturday 15th.

Set out this morning 45 minutes after eight. Traveld over very fertile & gently rolling prairies for 6 miles & came to a creek [Switzler] of Osage where the Santafeeans last spring had thrown a Bridge. This stream bold—about 15 or 20 feet wide, thin or narrow skirt of timber on each bank—oak, walnut, Mulberry Honey locust &c., undergrowth Hazle. Passd on over a rich prairie 7 miles & came to another fork of Osage [110 Mile Creek] about the same sise, timber more plenty—growth the same. From this creek to Ft Osage 110 miles. Distance today 13 miles. Encamped.

Sunday 16th.

Set out this morning about 9. Was somewhat difficulted in finding our Horses. Traveld a few miles & took the Divideing ridge between Osage & Kaw. Country high, small skirts of timber in sight on each side of us, but none near the road. Prairies of a good quality. Traveld about 10 miles, no wood nor water in view, except a small skirt of timber on a branch of Osage about 1&½ miles to the south of us which we was compeld to turn to. Campd for the night which was cool. Large white frost.

Monday 17th.

Clear & cool, large frost. Traveled over prairies that was gently rolling for about 6 or 7 miles & came to a small fork of Osage—our old encampment where we lost our Beeves as we went out & where Mr. Gamble left us when he went to the Osage villages. This is a creek of small sise but constant water, clear & pleasant—rocky bottom in places & in others remarkable mirery. Timber, Hickory, oak, Sycamore walnut &c. Killd 2 Deer & found Bees. Most excellent feasting, our stock of provisions being exhausted.

Tuesday 18th.

Our Horses being much exhausted, we let them rest. Our young men out in pursuit of game, which is exceedingly scarce here. Found none, but succeeding in getting some most excellent Honey.

Wednesday 19th.

Set out at 45 minutes past 8 this morning. Left one of our Horses, in a manner dead. The animal could not stand. Worn out with poverty & fatiegue. Passd over high prairies, almost without wood or water. In one place crossed a little woodless branch of Osage where we found one *hole* of watter which was clear & well tasted. Timber in sight on both sides of the Ridge. Arrived at 4 o'clock in the afternoon at what is called the narrow divide between Osage & Kaw at which place the waters of these two streams interlock. Traveld 15½ miles to our encampment which we made as we went out & where we first lost one of our Horses—which is on the Kaw side of the ridge. Killd several deer & one Elk today. Several of the Kaw Indians came to us—Their encampment not far of[f]. Manifested great friendship. I gave them a few twists of Tobbacco with which they was much pleased.

Thursday 20th.

Was much difficulted in finding our Horses. Set out at 10 in the forenoon. Traveld over high prairies for about 1&½ miles, then took the divide between Kaw & Osage. Timber & water Scarce. Was compeld to leave the Ridge on the Osage side & traveld off our course near 2 miles before we could get timber & water to encamp at. The prairies generally burnt. The Indians hunting & comeing to us from every direction. Succeeded in getting good grass timber & water to encamp at. Distance today about 12 miles.

Friday 21st.

The extremely reduced state of our Horses compeld us to rest today. In hunting up and examineing our Horses, one of them was found to be missing. One of our young men, L[evi] Cornelius, out from Camp about 1&½ miles in pursuit of game discovered a Horse trail—followed it a short distance & discovered the animal we had lost with its feet closely tied with an Indian tug in a thicket. He reclaimd the animal & brot it to camp. This is a proof to me of the Indian perfidy. They had been frequently with us. I gave them small presents of tobacco, with which they seemd much pleased & treated us with much Respect— & that night stole one of our Horses, which in all probability we should have lost, had it not have been for the vigilence of Mr. Cornelius. About 2 oclock p m H. Cooper Cap Becknal & Jo & Joel Walker met us with a Beef, some salt & a supply of oxen & Horses for the draft, which was a very seasonable relief to us. The exhausted state of our Horses in all probability would have compeld us to have left the waggons & traveld in on foot. We set out in the evening—traveld about 2 miles to another fork of Osage & encampd for the night, about 2 or 3 miles south of the divide.

Saturday 22d

Set out ½ past 8. Traveld on the Osage side of the Ridge for some miles—turned upon the Ridge & came in sight of Big *Blue* timber. A short distance farther & came to a small grove near the divide called the "Round Grove" which is on Kaw waters. Turnd down on the Kaw side & encamped. Distance 15 or 16 miles. Raining & wet evening.

Sunday 23d.

We lay last night a few miles west of where Patrick first broke his waggon tounge. Came over high prairies on the Divide between Kaw & Blue, without timber or water untill we came to Big Blue. Distance 18 or 19 miles—within a mile or two to either hand, timber & water. Encamped. Some of our Company found a Mule & a Horse supposed to belong to the St Fee traders who returnd this fall. Left one of our Horses, which is so far reduced that the animal is unable to travel. We passd the "Sauk" vilage today which I visited as we went out. The Indians had all left it whether for their fall Hunt or permanently removed I am unable to learn.

Monday 24th.

Set [out] early. Crossd Big Blue & rose the Hill which was Steep & rocky in safety & came in sight of Mr. [John] Youngs—The first white Mans Habitation which I saw since 18th July & arrived at Mr. [Henry] Burris by sunset where we encampd. "Big Blue" is from 45 to 60 feet wide—rocky bottom.

Tuesday 25th.

Set out about 10. Came on to "little Blue" by 12 oclock. This Stream is about 50 feet wide & affords more water than Big Blue.

*J*ournal of George C. Sibley on correction of the survey and making of Report, May 12 to October 27, 1827.

Saturday May 12th.

Today the Men engaged assembled at my House[154] and Signed an Article[155] drawn up by myself, containing every necessary Stipulation—which See on file. The men thus engaged are

1. Jno. Walker[156]
2. Jacob Gregg[157]
3. Andw. Carson[158]
4. Wm. Baxter[159]
5. David R. Cameron
6. Jno. Cameron[160]
7. Bryan Baxter
8. Jas. Baxter
9. Joseph D. Hardin[161]
10. C. B. Richardson[162]
11. R. D. Collins[163]
12. Wm. M. Owen

The Mules were collected, & each Man (except Collins who is the Waggoner) took one in charge. These Men are now on Wages at $20 p[er] Month, and were directed to prepare themselves for Service against Monday. There is a Small Company of Traders assembling 10 Miles below this on their Way to New Mex[ic]o and will probably get on the Road about the time I shall. But I am inclined to avoid this, and every other Party if I can; because it will be inconvenient for too many to travel together on Acc[oun]t of the Scarcity of Game.

Two of the Mules Sent up by Col. Reeves are unfit for Service; and

I have Substituted two of my own (better ones) for them; as it is impossible to get on without them. A Small Brown Mule (unfit for the Waggon) I exchanged for a Horse, even Swap, to go in the Waggon as a leader before.

Thursday May 17.

Today had the Waggon loaded as follows—

2 Bags of Rice—76 lbs. ea[ch]	152 lbs.
5 " " Flour—in all	614 lbs.
2 " " Corn Meal	300 lbs.
1 " " Salt	60 lbs.
1 Keg Whiskey	
1 Keg Sund[rie]s	104 lbs.
1 Box Candles	
1 Trunk Medicine & Powder	55 lbs.
4 falling Axes	
2 Spades	
1 Draw Knife	40 lbs.
Compass & Chain &c.	
1 Box Bacon	400 lbs.
3 Tents—Baggage &c.	275 lbs.
	————
	2000 lbs.

Friday May 18th.

At ab[out] 12 O'Clock today I Started my Party—12 Men, 14 Mules, 1 Horse & 1 Waggon in the charge of A[ndrew] Carson, who has directions to go on to the Upper Settlement on the Big Blue, and there wait for me.

I cannot leave home before Sunday, having much writing & other business to do first.

Tuesday 22d.

The arrival of Mr. [Paul] Baillio from N. Mex[ic]o on Saturday evening prevented my Starting on Sunday. Today I Set off from home at 9 o'Clock. Overtook the Party at R. Fristoe's[164] & camped with bad headache.

B. Majors[165] joined as a hand yesterday morning as agreed on, with his two cows.

Wednesday 23d.

Fine M[ornin]g. Headache bad. Engaged Jo. Walker[166] as a hand to join day after tomorrow. Majors agrees to let me have the use of his two cows on the trip for $5 if Returned to him at Big Blue—if killed or lost on the trip I am to pay him $9 a piece for them.

Broke up Camp and Started on at 10 O'Clk.; had not got 2 Miles before the Waggon broke down in crossing a branch near Fristoe's; to Repair this detained 'till after Noon, when we again got under way, & reached Big Blue at Night & camped. 26 M[iles] 41 Ch[ain]s from Ft. Osage. So far I believe the Road is located on the best ground.

It Sh[oul]d pass thro' the C[ount]y Seat of Jackson & then go by Mr. [John] Cook's[167] to the Prairie, then bear Southward & get on the Survey'd line, Saving perhaps ½ Mile.

Thursday 24th May.

Fine M[ornin]g. My headache Still plagues me. One of the Mules Ran off, and detained 'till late. M[ar]k[e]d the distance on a Tree, a Large Sycamore. Had Some Posts made to Set up today on the Prairie. Did not Start 'till after Noon. It is 5 Miles from Big Blue to Hycory Grove, or perhaps more properly Fish Cr[eek]. The Grove is off to the left of the Road nearly a Mile. We got there before Night & camped, having Some Posts to put up near this place.

Friday 25th May.

Fine M[ornin]g. All the Mules Ran Back to the Blue last night tho' Hobbled. Did not get to work 'till late. Put up Six Posts today, one of which is on the State Line & M[ar]k[e]d—"31 M. State Line." All the Posts have Large Mounds Round them.

The Hycory Grove at our camp last Night is a Mile, a little South of West from the Post on the State Line. In the evening of a very hot day, halted in a Pretty grove on a Small Branch nearly a Mile to the Right of the Road; after which, went out and put up Some Mounds.

The Prairie & whole country here is beautiful—the Land Rich, Timber good & Plenty & Water good, Prairie excellent.

The Road passes on a high Ridge about equidistant from two considerable Groves of timber, which are in Sight for Several Miles. From the State Line to this Grove at our Camp, the distance is 6 Miles by the Road. The Road So far is on the best ground, I am Satisfied.

Saturday 26th May.

Very fine Morning. Started early. Put up two Mounds & Posts, and then 3 very Large Mounds of Sod & then near our camp for the day a M[oun]d & Post or Bush. The M[ar]ks today Point out the most direct Route & conduct the traveler over very good ground. There are Several P[oin]ts of timber on either Side of the Road. At the one we Stopped at today is good Water & a pretty place, and near the M[oun]d on the hill a little Northward of Camp is a fine Large Spring. The Road Runs today on the Dividing Ridge between Kansas & Big Blue. Camp is at the upper P[oin]t of timber of Blue on the Road. A. Carson and Joel Walker overtook us last Night. Carson went back from Fristoe's on 23d. for Some Powder. Joel Walker has come to join as a hand in place of his Brother Jo—his time commences on the 25th & he is in other Respects on Same footing as the others.

Sunday 27 May.

Another fine Morning. Started after early Br[ea]kf[as]t. Our course is direct to the Round Grove—at about 2 Miles from which, and about ½ Mile North[war]d from the fork of the Road, put up a Large Mound & a Post upon which M[ar]k[e]d "To Big Blue 18 Ms.," after which went to the Round Grove, & halted about an Hour to Water—then went *down* the Cr[eek] nearly a Mile & found a good Crossing place, then out from Cr[eek]. ½ Mile or So, in line with Said crossing and last noted put up another M[oun]d, then Southwardly to a high Ridge near which the old Road Runs upon which I intended to have Raised another M[oun]d in line with the 2 last so as to cut off a Mile or So. Found that a much greater Saving of distance may be effected by turning off more Northwestward from the M[oun]d near our Camp of last Night leaving the Round Grove about 2 or 3 Miles to the left. This I deemed it fit to effect, and turned off to a Small P[oin]t of timber on a Br[anch] of Osage 1½ Miles from the Old Road & camped. Day very hot. I propose to go back tomorrow about 7 Miles and mark the cut off noticed above.

Monday May 28.

The M[ornin]g cloudy, foggy & quite cool. Started the Waggon on with 3 Men to find a Camping place on the old Road; and with the Rest Set off to Mark the Cut off. Went back & took down the Mound near our Camp of 26th and the next one back from it—then M[ar]k[e]d the Road to Run from the next M[oun]d ab[ou]t S.S.W., crossing the old Road to 2 large M[oun]ds put up today, thence ab[ou]t S.W. till it falls into the old Road on the high Ridge, crossing the Cr[eek] at a very good ford ab[ou]t 3 Miles *below* the Round Grove. This alteration throws the Road more Northward, & probably Saves 4 Miles, and is over good ground. Where it Crosses the Creek is a handsome grove & a very good place for camping, having plenty of Wood Water & Pasture. I Sh[oul]d Say that this crossing is about 19 Miles from the ford of Big Blue by the Road. Altogether this is an advantageous alteration in every point of view.

Finding that large M[oun]ds of Sod make excellent M[ar]k[er]s & that a good many will be necessary Sent two Men back to Ft. Osage for two more Spades. Having finished the M[ar]k[er]s which employed us busily nearly all day, Rode on briskly & overtook the camp, on a Small branch off to the left of the Road. The day cool & cloudy & pleasant. The Prairies are generally extremely Rich & beautiful So far.

Tuesday May 29th, 1827.

A cool & cloudy Morning. Started pretty early, and Soon Reached the *"Narrow divide"* a high Ridge so called between the Waters of Osage & Kansas Rivers, upon which the Road has heretofore passed, & in thus passing is necessarily extremely crooked.

By taking a course more Northward, it is Supposed quite as good a Road may be had, and about two Miles Saved out of five; to effect this however, the Road must pass two or three Creeks, & thro' Several Small Groves of timber, & will Require Some Labour perhaps. I Spent this day making the necessary examinations, which Result in the determination to Mark out the Road So as to effect the cut off.

Wednesday 30 May 1827.

Fine day. Employed the whole of it Marking the Cut off, and bridging the Small Creeks and did not complete the whole. In the meantime my Camp Remains at a P[oin]t of timber near the Prairie about ¾ of a Mile So.E. from the termination of the Cut off. Tomorrow I Shall finish this work and proceed on the Way.

Thursday 31t May.

Fine M[ornin]g. Went to work pretty early—and finished the Cut off by 1 O'Clk. Vizt. Turn off at a Large M[oun]d near the left hand side of the Road—pass 3 Smaller M[oun]ds which lead to Blazed Oak, follow Blazes to Bridge over Hungry Creek—then follow 4 Mounds & See blazes on the 4 Oaks at Crossing of Dove Creek—then follow 4 Mounds to Gooseberry Creek—then follow 3 M[oun]ds to the edge of the timber—then thro' the open woods by the blazes to Grindstone Creek[168]—then follow blazes to a high point of Prairie—then fall into the Road again at a Mound. This alteration is advantageous in this: it Shortens the distance nearly 3 Miles (& the Road is good) and affords Several excellent camping places Right on the Road. Just as we were Ready to Start, [Andrew] Carson & Kit [Richardson] joined us again with the Spades &c. they went for on Monday.

We Set off, and traveled Round the Circuitous Ridge to a P[oin]t of Timber a little off the Road and halted for the Night again, there being no other timber farther on that we can Reach. I think the Road must always pass *Round* on this Ridge; the ground across which a more direct Route would pass is low & flat, and is crossed by Several Muddy gullies. The view from this Ridge is truly beautiful, & amply compensates for the loss of half a Mile or So of distance, especially as the Road is excellent all the Way.

Friday 1t June 1827.

A Rainy cool Morning—it Rained a good deal Since Midnight. The high narrow Ridge along which we traveled last evening (& which is in fact part of the Narrow divide) affords Some of the finest views I ever beheld. On the Right is Seen a very extensive Valley of Prairies & forests intersected by a number of Streams which flow into the Kansas River, which terminates the view Northward. On the left at a greater distance are seen the fringes of Woods that Mark Several branches of the Marais Des Cygne. My Hunters who passed thro' the country of the Valley on the Right Report it to be extremely fertile & beautiful, & I Should judge from all that I can See & learn of it that it would afford Room for Several Hund[re]d families of thrifty farmers & it is finely watered with Springs & has abundance of Lime Stone, good timber, and the adjoining Prairie is very fertile & pretty.

The Rain detained us 'till after Noon, when we broke up Camp & traveled on ab[ou]t 5 Miles & again Camped at Some timber ½ Mile from the Road on the Right.

The Road bears much more South[war]d and for the first 3 Miles or So Runs unnecessarily crooked. At the termination of this crook, I Set up a Mound to Shew that a Straighter way may be traveled. We are Still on a dividing Ridge, the timber of the Kansas Waters on the Right, that of the M[arais] D[es] Cygne on the left. Prairie Still fertile and beautiful.

One of the Hunters killed a Deer today & another bro[ugh]t in 2 or 3 Gal[lon]s of Honey.

Saturday 2d June 1827.

A violent thunder Storm at daylight and Rain 'till nine O'Clk. After drying our baggage, Set out again—traveled about 9 Miles & halted on a Small Creek of Kansas. Erected two M[oun]ds today to Shew the proper direction from P[oin]t to P[oin]t at a very crooked place. Generally the traveled Road Runs very well, & cannot be bettered.

The Prairie Still continues very fertile & pretty. Our Camp toNight is 94 Miles from Ft. Osage by the Survey.

Saw a Number of Prairie Flies today & Some Musquitoes were *felt* last Night.

Sunday 3d June 1827.

A pleasant Morning—fair weather. Started early—traveled over a very pretty country today, Prairie Rich, Sufficiently Watered, and points of timber appearing frequently on either Side. Made Several corrections of the Road So as to Straighten it probably 2 Miles in all. Reached a Br[anch]of M[arais] D[es] Cygne before Night & camped, having traveled today about 15 Miles. This Cr[eek] is M[ar]k[e]d by Mr. B[rown] 111 Miles from Ft. Osage; It may now be reduced to 100 Miles as the Road is Marked, and called 100 M[ile] Creek. It affords Some pretty groves of timber & good Land. A Kansas Ind[ia]n came to our Camp; he Says 5 families are Hunting on the Creek about Six Miles off. Day very hot. Some flies.

Monday June 4th 1827.

M[ornin]g cool & pleasant—a thunder Storm about Sunrise which detained us. A small party of Kansas met us on the Road this M[ornin]g for the purpose of begging.

To Bridge Cr[eek] [Switzler] the Road Runs very well in general, & over a pretty country; only two Mounds necessary. From Bridge Cr[eek] to Muscle Cr[eek] [branch of Dragoon] at a Rocky ford the Waggon Road is extremely crooked. I Marked a Straighter Road, which Saves about 2 Miles out of 7, but from the broken Nature of the country, I doubt if Waggons will take it, tho' the old Road is also over very bad ground. The country is much more broken now as we advance. Prairie very Rich, tho' Stoney & comparatively poor in Spots. Muscle Cr[eek] is M[ar]k[e]d 124 Miles from Ft. Osage. It is a pretty Cr[eek] & affords good Land & considerable timber & fish. We Camped at a Spring.

Tuesday June 5, 1827.

M[ornin]g Fair and Somewhat Sultry—the Night was very Warm & close. Musquetoes troublesome. Started pretty early—the day excessively hot. We got to Elk Cr[eek] [142 Mile Creek] and halted for the day, having traveled 18 Miles. The traveled Road Runs well enough today except at two places which I straightened & Marked. The Prairie is Rather more broken than yesterday, and the Soil not So good on the high Ridges, Some of which are Stony. Still the land is good, & in the low level places *very good*. Between Muscle Cr[eek] & Elk Cr[eek] the Road crosses 4 other Small Creeks[169] all of which have Small patches of timber. Elk Cr[eek] is the largest & has most timber; it is the most Western Br[anch] of M[arais] D[es] Cygne of any Note. Game is very Scarce thus far.

Wednesday June 6, 1827.

M[ornin]g clear and Sultry. Started pretty early. From Elk Cr[eek] to Hycory Cr[eek] [Bluff Creek] is 6 Miles. The Road is as well M[ar]k[e]d by the old track as it can be, except in one place, which I M[ar]k[e]d by Mounds. From Hycory Cr[eek] to Rock Cr[eek] 7 Miles the Road is very Crooked, but cannot be altered for the better. The Prairie is very much broken for the whole distance, & the Road Runs on the high Ridges. Between Elk Cr[eek] [142 Mile Creek] & Hycory [Bluff] Cr[eek] we cross the high dividing Ridge which divides the Waters of the M[arais] D[es] Cygne from those of Neeozho. Hycory Cr[eek] has but little timber. Rock Cr[eek] has more. This is a beautiful Cr[eek] & might afford Room for a Number of families near the Road. Land on the Ridges poor—in the bottoms good. It is Stoney on the Ridges generally.

Thursday June 7, 1827

A cool pleasant M[ornin]g. A thunder Shower Soon after we halted yesterday evening. We got under way pretty early this morning—7 miles to Council Grove. Here we halted for the day, there being Some corrections to be made near. The Prairie is more & more broken and the Road necessarily crooked. The day Warm. Rain at Night.

Friday 8th June

It Rained all the day, & frequently after Night. Staid in Camp. The distance from Ft. O[sage] to C[ouncil] Grove by the Survey is 162 Miles. I believe that the corrections I have made & m[ar]k[e]d will

Reduce the distance 13 Miles at the least, and I have accordingly Marked it on a Tree 149 Miles. I was indisposed today & have been for three days past.

Saturday June 9th. 1827

It Rained this Morning; but cleared off partially about 9 O'Clock So that we could dry our Baggage &c. The Range is uncommonly good here at present. Game is extremely Scarce. Musquetoes troublesome. No Prairie flies. I feel badly this M[ornin]g. Set off at Noon & went on to the next Creek on the Road & camped for the day. The Road thus far from C[ouncil] Grove is on the best ground & Runs very well. I only had to Straighten it on the eastern Side of the Creek a Short distance. Land very good in the bottoms. Poor & Stoney in the Hills generally. I am unwell all day.

Sunday 10 June 1827

M[ornin]g fair and pleasant—feel better. Started early. Went about 20 Miles to the Spring [Diamond] and halted for the day. M[ar]k[e]d the Road to go close by this Remarkably fine Spring, which is on Otter Creek—165 Miles from Ft. Osage. The Creek affords Sufficient Wood for fuel. At the Spring is good camping ground & good pasture. This Spring is very large, Runs off boldly among Rocks, is perfectly accessible and furnishes the greatest abundance of most excellent, clear, cold Sweet water. It may be appropriately called "The Diamond of the Plains"[170] and So I had it Marked on an Elm which grows near & overhangs it.

Monday 11th June 1827

A Wet Rainey Morning. Staid all day in Camp. Urged by various considerations, I determine to Return home from this Point, and will Start back tomorrow Morning. I Shall make the necessary Surveys as I Return, & connect my late alterations of the Road with the old Survey.

I do not think there can be any alterations made farther West of Sufficient importance to justify the expense. The Road as traveled is already well enough Marked by the Waggons, any Mounds put up would be Soon thrown down by the Buffalo and Indians, & I fear if I go any farther I Shall be obliged to go to W[alnut] Creek before I can find Meat for Subsistence.

Tuesday 12th June 1827

Morning cloudy, Windy and cool. After B[rea]kf[as]t We Set out homeward—the day very Windy & unpleasant. Reached the Council Grove after noon and halted for the day. I feel unwell.

Wednesday 13th.

It Rained this Morning, & was cloudy 'till Noon & threatening a Storm. Set out however after late B[rea]kf[as]t. Coursed and chained the Cut off from C[ouncil] Grove to Gravel Creek [Big John Creek]—distance by the New M[ar]k[e]d Route, which is the best, 586 Poles, or 1 Mile 3 quarters and 26 Poles. Here halted for the day to make Some further examinations. Found an excellent Spring near Camp—which I had Marked *"Big John's Spring"* as it was first discov[ere]d by John Walker.[171] It Rained frequently today.

Thursday 14th June 1827

Morning fair and pleasant—it Rained last Night. After doing Some work here (which the Rain prevented yesterday,) Set forward again. Halted at Rock Cr[eek] for the day—day excessively Hot, and traveling in the Prairies very oppressive. With the Symptoms of illness that I feel, do not choose to expose myself more than I can help just now. Heavy thunder Storm with Rain & Wind this evening.

Friday 15 June 1827

Heavy Storm of Wind & Rain this Morn[in]g. Showery all the day—yet we got on 7 Miles to Locust Creek,[172] and Marked a Cut off there, & cleared out a fording place.

Saturday 16th.

A good deal of Rain fell last Night & this M[ornin]g So that we could not get out of Camp 'till late—then I Surveyed & Meas[ure]d. the Cut off—and after dinner Went on to *Elm Cr[eek]* [142 Mile

Creek] Measuring & Marking the best Route. The day was quite cool, So that my Capot [was] agreeable.

Some Indians Seen today at a distance Southward. At Night the Mules took fright but were Soon headed & Stopped. This Cr[eek] [142 Mile] is 3 Miles East[war]d of Elk Creek [branch of 142 Mile Creek].

Sunday 17th June 1827

A very fine Morning—very heavy dew. Started on pretty early. Got to Muscle Cr[eek] [Marais Des Cygnes] in good time and camped about ¾ Mile above the old ford. Marked & Coursed & Chained two Crooked Places So as to Straighten the Road materially.

Monday 18th.

Rain last Night & this Morning. Spent this day examining a near way from Pat's Cr[eek][173] to Bridge Cr[eek] [Switzler's], and find that the Road can be very much Straightened by Crossing Muscle Creek about 1½ Miles lower down. Tomorrow intend to Mark this Cut off, and Survey it So as to connect it with old Survey at Bridge Cr[eek] [Switzler's]. Day very hot. Flies are getting pretty bad.

Tuesday 19th June 1827

Morning fair and Windy. Set to work after B[rea]kf[as]t. Marked, coursed, & chained the cut off from Pat's Creek [Soldier] to Bridge Cr[eek] and halted at the Bridge for the day. This new Route is generally over good ground, the ford of Muscle Creek is good, and there is no place that can be called bad. The distance across is not half as great as it is by the Road as now traveled. The day very oppressively hot tho' Windy—the flies getting more & more troublesome as we go Eastward.

Majors, Cameron & Joel Walker left me this evening, by permission, for home. By Walker I wrote a few lines to Mrs. S[ibley]. Showery in the evening.

Wednesday June 20, 1827

It Rained nearly all Night and 'till half past 11 this Morning, So that we could not Make fires 'till about 10 o'Clk. The Creek Rising fast this Morning. We Started on after Noon and got across 100 Mile Creek [110 Mile Creek] (6 Miles) and again camped. From here homeward I propose to make Some very material alterations of the Road and Survey; if the flies do not prevent. Those pests are very troublesome today altho' it was mostly cloudy & all the Prairie completely drenched with Rain.

Thursday 21 June 1827

A fine fair pleasant Morning. Set off after Breakfast. Chained from the ford of 100 Mile Creek, from Mound to Mound as Marked on the way out, and Set up Several New Mounds. Finished 11 Miles, and then turned off nearly 3 Miles to Some timber Southward, on a Small Creek of M[arais] D[es] Cygne. Sh[oul]d have turned off Sooner (if any timber had Sooner appeared in Reach) to get Shelter from the flies, which are today extremely troublesome. Game is Still very Scarce, so that we get but little, and that Little Rather indifferent. The Hunters must exert themselves more hereafter, as we are nearly out of Meat. Some Honey got on this Cr[eek].

Friday June 22d. 1827

Morning fair and *very* cool. Started on after pretty early Breakfast. The flies were So very Severe that we could only chain 3 Miles, & make Some examinations before it was necessary to hasten to a Small patch of timber off Southward of the Road on a Small Creek of Osage. I fear the flies will So annoy us as to prevent our getting on but very Slowly with the Work. It was quite cool and pleasant all day.

Saturday June 23d. 1827

M[ornin]g fair & quite cool—very heavy *cold* dews every Night. Roused the Camp early, got B[rea]kf[as]t & Set to work at little after Sunrise. Went back 6 Miles with a Working Party, & Sent the Waggon on with two Men to a Cr[eek] 3 Miles off, where a ford is to be found and cut out. I completed nearly 9 Miles of Surveying & *Mounding,* and then halted for the day in a pleasant Grove of Trees at the ford of the Creek. Found the flies excessively bad today; So that I was obliged to defer Some work 'till tomorrow Morning on the New Route just Marked and Surveyed. Sent all the Hunters out this evening. Rather a pleasant day.

Sunday June 24th. 1827

A fine pleasant Morning. The Flies became So bad after I had completed what was left behind unfinished yesterday that I did not again leave Camp. The Hunters are all unsuccessful; they have failed to kill any game except an old Turkey, for Several days. Game is Scarce, but Still I think *Some* might be killed with proper industry on the part of the Hunters. No Meat in camp this Morning or all day.

Monday 25th. June 1287

Rainy Morning—did not get off till late. Tho' the flies were very bad, I made out to complete Six Miles, and finish the Cut off, which brought us to the Narrow divide not far from our camp of 30th & 31t. May. This was effected by 2 O'Clk. when [I] Sent out all the Men but Two to hunt, there being no Meat at all in camp.

But the Hunters were again unsuccessful. They got a little Honey, which, like children they eat up all at once.

The day quite pleasant, tho' cloudy for the most part.

Tuesday 26th June 1827

A fine cool pleasant morning. Set off after Breakfast, Surveyed the cut off as Marked on the 31t May, and camped for the day on Hungry Creek [branch of Coal Creek]. Had Some of the brush bridges to Repair. The day very Warm, and flies bad. The Mules and Horses are already the worse of these torments, and will I fear be greatly Reduced before I get through with my Work—which may yet employ me ten or twelve days probably, as I propose to Survey the Route round by the Blue Spring and Shall have to Resurvey the Road as far back as the State line.

I am most heartily tired, and wish myself at home an hundred times a day.

Wednesday June 27th. 1827

Morning cool and cloudy. Started a little after Sunrise, and completed 13 Miles of the Road to Caravan Grove.[174] Altho' cloudy & cool when we Started, it Soon became clear and almost unsupportably hot, and the Green flies Swarmed around us like bees. I never Saw the flies half as bad as today; they Stuck to the Mules 'till near Night. After Nightfall, we had a thunder Shower which cooled the air a little and made the Night passably pleasant.

Thursday June 28th. 1827

Morning clear and *coolish*. Had B[rea]kf[as]t early and Set forward to work. Finished 9 Miles, and halted for the day on Flat Rock Creek [branch of Indian Creek] in a Grove of Saplings, which afforded excellent Shelter from the flies and heat. The day was extremely warm— but flies not very bad today. Killed a very large Rattlesnake of the Black kind, at the mouth of my Tent this evening—the first Rattlesnake I have Seen or heard Since I left home. This Cr[eek] Runs into Big Blue and affords Some good Land and Timber.

Friday June 29th. 1827

The Morning fair and cool and pleasant. Started after Breakfast, and went on 4 Miles to a point of Woods, (where we Staid on the Night of the 25th May) on a Small branch of Kansas, which affords very good *cool* water. The Grove is a pretty one and the Spot good camping ground. Having to turn back from here to Survey the Road by the Blue Spring and to Send to the nearest Settlement (about 8 Miles off) for Some Bacon—halted 'till I get Ready to proceed. I here discharged four of my Men having more than I want, and they wishing to Return, Jas. Baxter, Wm. M. Owens, D. Cameron, & C. Richardson went in. I Sent by them 2 Horses and 5 Mules, which I directed Richardson to take care of at my House 'till I get home. I wrote by Kitt [Richardson] to my Wife, to Say that I shall not be at home before the 10th of July.

The day very *very* warm. Met 5 Kansas Ind[ia]ns Returning from a Hunt.

Saturday June 30, 1827

Fine Morning. Rain last Night. The Men did not come with Bacon 'till after Noon (having to go nearly down to the County Town for it), So that I did not get out to work today.

I felt quite unwell, and Should have kept my Tent at any Rate. The day was warm & close.

Sunday July 1t. 1827

Spent this day Marking & Surveying the Road to the State Line, and in making Some necessary observations to ascertain whether a better Route may not be had more North[war]d passing by Patterson's & crossing Big Blue Some 3 or 4 Miles lower down than the old Ford. This kept me busy nearly all the day. The day was Rather a Pleasant one. I feel better today than yesterday, tho' Still unwell.

Monday July 2d. 1827

Morning cloudy and Warm. Set out pretty early and went back 12 Miles to Caravan Grove: Repairing and building Some Mounds. The day was Warm and the flies excessively Severe on the Mules.

Tuesday 3d. July

Morning cool and cloudy. Set out early, but were caught in a pretty heavy Shower of Rain which obliged us to halt at the Round Grove early in the day. Got completely wet. I completed Survey of the old Road about 6 Miles however, and finished Mound Making. I am now thus far on the Road Round by the Blue Spring—and hope to get on pretty briskly.

Wednesday July 4th. 1827

Fine Morning. Started early; chained and coursed the Road to the ford of Big Blue, which I find to be 13 M[ile]s & 22 ch[ain]s from the Round Grove. The Road passes over Some Rough ground & Some Rather bad places.

The ford of the Blue is a very excellent one, the bed of the Creek being on Smooth flat Rock, & the banks good. There is considerable timber along here in Strips; Some very pretty groves, & excellent land. Camped at the ford.

Thursday July 5— 1827

Sultry Morning. Started pretty early. When we had proceeded about 3 Miles it began to Rain, and continued pretty Steadily to Rain nearly all day—and Sometimes very hard. I had to get off my Horse so often [to] take the courses that I got wet through all my clothes. I continued however to Survey the Road about 4½ Miles farther, and Stopped for the day just after we had crossed a fork of the Little Blue and got out of the bottom upon the high Prairie. I had my tent pitched, changed my Clothes, eat a Biscuit, drank a *Mint Sling,* and took a nap, after which I felt pretty well again, and Spent the rest of the day Reading Stern.

Friday July 6th. 1827

It commenced raining hard before daylight, and continued with Some Short intervals 'till night. So that we were confined to our Tents. The country here is very *high,* and a good deal broken affording however on the Streams Some very beautiful Situations—Groves of open Woods, fine Springs and Rich Land.

Thus far this Route is decidedly worse than the other however—the country is more broken, camping grounds not so good or convenient, and the Road necessarily more circuitous.

At about 5 P. M. during a thunder Storm, a flash of Lightning Struck our Camp. The facts of this incident are as I should conceive Singular. The Camp Stands on a high point in the open Prairie, no trees near except a Small Clump of Small Oaks on the descent of the Hill about 50 yds. from my Tent, the tops of these Trees probably 10 or 15 feet higher than any object in camp. The camp is arranged nearly thus

1 My Tent.
2 Waggon 10 feet from 1.
3 a Tent close to the Waggon.

The flash Struck my Tent on one corner, Splintered the upright, passed thro' a leather Iron framed Trunk, which it tore considerably, melted the case of a Pocket Compass in the Trunk (Missing Some Powder) Scorched Some woolen Socks. It Split the other upright. I was lying asleep on my Pallet on one Side of the Tent, my feet near the Trunk & my Head near the Pole least damaged. The Shock awoke me to the most painful & alarming Sensations, for my Right Side which I lay on, was for a Minute bereft of feeling nearly, My foot Seemed Reduced to jelly, having no feeling. A whirring noise passed thro' my ears continually, & the Tent was filled with Smoke & Strewed with Splinters. In the other Tent were Six persons; one of whom was Standing against the front Post. He was Struck down, & was Senseless for Some time. The *top* of the Pole Split. One of the others was Severely Shocked, the Rest but Slightly. My own escape was wonderful indeed. Recovered the circulation in my foot & leg in about an hour; but am a little deaf, & Still having a Singing & whirring in my ear.

Saturday 7 July 1827

Morning damp and cloudy. An immense quantity of Rain has fallen, and all the Creeks are Swimming. I Slept pretty well last Night, and feel this Morning about as well as usual except that I still feel a kind of confusion in my head, with Sometimes a Whizzing Noise, much Such as I have felt when I had a bad cold. Collins & Carson, the two men who were the Most Shocked, Say they feel pretty well tho' they were quite unwell all Night.

Collins asked his discharge this Morning and Set out for Home by way of the Lower Settlements of Blue. On examining my Compass, I find that it Received material unjury from the Shock yesterday and is Rendered entirely useless—So that I am obliged to Stop the Survey here. We packed up, and Set out about 10 O'Clk.

About 4½ Miles crossed another fork of L[ittle] Blue, the way Rough, crooked, & Southwardly. Then it is about 18½ Miles by the Waggon Road, to the Blue Spring—where we arrived just at Sun Set. The Road is extremely crooked and the country very much broken, good camping places not frequent or convenient. Camped at the Blue Spring. The Spring is a pretty good one, tho' nothing extraordinary.

Sunday 8th July 1827

Fine Morning. After early B[rea]kf[as]t Set out. I traveled ahead of the Waggon & got home at 12 O'Clk. the distance about 14 Miles.

The Waggon & Men all arrived in the evening all Safe. And thus ends a most disagreeable trip; in which I have effected every object I had in view, & in less time than I expected to have done it.

Friday July 27 1827

Wrote to Col. Mather to Say that I am Ret[urne]d. Have finished the Road—have asc[ertaine]d there is a deficiency of funds of ab[ou]t $670 to pay up to this time—estimating the property in hands, including mules in Col. R[eeves]'s hands at $700—that there is due me for Services & advances $1370.91½. Asked him for Some explanation of 2 entries in Hoods Acc[oun]t and to State how many Mules, & what prices he & Col. R[eeves] bought at Walnut Cr[eek] and what am[oun]t Goods they Sold there.

Also wrote to Col. Reeves to the Same purport, nearly, at Elkton, Ky. Wrote also to Mr. Hood & Mr. Samuel of Franklin on business.

Saturday 18 Augt. 1827

Today had all the Mules Horses Waggon and all other Public Property in my hands Sold at Auction agreeably to advertisements. There was a considerable collection of People, & the Property went off Rather better than I had anticipated. The whole produced the Net Sum of $686.91 Cash—and this finally closes my care of Public Property—it is now all Sold. The particulars are Stated at Large & in detail in another book.

Thursday 20th Sept. 1827

This day wrote to Mr. Brown very fully in Relation to his Report of the Survey. I enclosed him in 6 bundles all the Papers in my possession that can be of use to him. Mr. Brown's Report is to consist of his field Book, and Maps drawn therefrom on a Large Scale. I have given him very particular instructions on this Subject, & urged him to have all Ready by 20th October.

Also wrote to Messrs. Reeves & Mather to Say that I Shall not be able to meet them in time at St. Louis on Acc[oun]t of Sickness in my family &c. But will endeavor to be at Fayette on the 8th Octo[ber] when I Shall expect to meet them & complete everything.

Mond[ay] 8th October 1827

Arrived at Fayette agreeably to App[ointmen]t but do not find Col. Mather. Went to Col. Reeves' where I Staid 'till the

Sat[urday] 13th

when I Set out for St. Charles, where I expect to Meet Colo. Mather and where it is agreed between Col. R[eeves] & myself that I Shall prepare the Report & Accounts as soon as practicable; and with Col. Mather Sign & forward them to Washington; Col. Reeves being unable to go from home.

Whilst at Col. R[eeve]'s and at the time of my departure for St. Charles I was quite unwell.

Tuesday 17th.

Reached St. Ch[arle]s and find myself Seriously unwell from a very ugly bruise under the left knee & which occasions Some considerable fever & pain.

Wed[nesday] 18th October

Having provided a Room & the necessary materials, I Set to work on the Report, Acc[oun]ts &c. Wrote to Col. Mather to meet me here as Soon as he can, as I am unable to travel to him. Also wrote to Mr. Brown to hurry his Report, & to have Ready all the Maps &c. ordered on the 20th Ulto. and to bring them here when Ready.

Sat[urday] 21t

My knee has been So painful (& is Still growing worse) as to make it impossible for me to make much progress in writing the Report. I have completed a Rough Sketch however, which will be corrected

194

and written out fair as Soon as I am able to do it. Colo. Mather will be here on Friday next.

Friday 27th Octo[ber] 1827

The Report has been Ready for Signature Since Wednesday. Today Colo. Mather arrived at St. Charles, and having examined & approved what I had prepared by way of Report, he & I Signed the Same & agreeably to Request of Col. Reeves (he having Seen the Rough Draft) we also affixed his name to it; and the Report was then forwarded to Washington City per Mail.

The Acc[oun]ts not being yet in Readiness, Col. Mather & I agreed to meet at St. Louis early in Dec[embe]r next, to complete & forward *that* Report.

The General Report, this day forwarded, is copied accurately on the following pages.

Vizt.

FT. OSAGE

Explanation

1. Blockhouses
2. Officers' Quarters
3. Soldiers' Barracks
4. Factor's House and Store
5. Factory
6. Sub. Agent
7. Soldiers' and Indian Traders Houses

*R*eport of the Commissioners.

To the Honorable James Barbour
    Secy. of the Dept. of War, Washington City

Sir,

The undersigned Commissioners appointed by the President to carry into effect the Act of Congress passed on the 3d day of March 1825 "to authorize The President of the United States to cause a Road to be Marked out from the western frontier of Missouri to the confines of New Mexico" have, after Some unavoidable delays, fully completed the duties assigned them, and now do themselves the honour to lay before you, for the information of the Government, the following Report.

Anxious to execute the intentions of Congress promptly, the Commissioners did not lose a moment, after the Receipt of your communication dated the 16th. of March 1825 (announcing their appointment, and conveying to them instructions) in making Suitable preparations for the work before them; aware that the Season would be far advanced before they could collect their Men and the necessary equipment on the frontier, and that they would probably be obliged to encounter the extreme heat of Summer, and the Still greater inconvenience of the Prairie flies. These apprehensions were fully Realized; for it was not 'till the 17th. of July that the enterprise could Set forward from Ft. Osage, the point fixed on for the commencement of the proposed Road; and the journey for the first 160 Miles, was attended throughout, with difficulty and embarrassment, arising chiefly from the annoyance of the green flies of the Prairies, which obliged the Party to travel much in the Night, frequently leaving the direct route in order to find Shelter from the flies during the day, in the Small groves that are Seen here and there Scattered like little green Islands, over the plains. This irregular way of traveling not only harassed the horses and Mules excessively, but Rendered a Satisfactory view and Survey of the country impracticable at the time, and a Subsequent examination necessary.

The only intervening Tribes of Indians whose consent it was deemed incumbent upon the Commissioners to obtain by Treaty, to the Marking out, and free use of the Road, were the Great and Little Osages, and the Kansas; and as it was known to be most agreeable to the wishes of the Chiefs and head Men of those Tribes (who were consulted by Mr. Sibley on the Subject at St. Louis in June) to meet the Commissioners at Some convenient places on their Route from Ft. Osage to the Arkansas River; it was believed to be unnecessary to postpone the Survey and examination of the Route through the Territory claimed by those Tribes, these being at most preliminary operations, necessary to the ultimate location and marking out of the Road.

On the 10th. and 16th. days of August, the Commissioners met Successively by appointment, full deputations of the Chiefs and head Men of the Osages and Kansas, and after carefully explaining the object and wishes of the Government, So as to be prefectly well understood by them, concluded and Signed the Treaties that have been already Reported to, and duly Ratified by the competent authorities.

Having thus concluded their negotiations with the "intervening Tribes of Indians" within the limits of The United States, The Commissioners proceeded with their Survey and examination, without any further interruption, to the Boundary line between the United States and Mexico, at the point (as nearly as they had the means to ascertain it) where the 100th degree of Longitude West from London, intersects the Arkansas River; which point is in North Latitude 37°-47'-37", is distant from Ft. Osage by the Survey 386 43½/80 Miles: & which they reached on the 11th day of September.

When the Commissioners Set out from Ft. Osage, they entertained the expectations of being able to carry their Surveys and examinations quite through to the frontier Settlements of New Mexico before the Winter Set in, So as to enable them to locate and Mark out the Road as they Returned home early the next ensuing Summer; and to this end, were all their preparatory arrangements made, and all their exertions pointed—and they were fully justified in indulging this expectation, by the assurance of your letter,[175] that measures had been taken to obtain the co-operation or consent of the Mexican Government, which it was hoped would be effected in time to prevent any delay at the boundary line; and by the well founded belief that the Govt. of Mexico would promptly accede to a measure, which was obviously quite as much, if not more, to her advantage, than to that of the United States.

Great was the disappointment of the Commissioners, therefore, when on their arrival at the Line, they were obliged to Suspend their operations for want of the expected authority to proceed through the Mexican Territory. They waited until the 20th. of September, in the daily hope that they might Receive the permission to go on with their Survey, but in vain: and the Season being now So far advanced, it was believed, that go which way they might, there was but barely time left to Reach the Settlements before the Setting in of the Winter, especially with Reduced Horses & Mules. It was obviously necessary therefore to determine immediately what to do, and promptly to Set about it. After much deliberation, the Commissioners at length concurred unanimously, in adopting the following plan of procedure: That one of them, accompanied by the Surveyor and a Small party of the hired men Should proceed to New Mexico as expeditiously as possible, to find winter quarters, at or near the City of Sta. Fee. The other two Commissioners, with all the Remainder of the Men and equipment, Should Return to Missouri as Speedily as they could. That if the Government Should So direct, the two Commissioners Returning Should join the other in New Mexico as early as practicable the ensuing Summer, while the one in New Mexico Should possess himself of Such information within his Reach, as might be desirable, to enable the Board properly to locate the Road, or in any event, that portion of it within the limit of The United States, it being considered indispensibly necessary for the Commissioners to possess Some previous knowledge of the Country and the Route between the Arkansas and the frontier Settlements of New Mexico, to enable them even to make a definitive location of the

Eastern Section of the proposed Road. This arrangement was considered at the time it was adopted, decidedly the best one that could be made; and Subsequent events have proven that it was the only one that could have been carried into effect, by which The Commissioners could possibly have completed the Road, even as Soon as they have done it. It has also been the means of Reducing the expense Somewhat, that was necessarily attendant on the unlooked for delay of the Mexican Government.

To Mr. Commissioner Sibley was assigned the duty of proceeding to Sta. Fee it being understood that he was to Remain in New Mexico no longer than 'till the 1t. of July, unless he Should have Substantial Reasons to justify a longer Stay.

On the 22d. September, the two parties took leave of each other, and proceeded on their Respective journeys. The Returning party completed theirs early in November—the other arrived Safely at San Fernando, in the Valley of Taus, on the 31t. day of October.

Very Soon after his arrival, Mr. Sibley inquired of the Govr. of the Territory (Resident at Santa Fee) if the Government of Mexico had taken any order in Relation to the Road; and was answered, that none had been communicated to him. Mr. Sibley immediately addressed a Note to Mr. Poinsett, informing him of the progress already made by the Commissioners Stating the Serious inconvenience and expense of delay; and urging him to obtain the necessary order, if possible, in time to enable The Commissioners to complete the Road early the next Summer.

This note was dispatched to Mexico in a few days, under the Governor's envelope, by the Monthly courier, was duly Received by Mr. Poinsett, who answered by Return of the courier, that he had not been able to effect any arrangement with the Government at Mexico for the continuance of the Road through the Territory of that Government, but entertained hopes that he Should Soon obtain one.

Mr. Sibley also addressed Govr. Narbona on the Subject verbally and by note; who professed himself to be most favorably inclined towards the establishment of the projected Road, and promised to Represent to his Government his views of its importance which he Said he could Strikingly Set forth in the fact, that the Trade from Missouri already yielded an annual Revenue of Twenty thousand Dollars, besides many other great advantages.

Notwithstanding these flattering hopes and promises, no order was Received from Mexico on the Subject of the Road, until the 16th. June, 1826, when Mr. Sibley Received a Note from Mr. Poinsett, informing him that on the 13th. of May he had obtained from The President of The Mexican States an Order to the Governor of The Territory of New Mexico "to permit Mr. Sibley Commissioner of the United States, to make an examination of the western part of the Road to Sta. Fee from Missouri, without marking or cutting it out, or establishing any works of any class"— and on the same day Mr. Sibley Received an official notification to the Same effect, from Governor Narbona.

Altho' this permission fell very far Short of what might have been Reasonably expected, and could not indeed have been deemed Sufficient to Warrant The Commissioners in accepting it, without further instructions, if it had been communicated and Received otherwise than it was; yet from the knowledge Mr. Sibley possessed of the country through which "the western part of the Road" *must* pass, he did not entertain a moment's doubt as to the propriety of its being accepted & acted on by the Commissioners, all the circumstances being duly considered.

The following extract of a Letter from Mr. Sibley to Mr. Poinsett dated "Valley of Taus in New Mexico June 19, 1826" will Sufficiently Illustrate his views, (and those of all The Commissioners) on this Subject.

"This very Restricted permission would avail the Commissioners but little indeed, if it were not for the fact, that there is no 'marking' or 'cutting out' or any 'works' necessary, or indeed practicable to be done on any part of the Road within the Mexican Territory. From the crossing of the Arkansas to this Valley and to Santa Fe, the Road will not pass over timbered land exceeding one mile in the whole, and that is So Scattered and open, that it can be passed without the least difficulty with carriages, with no other Labor than Removing a few logs, poles

&c. and as it will be labour and time lost to attempt to 'mark out' the Road by any artificial means that The Commissioners can devise and effect, we Shall probably not otherwise mark it than by furnishing a chart of the Route, founded upon an accurate examination & Survey, upon which will be noted, with great care, all the prominent land marks already Set up by the hand of nature, which are numerous, and now Serve as admirable guides to the traveler.

"Any artificial hillocks or mounds thrown up, unless of much greater magnitude than our limited means will justify, would be destroyed in a very Short time, by the immense herds of Buffaloes that are continually passing to and fro over the plains; and what they might be unable to destroy would assuredly be levelled by the Roving bands of Indians, who are always Sufficiently inclined to commit wanton mischief. I have no objection then, myself, and I presume the other Commissioners will have none, to proceed with the 'examination' as permitted; inasmuch as we can effect everything under that permission, that we could do, if it were as ample as our Government wished or expected.

"It is certain, that if The Commissioners Shall determine to proceed as above Suggested, their Report of the Road will be Such as to make it entirely unnecessary for the Government of The United States ever to take any further order or interest in the Matter. I have deemed it proper for me to communicate to you these facts for your information."

Meanwhile, the Commissioners who had Returned to Missouri were officially advised that no arrangement was likely Soon to be made between the two Governments for the continuation of the Road through the Mexican Territory; and they consequently determined not to join Mr. Sibley in New Mexico, but wrote him by the Spring Caravan on the 19th. of May 1826 to urge his immediate Return home. This communication was received by Mr. Sibley on the 1t. day of August, who immediately made Such preparations as were necessary for his Return, determining to make a complete Survey & examination of the Route from San Fernando in Taus, to the boundary line, and connect it with the Survey Recently made from Ft. Osage to the Same point.

Mr. Sibley adopted this course without the least hesitation; because it was authorized by the Mexican Government, would be attended with little or no additional expense, and would in effect enable The Commissioners to complete the whole Road from Missouri to Taus, as perfectly as it could be done under any arrangement, however formal, that the two Governments might ever enter into on the Subject. He accordingly commenced a Survey at San Fernando on the 24th. of August, Ran it through the Mexican Territory, and on the 16th of September, connected it with the former Survey at the line, on the Arkansas River. On the journey from the boundary line to Ft. Osage, Mr. Sibley made Some necessary corrections of the first Survey, but had not time, or indeed the means, to "mark out the Road" or in fact, to complete all the necessary alterations in the Survey of the first 160 Miles from Ft. Osage, which, as has been already Stated, was passed over at first, under circumstances that made a Satisfactory Survey of it impossible.

Mr. Sibley went out in May last, with a Small party, to make the last mentioned corrections of the Survey, and to "mark out" by Suitable mounds, so much of the Road as extends from the western boundary of Missouri to the Buffalo Range; beyond which, it was entirely useless to incur any expense in Setting up marks.

This last object was effected in a very Satisfactory manner (notwithstanding the journey was extremely unpleasant) and was completely finished early in July.

The Commissioners had the honor, on the 10th. of January last, to Submit to The President the opinion (which they Still entertain and beg leave here to Repeat) that it is unnecessary for The Government of The United States to do anything further in Relation to that Section of the Road that has been Surveyed thro' the Mexican Territory. Even if it were *practicable* to "mark out" that portion of the Road by permanent artificial "works," they would deem it a very useless expense of Money & labor, for the Reason already given in another part of this Report.

In the belief therefore, that they have effected all the objects proposed by the Act of Congress, under the authority of which they were appointed, The Commissioners Report

That they have Surveyed, located and Marked out, a Road from the Western frontier of Missouri, to the confines of New Mexico, and from thence to the frontier Settlements of New Mexico. That they have located the Road upon the best practicable Route that exists; and that the whole is Sufficiently marked out by natural and artificial conspicuous objects, and by the tracks of the numerous caravans that have passed on it, to prevent in future, any the least difficulty in the commercial intercourse between the western parts of the United States and New Mexico, Sonora, and Chihauhua; in So far as a direct and most excellent Road from Missouri and the Mexican Settlements is considered useful in promoting that object.

From Ft. Osage on the Missouri River (In latitude 39°-10'-19" North, and Longitude 93°-51'-05" west from London) to the Village of San Fernando, in the valley of Taus, in New Mexico, a few miles eastward of The Rio Grande del Norte, and about 65 Miles North 25 east from the City of Santa Fe (in Latitude 36°-24'- North and Longitude 105°-31' West from London) the whole distance, ascertained by actual measurement, upon the courses of the Road, as located and established is 746 15¾/80 Miles. 425 78¾/80 of this distance, by way of the Road, lies within the limits of the United States; and 320 17/80 Miles within the Mexican Territory.

The Road, in nearly its whole extent passes over open, grassy prairie; the forest or timber land, over which it Runs does not exceed altogether, twenty Miles—Water, fuel, and pasturage, are Sufficiently plentiful, and, with but few exceptions are good. Caravans may obtain their chief Supplies for Subsistence, without difficulty or delay, from the numerous herds of Buffaloes that are almost continually passing and repassing over the plain, crossing the Route everywhere along the greater part of the way; and many years must elapse before this great Resource will fail, or materially diminish.

Between Ft. Osage & San Fernando, there does not exist a Single Serious difficulty or obstacle to the passage of carriages of any description. Even the Mountains near Taus (where Scarcely any effort has ever yet been made to form a Road) are crossed without any great difficulty; and whenever the authorities there Shall think fit to order it, an excellent Road may be made at a very trifling expense. Caravans, with or without carriages may either go direct to the City of Santa Fe, without crossing the Mountains at Taus, or they may go down through the Settlements from San Fernando. Both Routes are, or may very easily be made, perfectly Safe and good; and from Santa Fe to the City of Mexico the *Road* is Said to be "nearly equal to turnpike."

In Short, it may Safely be assumed that there are fewer natural obstructions to the passage of loaded carriages (as Respects the Road merely) between Ft. Osage and the City of Mexico, a distance not much Short of 2500 Miles, than there are on the established Road from Ft. Osage to St. Louis, which is probably not inferior to any (except turnpikes) in the Union, of the Same extent, about 260 Miles.

Upon the whole, The Commissioners may congratulate themselves and all concerned, that they have Succeeded in locating and marking out a very direct and permanent highway across the immense desert plain that intervenes between the Settlements of the Missouri River and those of the Rio Grande del Norte, which, until Recently subdued by the enterprising Spirit of our Western Citizens, has been considered an impassable barrier to any direct or profitable commerce.

That barrier is now Removed; the way is open, plain and direct; and a Stream of Commerce is already flowing upon it, which it is believed will grow into Some considerable importance, and is certainly entitled to the favourable consideration of the two Governments whose citizens are mutually benefited by it.

Altho' this is a Subject that does not Strictly come within the official duty of the undersigned to mention in this place, they cannot Suffer the present occasion to pass without expressing their opinion of its importance. They could not *mechanically* locate and Mark out a Road of Such extent, through Such a country, and for Such an object, without feeling Some interest in, and forming Some estimate of its probable future usefulness—nor can they now omit to Suggest what, from the view they have been able to take of the whole ground, they consider necessary yet to be done, in order to Render this *highway between Nations*, what it evidently Should be, not only open, plain and direct; but free in its whole extent from every obstruction.

It has been already Stated, that no natural obstructions, worth notice, exist on the Road. The only danger to which it is now liable, is from the Roving bands of Indians that Sometimes beset Small parties of our Traders, and either Steal or forcibly take away their Horses, Mules, and other property. Such outrages most frequently occur on the journey homeward from New Mexico, and most generally on the Mexican Side of the Arkansas; though Some of the depredators are known to have their Villages within the Territory of the United States and Receive presents & other favors from the Government.

The Indians who are most commonly engaged in these Lawless practices belong to the Nations or Tribes called Pawnees, Arapahoes, Kiaways, Comanches, Appaches and Yutahs; the first, & probably the second named are within the agencies of The United States; the others Reside within the Jurisdiction of the Mexican Government. It is not Supposed that the irregularities of Mere Savages can be Suddenly Suppressed; but it is very confidently believed they may be materially checked, and ultimately entirely prevented by a Seasonable interference of the two Governments; while it may well be apprehended, that unless this is done, Some of those Tribes may be tempted to form combinations, and establish Something like a System of highway Robbery, that may be extremely difficult to Suppress, if too long neglected.

Individual losses have already been Sustained on this Road from Indian Robberies to a large amount, to say nothing of the personal Suffering consequent upon them. As there is no position on the whole Route except near the Mountains, about 36 Miles from the Settlements of Taus, Suitable for a Military post, having for its object the protection of the Road; no other fit means of protection can be Suggested, than occasional escorts of Troops from the nearest Military posts, and proper admonition to the Indians.

With the exception of the Pawnees, the Tribes that have been mentioned, have but little knowledge of our Government and People; and *none* of them have *any* Respect for the Mexican authorities. It is presumed, however, that a very Salutary change might easily be effected in the disposition and conduct of those Indians if the two Governments were to act in concert; and announce in a Suitable manner their determination to protect their commerce on this Road; and occasionally

206

detach light parties of Regular Soldiers to Scour the country, and detect, & arrest for punishment all those who Should presume to infringe the Rights of the highway.

A very brief notice of the country examined by the Commissioners, will here Suffice. The field notes and maps presented by Mr. Brown, the Surveyor of the Road, which accompany and belong to this Report, furnish in detail, whatever it is Supposed may be at all useful or interesting in Relation to the Survey and location of the Road, and of the Streams, Ridges, hills, Mountains &c. that it crosses.

A Rapid glance, confined as much as possible to the Scope taken in the Surveys and examinations, will be given in the belief that it may Supply Some facts not heretofore very generally known.

It has been already observed, that the Space between the Missouri River and the Rio Grande del Norte is occupied by an almost unbroken plain or Prairie. Taken as one great whole, this vast expanse of open named Wilderness, presents but little more variety of Surface, than the face of the Atlantic Ocean. Its features are generally proportioned to its great magnitude, except as to its Streams. Numerous Rivulets, Creeks & Small Rivers flow through it, the most of which are marked in their courses by narrow fringes of forest Trees, & thickets of underbrush. Prominent Ridges frequently occur, which give direction to the flow of the Streams and Serve to Relieve in Some degree, the dull *monotony* of the Scene. These elevations are usually *poor* in point of Soil, compared with the interjacent level vallies & bottoms, which are in general tolerably fertile.

The Herbage of this Plain is in general Rich & luxuriant, consisting chiefly of Strong and Succulent Grasses, of many varieties; Some of which would doubtless prove valuable additions to the cultivated grasses of the United States. In the Season of flowers, a very large portion of this great plain presents one continual *carpet* of Soft verdure, enriched by flowers of every tint—these beauties afford pleasure for a time; but the traveller is apt Soon to lose the Relish for them, as he pursues his tedious way, under a cloudless Sky, and exposed to the unbroken Rays of a burning Sun, which, but for the brisk flow of air that usually prevails, would be Scarcely Supportable.

Except the Arkansas, the Road does not cross a Single Stream that is an hundred feet wide (at or near the crossing) very few of them are half that width, and none of them are deep, or difficult to cross; one only it has been found necessary to bridge, with poles and brushwood.

The Arkansas flows over its Sandy bed, through a very broad, level, naked Valley; the Soil of which is generally extremely fertile, having a Slight Saline empregnation, which Renders the pasturage peculiarly nutritious and inviting to the Buffaloes, of which great numbers Successively occupy it in their migratory passage to and from the upper Regions of the Missouri. The qualities of this pasturage are found also to agree well with the Horses, Mules & other animals used on the Road, Restoring them to health and vigor with Surprising Rapidity.

The Road Strikes the Arkansas (going westward) ten Miles below the extreme of the North bend, at the Mouth of Walnut Creek, in Latitude 38°-21'-10" North; and by the Survey, 271 1½/80 Miles from Ft. Osage, and then pursues the course of the River, and never far from it, about 170 Miles, to a large Island [Chouteau's] (in Latitude 37°-35'-18") where it finally leaves it, having crossed about Twenty Miles below. In that distance, and for full 50 Miles below the North bend, the character of the River varies but very little indeed. It bears a uniform width of from 400 to 500 yards, a depth of from 18 Inches to 4 feet—velocity of current, 2¼ Miles an hour—its bed Sand—banks, low and loose—Water turbid, Sometimes filthy—channel crowded with Sand banks and Islets—forest growth very little, and that little chiefly on the Islets and is principally of the Species of poplar called Cotton Wood.

Its annual floods occur in June, and frequently inundate much of the adjacent flat land. In its ordinary Stages, it may be crossed by carriages without the least difficulty, or a moment's delay.

At the mouth of the Walnut Creek, the Arkansas approaches within 20 Miles of the "Smoky Hill Fork" of the Kansas River, and if there is any point upon the Road within the Territory of the Union, where a Small Military establishment might for a Short time be maintained at a great expense and for Some useful purpose in protecting the Trade, it is here. But the Commissioners cannot Recommend it.

Whether the "Smoky hill Fork" of the Kansas is navigable and to what extent, or how far it is capable of being made So, could not be ascertained. Except during its floods, the Arkansas has no navigation within 200 Miles of the North bend, or Walnut Creek.

After leaving the Arkansas, there is a Striking difference in the general aspect of the Country. It is more broken, Sterile, Sandy and dry. Its features are more bold and various, especially after arriving within an Hundred Miles of the Mountains, when they become more and more grand and interesting.

The distance across the mountains is 34 64/80 Miles—of this about 10 Miles is Somewhat Rough & precipitous, the Rest is level enough; in fact, the greater portion of it is open and Rich Prairie. The forest growth on the Mountain Sides is chiefly Pine of various kinds, but thinly Scattered, and of very inferior Size and quality.

On the whole distance, from the Western boundary of Missouri to the Village of San Fernando in New Mexico, the Road does not pass over any body of Woodland exceeding one Mile in depth; there is but one that exceeds 500 yards, and the whole united, (in a distance of 715 Miles) would not make a forest of three Miles in depth. Yet, good camping places are to be had, at convenient intervals, the whole way; with Water, fuel & pasturage, generally good and Sufficient.

From the Missouri to the Arkansas, with one or two exceptions only, Wood for fuel is abundant at the usual camping places; and the annual deposits of drift wood furnish ample Supplies during the journey up the Arkansas. After leaving the river, there is, in Some places, a deficiency of wood; but wherever this occurs, upon the whole journey, the *Ordure* of the Buffalo is found in great abundance, which is a very excellent Substitute for wood, as fuel.

While in New Mexico, Mr. Sibley was able to ascertain Satisfactorily Some facts, which, as they concern the *utility* of this Road, may be mentioned here without impropriety. *First*—the Stream that issues from the Mountains North of Sta. Fe, commonly called there "Rio Colorado," and which has been heretofore laid down on the Maps as a principal head branch of the Red River of Natchitoches, is now well ascertained to be the Main branch of *Canadian* that Runs into the Arkansas about forty Miles below Fort Gibson. The Canadian is navigable only a Short distance above its mouth; the whole River being frequently lost for miles together in the deep Sands.

Second. The Red River of Natchitoches has none of its Sources in the great Range of the Shining Mountains, as has been Supposed, nor is there any branch of that River that is navigable, even for canoes, within 300 Miles of Sta. Fe or any of the Settlements of New Mexico.

Third. The Rio Grande del Norte does not, and will not probably for ages to come, afford any Safe or certain navigation, exceeding *two hundred* miles at most, upward from its mouth. In its whole course, from the mountains near Taus, to its entrance into the Gulf of Mexico, its channel is more or less choked with Rocks, Ripples, Sand bars &c. Its tributaries are few and insignificant and this *"great River of the North"* as it is called, even if cleared of the innumerable obstructions in its channels, would only Rank among the third or fourth class of Rivers in the United States.

In fine, it may be Safely asserted, that the nearest approaches that can be made to Santa Fe or the other Settlements of New Mexico, by *Water,* for the purposes of Commerce, are by the Missouri and Kansas Rivers, and the Gulf of California at Guaymas.

When the highway, now opened from Missouri to Santa Fe Shall be cleared of the *Pirates of the Plains,* there is good Reason to believe that the Trade between the two countries in that direction, will assume a character, & employ an amount of Capital, not only greatly advantageous to those immediately engaged in it, but beneficial in no trifling degree to Some of the manufacturing interests of the United States.

> With great Respect we have the honor
> to be Sir Yr. Obt. Svts:
> B. H. REEVES
> G. C. SIBLEY
> THOM. MATHER

St. Charles, Missouri
October 27th, 1827.

It may be proper to State, that the Longitudes given in the preceding Report have been from necessity, deduced from the Results of the Survey Westward from Ft. Osage, which place is assumed to be in 93°-51'-5" upon the presumption that the Ranges of the Public Lands are correctly Surveyed between that point and the mouth of the Ohio River, where it is believed Mr. Illicott fixed the Longitude accurately. This method of ascertaining Longitude must obviously be attended with Some uncertainty as to the Result. Great pains were taken however, to test the accuracy of the Survey and measurement by observations—but, as these were taken by one observer only, with a single Sextant, and by common time, there is no Reason to Suppose that the Longitude has been accurately found in a Single instance, though it is probable they are all nearly correct.

As to the Latitudes, of which a great many parallels were taken at Remarkable points along the Survey & elsewhere, they are all believed to be critically true, and may be Relied on, having been taken with very great care, in the best manner and with the best Instruments.

The following Table exhibits Some of the Latitudes and Longitudes ascertained at Remarkable points on the Road from the Missouri to Sta. Fe in New Mexico.

Names of places

Names of places	Latitude	Longitude		
Fort Osage, on the Missouri River	39°-10'-19"	93°-51'-05"		
West boundary of Missouri	38°-54'-28"	94°-17'-22"	31	31
Council Grove, Neeosho	38°-40'-00"	96°-12'-22"	109	140
Diamond of the Plains, a Fountain			17	157
Walnut Creek, No. bend Ark. R.	38°-21'-10"		114	271
Mulberry Creek, So. Bend, Ark. R.	37°-38'-52"	99° about	83	354
U. S. & Mexican boundary line	37°-47'-37"	100°-00'-00"	32	386
Chouteau's Island, Arkansas River	37°-53'-18"		59	445
Lower Semerone Spring	37°-24'-00"		32	477
Upper Semerone Spring	36°-51'-40"		73	550
Rabbit Ears (a detached Mountain)	36°-33'-00"		45	595
Point of Rocks	36°-25'-42"		47	642
Foot of great Mountain Range	36°-10'-20"		69	711
San Fernando Village, in Taus	36°-24'-00"	105°-31'-00"	35	746
Santa Fee City	35°-41'-00"	106°-10'-00"	65	812

*A*ppendix — *Correspondence, prior to, during, and after the Survey.*

Thomas H. Benton

to

George C. Sibley

St. Louis, April 12 1825

D. Sir,

In executing the late act for marking a road to N. Mexico, you will have an opportunity to become intimately acquainted with the intervening country. I would, therefore, suggest the propriety of keeping a Journal in which the soil, timber, water courses, grasses, minerals, fossils, fall of the country, and every thing calculated to increase of geographical information, should be carefully noted. Such a work may be advantageous to yourself as well as to the country, and if published among the documents, would be a lasting monument. If forwarded to me, my well known desire to develope the resources of the west would be a guaranty of my good offices. A problem, yet to be solved, is to ascertain how much water transportation can be had between M[issou]ri & Mexico. The trade carried on between them will not be in heavy and bulky articles, such as tobacco, flour, whiskey &c. which require large boats and deep rivers; but it will be in dry goods, and light articles, and small boats and shallow streams may be useful. In this point of view it would be well to ascertain the character of the Kanzas, Osage, Arkansas, and of the Rio del Norte as far as the Passo; the periods of high and low water, [and?] ultimate rise and depression; whether from snow or rain; how near their navigable points approach each other, &c. I should think that a stream which would float small light boats of 5 or ten tons will be found very valuable when the trade becomes more considerable.

Yours respectfully,

THOMAS H. BENTON

From the Lindenwood College Collection of Sibley Papers.

Thomas H. Benton

to

George C. Sibley

St. Louis June 30th. 1825

Sir,

On my return home, I found your Letter of the 24th Inst. The dispositions which have been made for carrying into effect the Act of Congress for marking out the Road to Mexico, are, in my opinion, judicious, and well calculated to ensure the satisfactory execution of the Work.

The appropriation of $30,000 was not made as a *limit* beyond which, the expenditure was not to go. I put it in myself, and if I had said 10 or 15,000 more it would have passed just as easily. If further appropriation shall be found to be wanting, it will be made, without the least hesitation. In executing the Work, I would wish The Commissioners not to consider themselves limited, either as to time or money. It is not a County or State Road, which they have to mark out, but a highway between Nations, and which when once fixed, cannot be altered for Ages & Centuries to come.

The necessity of proceeding with due deliberation, & doing the work so as to need no alteration is therefore apparent.

The Secretary of War wishes information which will enable him to fix a Military Post at the Crossing of the Arkansas—facility of transportation by Land or water, number and character of the neighboring Indians, the capacity of the Soil to produce grains and vegetables, are among the points of his enquiry, and upon which, the Report of The Comm[issione]rs is expected to give the most exact information. Wishing to the expedition health & Success, I remain, Sir, Yrs. Respectfully

Signed, THOMAS H. BENTON

This letter is from a copy in the Lindenwood College collection. George C. Sibley in an appended note writes that he sent the original to Senator Josiah S. Johnston on January 4, 1833.

George C. Sibley
to
Owen Simpson

St. Louis, Mo. May 1, 1825.

My Dear Owen,

Having as you know, determined to accept the appointment of Commissioner on the part of our Gov[ernmen]t to carry into effect the Act of the last Session of Congress, which authorizes The President to cause a road to be marked out from the western frontier of Missouri, to the confines of New Mexico, and very cheerfully complying with your desire to be informed from time to time of my progress in this arduous undertaking, and of the result of my observations on the wild region through which the road is to pass, and on the trade which it is proposed thus to protect & encourage, I now commence for your amusement a series of letters, which I hope to continue from place to place as I proceed, and which may or may not afford you the gratification you seem to expect from my report.

It is not necessary to go into a very particular account of the trade from Missouri to Santa Fe in N. Mexico—suffice it to say that it began on a very small scale in the year —— and has been growing ever since in importance; the first adventurers were hardy enterprising men, who being tired of the dull & profitless pursuits of husbandry & the common mechanical arts on the frontier, determined to turn merchants or traders, and in the true spirit of western enterprise, directed their steps westward to the settlements of New Mexico, from whence many strange and marvelous stories of inexhaustible wealth in the precious metals, has long before, found their way to & were circulated and readily believed thro' our settlements on the Missouri. I believe the honour of the first enterprise of this sort belongs to William Becknell, a man of good character, great personal bravery, & by nature & habit hardy and enterprising. His pursuit immediately previous to his first trip to S[an]ta Fee was, as I am informed, that of a salt maker. He certainly had no knowledge of mercantile concerns, & is tho' very shrewd and intelligent, very deficient in education. His outfit consisted of a few hundred dollars worth of coarse cotton goods. His followers were about ——, in number all of the same description of persons or nearly so, & fitted out in the same manner. Their whole outfit of merchandise might probably have cost $—— in Philadelphia. They left our frontier at Ft. Osage, in —— and after suffering many hardships, and encountering many dangers, reached the settlements of Taos in N. Mexico where they were well received. In the following —— Becknell & his party returned home, having disposed of their merchandise to some advantage, the proceeds of which they brought home in specie, mules, asses, & Spanish coverlids or blankets. This successful (for so it may be termed) expedition instantly excited many others to adventure to S[an]ta Fee; and among the rest were some few who had been partially bred to the retailing of merchandise in the U. States. The result of the experiments & observations of those best informed in commercial matters who visited S[an]ta Fee the next 3 years after the return of Becknell, was reported, & seemed decidedly to discountenance any further trade. It was at once discovered that the precious metals were far less abundant in N. Mexico than was at first supposed, & that the other resources of the country were for want of enterprise & industry in the inhabitants yet very partially developed, that the inhabitants were generally extremely poor & ignorant, and the local gov[ernmen]t tho' a little emerged from its former servile state, & evidently fast improving in liberal principles, was yet very strongly biased against the proper encouragement of a liberal intercourse with our people.

Notwithstanding these discouraging circumstances, they had little or no influence except with the merchants. In fact they seemed to have had a contrary effect on those who had first adventured, and others of the same description. Still larger caravans were equiped, composed almost entirely of farmers' sons, mechanics, hunters and trappers; very few, if any were qualified as merchants. These caravans being better equiped, & much better organized, as well as more numerous were able to search for, and find out better routes than their predecessors—the journey was thus not only somewhat shortened, but was also rid of some of the dangers & difficulties that at first beset it. And thus this trade has gone on to increase, in such hands as I have described, and has at length aroused our commercial men, & our statesmen and our government to its importance. A large capital is ready to be invested the moment our merchants can see their way clear, and that the general government intends to extend its protection and encouragement to this trade. You are aware that a law passed at the last session of Congress, having for its object this very thing; providing for a survey of the country intervening between the two settlements of Missouri & Mexico, the marking a road, & negotiating with the intervening tribes of Indians for the free & unmolested use of the road by the citizens of the two republics. Since the passage of this law which is strong evidence of the fostering care of the Government, this trade to New Mexico has been carried on with increased vigour. A very large caravan is now assembling on the western frontier, which it is reported will consist of not less than 30 waggons & 100 pack horses & mules laden with merchandise. Several adventurers from Kentucky have gone on to join this caravan, which it is expected will set out from Ft. Osage some time in this month, carrying with them a much larger & better assortment of merchandise than has ever gone from here to N. Mexico before.

Congress appropriated the sum of $30,000 for the purpose of marking a road & obtaining the consent of the Indians to use it. The President has appointed Benjamin H. Reeves, G. C. Sibley, & Pierre Menard, Commissioners, to carry the Act of Congress into effect, & has instructed us to proceed in the duties assigned by the Act, & has given us discretionary powers, & entire controul of the fund appropriated. The Commissioners are allowed to appoint a secretary & surveyor & to employ as many men as they may deem necessary for hunters, chainmen, waggoners, &c. Their own compensation is fixed at $8 a day, that of their secretary $5 p. day & their surveyor & men at such rate as they may deem proper. I came from my residence at Ft. Osage to this place, upon my own private business, not being at all aware when I left home of this appointment, or even dreaming of such an honour, as I never applied for it in any way whatever. I am waiting here for Col[onel] Reeves, who

I understand accepts, that he and I may consult together and proceed as soon as we can to business.

Mr. Menard it is said will not accept. He is not here however, & is not expected for some days to come.

The detention here so much longer than I expected when I left home is not a little hurtful to my private business. If I continue here 'till the necessary preparations can be made to set out on this service, I shall probably not see home for two months to come; & as I left my affairs as a man merely going away for two weeks my farm and stock must necessarily suffer very considerably in my absence. I am embarked however & cannot now retract, tho' I must say that nothing but the force of circumstances could have impelled me to leave for a year my family & cottage, to undertake a service that I am persuaded must be fraught with difficulties & privations & hazards innumerable. A principal reason for my entering upon this duty is the hope & belief that it may be beneficial to my health, which tho' not exactly *bad* at this time, is & has been for 3 or 4 years indifferent.

Your friend

G. C. Sibley

Published by courtesy of the Missouri Historical Society of St. Louis.

G. C. Sibley

to

B. H. Reeves

Saint Louis, May 15, 1825

Dear Sir,

It was impossible to get a contract for the waggons to be ready sooner than the 12th of June. Even if I had taken second hand waggons for part, there could not have been a saving of more than 5 or 6 days, as the workmen say they can carry on six nearly as fast as they could 3 or 4, and besides, I did not think it prudent by any means, to depend upon second hand waggons for so long a journey through a wilderness country. The six waggons are in the hands of two makers (who have plenty of hands) and are to be complete on the 12th of June under penalty of $500 if they fail. They promise to have them ready sooner if possible. I shall have everything else ready as soon as the waggons are, so that they may be loaded and started without a moment's delay.

I can make no better estimate than the one we made here—none that will justify any increase of wages to the hired men. In truth, I am perfectly satisfied that we can obtain hundreds of the most suitable kind of men for the trip for $20 pr month. Several young gentlemen of the first respectability have applied to me to go out as hands; and I have no doubt I shall offend many such by refusing them. We do not want a party of gentlemen coffee drinkers, who cannot even cook their own victuals or saddle their own horses. Many such are anxious to be employed however, and are willing to engage to perform all the hard services that may be required of them. I shall not employ any such I assure you. I mention this, to shew that hardy men, accustomed to labour, & to live on substantial food, can easily be had. I can hire a hundred such here. Several mechanics have offered themselves, such as blacksmiths, carriage makers, and carpenters. You need not employ a smith; that is, not to give him any extra wages, as I shall be able to engage one here of excellent character (as one of the six waggoners) at the $20 p. month. I shall endeavor also to engage a man who can repair the wood work of the waggons if necessary; & have no doubt I shall succeed. I conceive it highly important that every man should be a rifleman & hunter, and at the same time qualified to serve as chain carriers, axemen, &c. and who can submit cheerfully to all the necessary privations of the trip. It should be well understood by every man, that from the moment he enters upon his duties under his engagement, he is to be subject to such proper regulations as the Commissioners may deem necessary; and I should wish (indeed I consider it absolutely necessary to prevent dissatisfaction) that each man be distinctly given to understand, that the 30 hands are to form messes among themselves, and are to be distinct and separate from the mess of the Commissioners in all things, and that it is not contemplated to furnish groceries for the 30 men except in cases of sickness: and that even in the article of bread, they must not look for a constant and regular supply, owing to the difficulty and expence of transporting flour for so large a distance. It is always best to be on the safe side in such matters. If the men are suffered in the outset to promise themselves a free use of the Commissioners' stores and an unrestrained access to their tents (which the very nature of the service absolutely forbids) we will most infallibly have to settle many unpleasant difficulties with them before the necessary order & camp discipline can be established. On the other hand, if everything is fully and candidly explained beforehand, all such difficulties may very easily be avoided, and we shall have it in our power on proper occasions to relax in our established rules, & again require their strict observance, and so on, from time to time, without any danger of producing insubordination or the least dissatisfaction among the men. Those engaged by me will assuredly have all these things fully explained to them; and be given to understand, that the Commissioners will be under no obligations to shew any favours to one more than another in consequence of their rank in society, but will be perfectly free to make such distinction or not as they may feel inclined.

I have deemed it proper to explain to you fully my views upon this subject, in which I am persuaded you will concur. I should perhaps further remark, that nothing is farther from my wish or disposition than to establish any other line of distinction between the Commissioners and those who are to serve under them, than such as is absolutely necessary for the service, and as are in fact naturally drawn by their respective duties.

In selecting a fit person to take the immediate charge of the men, you will oblige me if you will take Mr. Ira Emmons into your consideration; he has been twice to St. Fee and once commanded a party; and I have been informed gave general satisfaction. Please to understand that I suggest this merely as an individual & not officially; for I leave the selection of this officer entirely to yourself; and am persuaded that I shall concur with you whether you appoint Mr. Bynum or Mr. Emmons. I should be glad at any rate to have Mr. Emmons of the party if he can be induced to go for any employment we can offer him.

I have taken measures to secure Mr. Brown's arrival here in good time; he will receive his Letter of App[ointmen]t in 7 days from today. His friends say there is no doubt of his accepting (since some little excitement has been manifested here on the subject of his appointment) and nothing but sickness will be likely to delay his arrival here beyond the 10th of June.

A very strong recommendation has been forwarded from here to the President in favour of Judge Bent as Col. Menard's successor.

I shall be glad to hear from you how you progress &c. I have no idea that I shall be able to get away from here 'till in June.

Yrs. very Respectfully

G. C. SIBLEY.

P. S. Since writing this l[ette]r, I have received from the office of State, a joint commission in due form, addressed to Col. Menard yourself and me, which I shall retain 'till I see you. There is no bond or surety required.

Yrs &c.

G. C. S.

Published through courtesy of the Missouri State Historical Society, Columbia, Missouri.

George C. Sibley

to

Benjamin H. Reeves

St. Louis May 29th 1825

D[ear] Sir,

A Mr. James Logan of Wayne County is desirous to go out with our party as a Volunteer. He offers to serve as a hunter &c. without pay or any other compensation than the protection of the Commissioners and his provisions. His object is, as I understand, to visit Santa Fee. I have no acquaintance with this gentleman, and have only been applied to by him indirectly through Mr. Geyer, who has recently returned from below, where he saw Mr. L.

I am not at all disposed to encourage such applications as the above; because I do not think we can with propriety accept of conditional service, inasmuch as it would increase our expences and in some degree diminish the comforts and accommodations of our regular hired hands, and besides, it will be extremely difficult to fix any limit to the number, at least it would subject the Comm[issione]rs to an *unnecessary* and (at least to me) extremely disagreeable alternative of either accepting *all* offers of service, or of discriminating between a host of applicants; which latter, I have already become sufficiently tired of; and have no doubt you must be still more so than I am.

I have from the first anticipated that some such applications would be made to the Comm[issione]rs & that some traders would avail themselves of our escort to visit S[an]ta Fe; and I should have no objection whatever to permit any reasonable number to join our party, provided they find all their own supplies, and submit themselves to our camp regulations; and I would at all times be willing to afford such persons any assistance that we could *properly* give them on the journey not incompatible with the public service. But I would not consent to burthen our party with any persons whose equipment for the journey did not in the outset, hold out a reasonable prospect of their being able to go through.

I shall inform Mr. Logan of my views on this subject, so that he may go or not, as far as my consent is necessary, as he thinks proper. It will certainly afford me pleasure to be able to extend any personal civilities to such men as Mr. L. is said to be; but for the reason I have stated, I cannot consent to accept of any volunteer services, except on the conditions I have named.

My preparations progress fast enough. I am inclined to think that we might yet save much time, trouble & expence by concluding our negociations with the Osages and Kansas at this place; they will probably stay here 'till the 10th of June. I think I can have the waggons & outfit at St. Charles on the way up, by the 14th or 15th. I have employed Benjamin Jones, an old & experienced traveler, hunter &c. Benjamin Robinson—Mr. Jones' stepson, a good rifleman, waggoner, &c. James Wells—son of a respectable farmer near this place. James Brotherton—son of a widow near St. Louis, formerly from Pittsburgh. Dan[ie]l Murphy—respectable young man, who has been a surveyor &c. Harvey Clark—son of a respectable farmer, good rifleman & hunter. All young men except Mr. Jones, all good riflemen & of good families. Mr. Jones is a great acquisition; he is the man who piloted W. P. Hunt & party from the heads of the Yellowstone to Ft. Osage, & was formerly the compeer & favorite of the celebrated trader and Indian fighter, Robt. McClellan. I have selected the six men just named after very strict inquiry, from a list of more than a hundred applicants; and have given offence to many good but silly men; who *conceived themselves,* best qualified, and best entitled to the preference. This expedition of ours has excited a more general interest among the people of this & the adjoining states than any thing that has occurred for many years. The excitement is not only extensive, but very warm; It is in fact a mania; & I do not suppose that if The Comm[issione]rs had half a million at their disposal, they would be able to satisfy all the *good* men (to say nothing of others) who would apply for service.

I am sorry to see this thing so over-rated, and its importance so greatly magnified. There being necessarily so many disappointed applicants, we shall of course have every step we take noticed, and commented on; this I anticipated from the first; but altho' I have no particular relish for newspaper *abuse,* I confess I prefer it very much to newspaper puffing, in advance. In the first case, we have a good chance of doing more good than the noisy portion of the people expect—in the latter we should be certain of disappointing the public expectations.

For my own part I feel most sensibly that I have embarked in a service that will be found extremely arduous & in many particulars extremely unpleasant; that I shall necessarily make sacrifices of time, interest, comfort, & perhaps health (if the season sh[oul]d be very dry) not to be compensated by the pay allowed me. I will go on however without looking back; and if God gives me health and power, I will go through with the enterprise, & do all in my power to make it useful to the country & honorable to those concerned in it.

Among the silly articles that have appeared in the papers on this subject: I regret very much to find that of Mr. [T.] Boggs who has so far forgotten what he owed to his own standing as to indulge in some very unnecessary & exceptionable remarks, in his Letter to the Editor of the Advocate. In that letter Mr. B. permits himself to assert in the most unqualified manner, that I gave him my promise to support him for the app[ointmen]t of Sec[retar]y &c. which assertion I aver most peremptorily is not true; & I am sure that Mr. B. has greatly missed the mark, when he suffered his angry feelings to get the better of his reason so far as to charge me publicly with violating a promise to him, when a moment's reflection must have convinced him that he *may* have been mistaken.

There is a disingenuousness & want of candor & self respect in this silly procedure that has at once destroyed the good opinion I once held of Mr. B. which he can only recover by correcting his error in a public manner. Mr. B. might have infered from the note he carried from me to you from Franklin (if you informed him of its contents) that I did not consider that anything I had said to him amounted to a promise of support; & if he had deceived *himself* into such a belief he might then have been *undeceived*. At that time Mr. B. stood uppermost in my mind for the app[ointmen]t he asked. I had not then had any other application. Mr. B. met me in the Prairie on his way up to my house to solicit my support; which he did solicit very unceremoniously, & I promptly told him that if I had any part in making the appointment, he might rest assured that I sh[oul]d have no objection to him, as I considered him qualified, &c. This I am sure was the amount of what I said to him on the subject. I do not pretend to recollect the words, but this is the substance. It is possible that I may have expressed myself so as to have been misunderstood by Mr. B. and that his anxiety on the subject may have led him to construe into a promise, a mere expression of my approbation; however this may be, it is certain that I had not the most distant intentions of pledging myself, nor can I for one moment believe that I gave the slightest reasons to Mr. B. to think so. Mr. B. certainly made his application to me, very unexpectedly, and as I thought, very prematurely. He knew that I considered the report of my app[ointmen]t to be founded in mistake, & that I doubted at any rate whether I could accept; yet he thought fit to solicit from me a pledge to make an appointment that he knew I thought (& while in fact I *had* no authority) I had no right to make. I was surprised by his sudden application, & *answered* in substance as I have stated, & no more was said about it, except that Mr. B. told me that you had given him a favourable answer to a similar application to you. I know not whether you informed Mr. B. of the contents of the note I wrote you from Franklin.

If you did, Mr. B. has no colour of pretence for affecting to believe me pledged to him; and when I recollect the friendly manner (at least apparently so as you may have witnessed) he conversed with me just before he left St. Louis, I am forced to conclude that Mr. B. acted with great duplicity, or that he was not under the impression that I had violated any pledge to vote for him. When Mr. B. was informed that I preferred Mr. Gamble to him for sec[retar]y & meant to vote for Mr. G. he ought at once to have advised me of his impression of my pledge, so as to have had the matter properly explained; or he ought to have expressed his resentment of my (supposed) breach of faith the next morning when I saw him at the tavern. I must beg pardon for troubling you with this matter. I cannot properly enter into any quarrel public or private with Mr. B. He has certainly done very wrong in publishing his letter; and knows perfectly well how to make honorable amends; and I hope for his own sake he will do so. If I am obliged to make a public denial of the truth of Mr. B's statement, I shall accompany it with my solemn oath that I did not intend to, and do not believe I did, give him any promise &c.

Hoping to hear from you soon, & to learn that you are improving in health

I remain respectfully,
Yr Obt Svt.
G. C. SIBLEY

CONTRACT WITH THE MEN

We the undersigned having engaged ourselves to the Commissioners appointed to mark out a road from the western frontier of Missouri to the confines of New Mexico, Do each of us promise and hereby bind ourselves to serve the said Commissioners faithfully and dilligently and to the best of our skill and abilities. We will do and perform all such services as may from time to time be required of us by the Commissioners either as Chain Carriers, Axemen, Hunters, Waggoners, Hostlers, Packers, Labourers, or in such other capacities as the nature of the service may require. We will observe strictly such rules and regulations as may be established by the Commissioners for the proper government of the party, and in all things pertaining to the service obey their orders promptly and truly. And we engage to serve the Commissioners as above for and during the term of their Commission unless sooner discharged.

Signed at Saint Charles, this   Day of June 1825.

In presence of   *Names*   *Services commenced.*

Benjamin Jones
Benjamin Robinson
James Wells
James Brotherton
George West
Daniel Murphy
Harvey Clark
Joseph Walker
John Walker
John L. Davis
Antoine Long

From a copy in B. H. Reeves's handwriting in Lindenwood College Collection.

James Barbour
Secretary of War
to
G. C. Sibley & B. H. Reeves esqr.
Commissioners &c. &c.

Dept. of War
September 19, 1825

Gentlemen

The President has recently been informed that Mr. Poinsett our minister [————?] the Government of Mexico has not as yet been able to make any progress in the negotiation on the subject of a continuation of the road which you are now engaged in marking out, beyond the boundary line of the United States. You will, therefore, confine your operations to the said boundary agreeably to 1st Section of the Act of the 3d. March last, copy of which has been furnished you.

I have the honor to be

Yr Obt Servt

JAMES BARBOUR

Published by courtesy of the Missouri State Historical Society, Columbia, Missouri.

George C. Sibley

to

Benjamin H. Reeves

San Fernando, New Mexo.

12 Novr. 1825.

D. Sir,

I regret that I am obliged to write you in such haste as almost to preclude the possibility of giving you even such particulars as I think you ought to know.

I arrived here on the 30th Ulto. at noon with my whole party safe & sound, except 4 horses that I was obliged to leave over the mountain, & which I suppose will be lost; they were all sick & tired out.

Our journey from the time I left you 'till our arrival here was unmarked by any material accident; and was every way quite as prosperous as could have been expected. We did not see any of the natives, or any very recent signs of any.

Knowing that if I could winter my horses at all, it must be in this settlement, & that it would also be better & cheaper to quarter the men here for the winter, I determined to get thro' on over the mountains at this point & not take the waggons round to Santa Fe. This desirable object I effected without much difficulty with the assistance of Mr. Baillio, who came over the mountain to us with an Indian guide and some fresh mules. We found a very good way over the mountain and brought the waggons all over perfectly safe and with very little difficulty. I have been employed ever since I came here writing, and making arrangements for the wintering my men & horses; & was in hopes I sh[oul]d have been able to give you a much more detailed account of the route from where we parted to this place; but the party by whom I write, starts sooner than expected, & scarcely allows me time to write at all.

I enclose you a map, which Mr. Brown has partly prepared, from which you will be able to learn all that is material for the present. Mr. Young will start in, he says in February or perhaps sooner, & by him I will write you particularly.

I believe I shall be able to effect the wintering of the greater part of my horses here, pretty easily, & on pretty good terms; and you may rest satisfied that my expences here will not exceed at any rate (I am sure they will fall short of) the estimate made before I left you.

Williams is gone trapping 'till June, & Davis pays part of his wages by tailoring, so that I save at least $40 p. mo[nth] of wages, which will nearly pay the expence of provisions for the men. In the event of my not being able to write you before you start out in the spring, I beg you to bear in mind the following.

If the road is to be continued, it will be necessary to bring out with you [——?] 4 spades, 8 axes, 2 mattoks [sic], 20 good axe handles, no such thing can be had here, some files, nails, augers—also some rifle powder, lead, coffee, tea, sugar &c. If the appropriation is augmented, so as to allow a more thorough examination of the country before we finally locate the road, which I trust may be the case; it will require a larger supply of the above articles. As the waggons I have here are in good order, I do not think it will be necessary to bring out any of the others, unless our explorations &c. are much to be extended. Nor do I think it will be necessary, in any event, to employ many men. If you come out with a caravan of traders, the fewer men you can do with the better. Any number may be hired here at any time, & for less wages than $20 a month.

As I shall dispose of all the goods I brought with me, in barter for corn, wheat, mutton, &c. for the men & horses; I would advise that a few Indian articles should be bought & fetched out, such as 1 piece scarlet cloth, 1 piece blue ditto, 3 pieces ——[?], 12 lbs vermillion,

8 lb. blue beads, 6 doz. knives, some ribbons, awls, [————?] gartering & such little things. These may be very essential if we meet with any Indians, as no doubt we shall in the spring.

I wish it to be understood that I do not consider that a secretary will be proper or necessary; unless the gov't. should direct some further negotiations with Indians, & in that event, I hope Mr. Gamble may be again employed, or if he wishes to decline the service, I should then prefer Mr. Wilson McGunnegle, and last of all would I agree to the employment of Mr. Boggs. I do not appreciate however that any difficulty can occur in this matter, as no secretary will probably be needed.

Your communication from Walnut Creek was duly received. I have not yet learned whether the governor of this province has received any orders or not; I have addressed a letter to him on the subject, & also one to Mr. Poinsett, our Minister at Mexico, from whom I shall probably hear very fully on the subject of the road in February, and if I get his answer in time to forward you by Mr. Young, shall do so. Please to forward this l[ette]r & the map to Col. Mather, or copies; for tho' I wish it, I fear I shall not be able to write him. I hope you got home safe & well, & found all well. Mr. B. & I & all hands are well.

Yrs. very respectfully,
G. C. Sibley

p. s. I have enclosed a map to Col. Mather.

From the Leonard Collection by courtesy of the Missouri State Historical Society.

ARCHIBALD GAMBLE'S REPORT

from Missouri Republican, Monday,
October 24, 1825.

The road commences a mile or two south of Fort Osage, upon a line run some years ago as the boundary of the Indians lands, in Lat. 39° 10' 19" and Lon. 93° 51' 5" from London. It follows the neighborhood road until it crosses the Little Blue Creek; it then enters upon those extensive prairies which reach, without intermission, to the Mountains of New Mexico. At the distance of 26 miles from Fort Osage, the road crosses another stream of the Missouri, called Big Blue, a creek about 20 yards wide, and which, at the season of high water, might require a ferry boat. After crossing the creek, the route pursues the ridge which divides the waters of the Kansas from it, and which ridge continues on in a good direction, and becomes the divide between the Kansas and the Osage Rivers, and also between the Neeozho and the Kansas, and the Little Arkansas and the Kansas. It will be seen by a reference to the Map, that the Kansas River runs in the direction that the road must follow, to reach what is called the North Bend of the Arkansas, and where the Smoky Hill Fork of the Kansas and the Arkansas approach nearest to each other. It was ascertained by observations for latitude, taken by Mr. Brown, the Surveyor, that the distance between those points is 10½ miles. In surveying the route for a road, it was found advantageous to adhere to the ridge where it did not swerve materially from the direction. In some places, however, it was necessary to leave it to the right, and cross some of the head streams of the Osage. None of them, though, are difficult to cross, or likely to obstruct the traveller at any season. Upon the whole, the face of the country offers great facilities for a national way. The ridge upon which it runs is high and open, and the streams upon the opposite sides, (generally with a small fringe of timber upon them,) approach so near as to furnish wood and water without much inconvenience.

There is a part of the route, however, as you approach the Arkansas, that must forever be scarce of wood and water. It is a high and level plain, extending across from the Cotton Wood Fork of the Neeozho, nearly west, about thirty miles. The substitute for wood here is the Buffalo ordure, which answers a good purpose, and even in the driest season the traveller will be able to find a sufficiency of standing water.

The Commissioners in going out struck the Arkansas lower down than the road is expected to cross that river; they followed it up to the boundary line of the U. S. in lat. 37° 47′ 37″, and on their return will correct the road back so as to leave the Arkansas at the mouth of Walnut creek (the North Bend).

The expedition reached the boundary line early in Sept. and remained in camp until the 21st, waiting for authority to continue the surveys through the Mexican territory.

As the season was now advanced, and the means of subsisting horses becoming very precarious, the Commissioners came to the conclusion that it would not be safe to remain longer inactive. They, therefore, divided the party; one of the Commissioners (Maj. Sibley) and the surveyor, with ten men, were sent to Santa Fee to winter, with a view to obtain information of the country, and to make arrangements, if necessary, with the Commissioners on the part of the Mexican government for the completion of the road in the spring. The other two Commissioners, Col. Reeves and Col. Mather, with the balance of the party, are on their return, and are correcting and straightening the road, where it will admit of it. Mr. Gamble left the company at the North Bend of the Arkansas, all in good health—they stopped a day to kill and dry a sufficiency of Buffalo meat to last them to the settlements. Whilst there, a company of 20 adventurers, with a great many mules and horses laden with merchandize, arrived from Missouri, bound for Santa Fee; and an hour afterwards a company of 81 persons, returning from Santa Fee, also arrived at their camp. An intelligent gentleman of the returning party furnished a memorandum of the property with which the company started from Santa Fee. It is—

In silver			$13,568
Gold			182
Beaver Fur,	2044 @ $ 5		10,220
Mules	416		
Jacks & jennets	25		
Horses	139		
	628	@ $25	15,700
			44,679

The party lost about 100 head of stock on the Arkansas, having taken fright at the Buffalo. It is a curious fact, than when horses take fright at the herds of Buffalo that run by them, they universally run with them and not from them.

Benjamin H. Reeves

to

the Hon. James Barbour

Secretary of War

Fayette, Mo. April 15th, 1826.

Sir,

Early in Nov. last Col. Mather and myself had the honor of informing you of our arrival here with the greater part of our party, and that
Major Sibley with a fiew men passed on to the St. Fe to winter. I have
just received advices from Mr. Sibley on the 15th of February; he
dispatched six of his men with a returning carivan to Missouri. This
party in all about twenty strong was attacked by a large band of the
Pawnee (or Panis) Indians and sustained a considerable loss both of
public and private property. The precise amount of either I am unable
at this moment to say. I have deemed it my duty to give you this information so that the government may take such steps as is deemed
advisable for the recovery of the property taken at least; if not to
take such farther measures as the indignity offered the authority of the
government would seem to require. No lives were lost on this occasion,
the great object of those Indians seem to be more for the sake of
plunder than blood.

From information just received, and on which some reliance is
placed a large party of those Indians was lying in wait last fall for
the commissioners just beyond the line of the U. S. expecting to coerce
from them a rich booty; but they accidentally fell in with a carivan
returning from St. Fee and robed [sic] them of a large drove of mules
and other property. This prevented their attack upon us. The great
bulk of those roberies [sic] is committed on the Simiron, a branch of
the Arkansas. Why this particular spot should be selected for their
depredations I am unable to say; unless it should proceed from a belief
in them that they cannot be punished for an outrage committed beyond
our bounds.

Mr. Sibley is still at St. Fee and confidantly [sic] expects to be joined
this spring by the other commissioners to continue the survey of the
road beyond our line. Should the negotiation with the Mexican gov-

ernment have progressed so far as to induce a belief that such will be the result, if not incompatible with the state of the negotiations, I would be highly gratified to be informed.

I am with grt respt

Sir, your obt. servt,

B. H. REEVES

Hon James Barbour
Secretary of War
A copy of this letter in the Leonard Collection is published through courtesy of the Missouri State Historical Society.

S. Camancho
Secretary of State for Mexico
to
J. R. Poinsett

13 May, 1826

Most Excellent Sir,

I have communicated to his Ex[cellency] the Presidente the contents of your Note of the 17th April respecting a Road projected from Santa Fé to the Missouri and he has been pleased to direct me to inform the Governour of New Mexico to permit Mr. George Sibley to examine the western part of Said Road, without marking or cutting it out, or establishing any works of any class whatever, in consideration of this point having been submitted to the Authority to whom it exclusively belongs to determine it.

At the same time, I am commanded by the President to inform your Excellency, that at present it is not convenient for this Government to send an Agent to examine the Road in company with Mr. Sibley. And that he hopes when it may be thought necessary, that there will be no objection made by your Government to the Mexican Commissioners making necessary examinations and observations, within the limits of The U. States.

From a translation in the Lindenwood College Collection of Sibley manuscripts.

J. R. Poinsett
to
G. C. Sibley

Mexico, 13 May 1826

Dear Sir,

I regret exceedingly this delay, but beg you to be assured that it has not been on account of any neglect on my part. I knew that you were counting the days until you received my answer, and I have been unceasing in my applications to the Secretary of State for the final determination of the President.

By the date of his note, a copy of which accompanies this letter, you will perceive that it was received only to day.

With my best wishes for a pleasant Journey homeward, I am dear Sir
Yr. Obt. Servt.
J. R. POINSETT

G. C. Sibley Esq. &c.
From a copy of the letter in the Lindenwood College Collection of Sibley Papers.

A. Narbona
to
G. C. Sibley

Santa Fe 14th June, 1826

Under date of the 13th May last, His Ex[cellenc]y the Secretary of State and Dispatch for Internal & External Affairs, writes me as follows.

"El Excellentissimo Senor, The President in consequence of a Note of the Minister Plenipotentiary of the United States of the North, has been pleased to determine that you permit Mr. George Sibley, Commissioner of The United States, to make an Examination of the Western part of the Road from Santa Fé to the Missouri, without marking or cutting it out or establishing any work of any Class—in consequence of this point having been Submitted to the Authority to whom it exclusively belongs to determine it. I communicate this by order for your future Government."

And I insert this, that in the exercise of your commission, you may determine agreeably to the disposition of the Superior Government.

Signed   ANTONIO NARBONA

From a copy of the translation in Lindenwood College Collection of Sibley Papers.

George C. Sibley

to

J. R. Poinsett

Valley of Taus in New Mexico
June 18th 1826

To His Excellency
    J. R. Poinsett
        Minister &c.

Sir,

I have had the pleasure to receive your communication of the 13th Ulto. and on the same day (the 16 Inst.) I also received a Note from the Governour of this Territory, announcing that he has received directions to "permit Mr. George Sibley Commr. of the U. S. to make an examination of the Western part of the Road from Sta. Fé to the Missouri, without marking or cutting it out, or establishing any works of any kind whatever."

This very restricted permission would avail the Commissioners but little indeed, if it were not for the fact that there is no "marking or cutting out" or any "works" necessary, or indeed practicable to be done on any part of the Road within the Mexican Territory.

From the crossing of the Arkansas to this Valley, and to Santa Fé, the Road will not pass through any timbered land exceeding in the whole, one Mile, and that is so scattered and open that it can be passed without the least difficulty with carriages, with no other labour than removing a few logs and poles, &c. And as it will be labour and time lost to attempt to "mark out the Road," by any artificial means that The Commissioners can devise and effect, we shall probably not otherwise mark it than by furnishing a *Chart* of the route founded upon an accurate examination & Survey, upon which, will be noted with great care all the prominent land marks already set up by the hand of Nature, and which on [occasion?] now serve as admirable guides to the traveler. Any artificial hillocks or mounds thrown up (unless of greater magnitude than our limited means will justify) would be destroyed in a very short time, by the immense herds of Buffalo that are continually passing to and fro over the plains, and what *they* might be unable to destroy, would assuredly be leveled by the roving bands of Indians who are always sufficiently inclined to do wanton Mischief.

I have no objection then myself, & I presume the other Commissioners will have none, to proceed with the examination, as permitted, inasmuch as we can effect every thing under that permission, that we could do, if it were as ample as our Government wished and expected. It is certain that the Commissioners shall determine to proceed as above Suggested, that their Report of the Road will be such as to make it entirely unnecessary for the Government of the U. States ever to take any further order or interest in the Matter.

I have deemed it proper to state these facts to you for your information.

I have the honor &c.

Signed   G. C. SIBLEY

From a copy in the Lindenwood College Collection of Sibley Papers. Sibley in a note indicates that the original accompanied the Report of the Commissioners, sent to Washington in 1827.

G. C. Sibley

to

A. Narbona

Taus, June 19, 1826

Sir,

I have the honour to acknowledge the receipt of your note of the 14th Inst. in which you inform me, that you are directed by your Gov[ernmen]t to "permit Mr. George Sibley Commissioner of The U. States to make an examination of the Western part of the Road from Santa Fé to the Missouri, without marking or cutting it out or establishing any works of any class."

As soon as my Colleagues, the other two Commissioners arrive here, who are expected in a short time, I shall lay your Note before them, and we shall then determine what course it will be proper to pursue in relation to our duties, under the restricted permission granted by The Government of Mexico—which determination will be made known to Your Ex[cellen]cy in due time & form.

I have the honour &c.

Signed   G. C. SIBLEY

To His Excy. A. Narbona
Govr. of N. Mexico.
From a copy in the Lindenwood College Collection of Sibley Papers.

Footnotes

1 George C. Sibley, Fort Osage, Jan. 18, 1809, to Samuel H. Sibley, Fayetteville, N. C. Sibley Papers, Mo. Hist. Soc., St. Louis.

2 *Debates and Proceedings of the Congress of the United States,* 18th Cong., 1st Sess., Washington, 1856, p. 2703.

3 *Ibid.,* p. 260.

4 Ex. Doc. No. 79, Serial 116, 18th Cong., 2nd Sess., p. 6.

5 *Register of Debates in Congress,* Gales and Seaton, 1824-25, p. 6.

6 David Barton, Washington, Jan. 24, 1825, to Abiel Leonard, Fayette, Mo. Leonard Collection, Mo. State Hist. Soc., Columbia, Mo.

7 Gales and Seaton, *op. cit.,* pp. 109-110.

8 *Ibid.,* pp. 347-348.

9 Pierre Menard, Kaskaskia, Ill., May 4, 1825, to James Barbour, Washington. Retired file, Indian Office, Santa Fe folder.

10 Sibley, St. Louis, Feb. 5, 1825, to J. S. Johnston, Washington. Hist. Soc. of Pa.

11 Most of the material for George C. Sibley's early life comes from an autobiographical sketch he wrote for his cousins Cyrus and Origen Sibley of Blakeley, Alabama. I have my copy through courtesy of Dr. Wm. S. Sibley of Little Rock, Arkansas.

12 The family Bible was in possession of Miss Laura Brown, since deceased, Point Pleasant, Mo.

13 John L. Thomas, "Some Historical Lines of Missouri," *Mo. Hist. Rev.,* 3:228.

14 *Ibid.,* pp. 216-217.

15 Commissioners Clark, Edwards, Chouteau, St. Louis, Nov. 4, 1816, to Wm. H. Crawford, Sec. of War. Photostat, Mo. Hist. Soc.

16 Plat of Survey in 1820, by Brown, of Incorporation of St. Louis. Mo. Hist. Soc., St. Louis.

17 John L. Thomas, *op. cit.,* p. 7 and Joseph C. Brown, *Field Notes of West Boundary of Missouri, south of the Mouth of the Kanzas River,* surveyed 1823. Mo. Hist. Soc., St. Louis.

18 In reply to accusations that friendship and relationship influenced appointment of Gamble and Brown.

19 Thomas, *op. cit.,* pp. 260-261, 271.

20 *History of Franklin, Jefferson, Washington, Crawford, and Gasconade Counties, Missouri,* Goodspeed Pub. Co., 1888, p. 223.

21 Landon C. Bell, *The Old Free State, a contribution to the History of Lunenburg County and Southside Virginia*, Richmond, 1927, p. 456.

22 From Miss Laura Brown, grand-daughter of Joseph C. Brown, School of the Ozarks, Mo.

23 St. Louis *Republican*, Feb. 23, 1849.

24 Sibley, St. Louis, May 29, 1825, to Reeves, Franklin, Mo. Leonard Coll., Mo. State Hist. Soc., Columbia, Mo.

25 Sibley, Franklin, Mo., Apr. 13, 1825, to Reeves, Franklin, Mo. Same collection.

26 Benton, St. Louis, Mo., Apr. 12, 1825, to Sibley, St. Louis. Sibley Coll., Lindenwood College. See appendix.

27 Sibley, St. Louis, Apr. 25, 1825, to Reeves, Franklin, Mo. Leonard Coll., Mo. State Hist. Soc., Columbia, Mo.

28 Sibley and Reeves, St. Louis, May 11, 1825, to the Hon. James Barbour, Washington. Sibley Coll., Lindenwood College.

29 Sibley, St. Louis, May 29, 1825, to Reeves, Franklin, Mo. Leonard Coll., Mo. State Hist. Soc., Columbia, Mo. See appendix.

30 Logan, Jackson, Mo., May 25, 1825, to Reeves. Same collection.

31 *Missouri Republican*, May 16, 1825.

32 *Ibid.*, May 23, 1825

33 Sibley, St. Louis, May 29, 1825, to Reeves. See appendix.

34 Sibley, St. Louis, May 15, 1825, to Reeves. Leonard Coll., Mo. State Hist. Soc., Columbia, Mo. See appendix.

35 Reeves, Howard Co., June 9, 1825, to Sibley. Sibley Collection, Lindenwood College. See appendix.

36 Some time previous to his expedition with the Astorians, Ben Jones had married Mrs. Margaret Robinson, who had at least three children, Ben, Marie, and Rowena. After he had departed on his long trapping and exploring expedition, Mrs. Jones gave birth to twin sons, whom Ben on his return promptly named after his late employers, Wilson Price Hunt and Ramsay C. Crooks. The primer given by the leaders of the Astor expedition to these twin sons of Ben Jones is still in possession of descendants in Montgomery City, Missouri. After his return from the Pacific, Jones bought a farm in St. Louis County, near the mouth of the Missouri, and for a few years led the life of a farmer. Whether the four years on a Santa Fe expedition, reported by Miss Stella M. Drumm in her account of Jones, preceded his trip to Santa Fe in 1825 or not, Sibley looked upon him "as a great acquisition," and made him one of the party of nine to continue into Mexican territory. When he returned to St. Louis in the fall of 1826, he had bad news for his family. Ben Robinson, his step-son, who had set off with Ewing Young

on a trapping expedition, had died of some sudden illness before they were fairly out of the settlements. Ben Jones died of the cholera in June, 1835, leaving his wife Margaret and five children. Wilson Price Hunt became the guardian of his three sons who were minors.

Stella M. Drumm, "More about Astorians," *Quart. Ore. Hist. Soc.* 24:357-360. Bryan & Rose, *Pioneer Families of Missouri,* St. Louis, 1876, p. 504.

37 See n. 36.

38 Daniel Murphy and his wife Catherine acquired property in Christy's addition to St. Louis. He died on Dec. 19, 1874. He may have been the Daniel Murphy who had a coffee house on the Levee.

39 Sibley, St. Louis, May 29, 1825, to Reeves. Leonard Coll., Mo. State Hist. Soc., Columbia, Mo.

40 Same to Same, June 5, 1825. Same Collection.

41 *Missouri Republican,* June 27, 1825.

42 Sibley, Fort Osage, July 27, 1825, to Owen [Simpson]. Sibley Papers, Mo. Hist. Soc., St. Louis.

43 See Sibley's Journal, p. 52.

44 *Missouri Iintelligencer,* July 9, 1825. Mo. State Hist. Soc., Columbia, Mo.

45 *Ibid.*

46 Sibley and Reeves, Franklin, Mo., July 4, 1825, to the Hon. James Barbour, Sec. of War. Sibley Coll., Lindenwood College.

47 See Sibley's Journal, p. 52.

48 On Oct. 14, 1847, the Boonville, Mo., *Weekly Observer* carried notice of the death of Richard Brannin, aged 72 years, a native of Virginia, but for twenty-six years a resident of Missouri. His life of many adversities may be traced through the Circuit Court of Howard County, Missouri, in two judgments against him for debt in 1822 and 1824, and in claims against the government for Indian robberies in 1826 and in 1827 or 1828. Litigation for debt did not militate against his character. Reeves chose him to be a wagoner on the survey; Sibley selected him to be one of the nine men to go with him to Taos and put him in charge of the six men he sent back to Missouri in the spring of 1826. In the fall of that year he became government agriculturist for the Osages and his wife became a teacher in the Mission school. On reorganization of the Osage Agency he lost his position and, on Dec. 17, 1831, complained to William Clark that he had not yet been paid for the corn he had had to leave on the Neosho and threatened to go to Washington for redress.

William Clark Papers, Kan. Hist. Soc., Accts with Agriculturists,

Blacksmiths & Supt. of Indian Affairs, 29: 3; 32:86, 400: Clark Letter Book—Letters of Agts. to Supt., 32: 86. Claims against Indians II:39.

49 Edward Davis was one of the Kentuckians from Todd County who had come to Missouri with Benjamin H. Reeves. He settled in the northeastern part of Moniteau Township, Howard County, and at the time of his death in April, 1844, possessed considerable property in land and slaves. He was the father of four sons and three daughters.

History of Howard and Chariton Counties, St. Louis, 1883, p. 240. *Government Plat Book,* Howard County, Mo. *Record of Wills, Bonds and Letters,* Howard Co., Mo., 3:142.

50 Joseph Davis was born in Christian County, Kentucky, in 1804, and came to Howard County, Mo., in 1816. At the age of eighteen he became a clerk in the land office of Gen. Thomas A. Smith at Franklin and spent his evenings studying English, Latin, and mathematics. After his return from the Mexican Boundary, he studied law with Gen. John Wilson and in the office of Edward Bates in St. Louis. About 1830 he opened a law office first in Old Franklin and afterwards in Fayette. He married Miss Sarah Elizabeth Green in 1839. He was a Whig member of the Missouri Assembly from 1844 to 1864; was one of the three commissioners to accept or reject the Missouri Pacific Railroad; commanded a brigade in the Mormon War; was Provost-Marshall of Randolph County during the Civil War. He died on Oct. 7, 1871, aged sixty-seven.

Joseph Davis kept a diary while on the survey. The second volume in possession of his grandson, Mr. Lionel Davis of Fayette, is the only part extant, and with the diary of Benj. H. Reeves is the source of information for the return from the boundary.

L. A. Kingsbury, *Index of Graves in Howard County.* Conversation with Mr. Lionel Davis of Fayette, Missouri.

51 James and John Davis were two brothers from Tennessee, who were reputed to have come to Upper Louisiana before its transfer to the United States. James, at any rate, was in the Boonslick early enough to have to run for his life from Indians. He and James Cole, out scouting, were preparing to return to the fort when they found that they were cut off by a large number of Indians. They started for John W. Johnson's trading house on the Moniteau, where they found safety for a few hours. In the night they escaped from the surrounding Indians and, though pursued, made their way to Cole's Fort to give warning to the settlers.

The James Davis who went as a hunter on the survey may very well be the James Davis who was wounded by Indians on Ashley's Expedition of 1823—perhaps the James Davis of Tennessee, who settled in Otterville Township, on what is now known as the McCullock farm. "He was an industrious farmer and a great rail splitter."

Levens and Drake, *A History of Cooper County, Missouri,* St. Louis, 1876, pp. 23, 24, 166. *History of Howard and Cooper Counties,* St. Louis, 1883, pp. 101, 102, 702. *Missouri Intelligencer,* Jan. 8, 1823.

52 Garrison Patrick, a wagoner on the survey, settled in Richmond Township, Howard County, Mo., as early as 1819. Very soon after his return from the Arkansas he started his farming career by buying 160 acres for $500. He married Mary Jane Carey on Sept. 23, 1832, and became the father of five sons and four daughters. The probate court, in making a partition of his estate after his death on July 24, 1851, leaves evidence that he had accumulated a considerable fortune.

History of Howard and Cooper Counties, St. Louis, 1883, p. 177. L. A. Kingsbury, *Index of Graves in Howard County. Missouri Intelligencer,* Aug. 7, 1824; Aug. 17, 1826; Feb. 1, 1827; June 28, 1828.

53 William Barbee bought land in Howard County, Mo., on Nov. 22, 1819.

54 Joseph H. Reynolds from Lincoln County, Ky., was an early settler of Jackson County, Mo. He ran for the office of coroner in 1830 and was elected sheriff in 1840. He was still living in 1881. *History of Jackson County, Missouri,* Kansas City, 1881, pp. 105, 111, 179, 297.

55 Bird Pyle was a resident of Ralls County, Mo., in 1826 and 1827.

56 Four men named Cornelius signed vouchers for the Commissioners—Benjamin, Jesse, Reuben, and Levi. Benjamin Cornelius, born Feb. 9, 1802, in Kentucky, came to Howard County, Mo., some time after the War of 1812, and resided in Moniteau Township until 1845, when with his sons he emigrated to Oregon and settled in the Tualatin plain of Washington County, Oregon, where he lived until his death on Dec. 13, 1864. This seems to be the Benjamin Cornelius who in Howard County married Elizabeth Means on Feb. 22, 1820; and Elizabeth Adams on Nov. 9, 1826.

Reuben Cornelius was a resident of Fort Kinkead in the Boonslick during the War of 1812. With some part of the money he earned on the survey he bought on Jan. 24, 1826, three acres in the outskirts of Fayette. But on Dec. 20 of the same year, in a sale of one acre of this land to Bird Pyle, he is described as of Ralls County. On March 8, 1850, Reuben and his wife Elizabeth are described as of Scotland County, Mo.

57 Levi Cornelius on Aug. 27, 1822, was married in Howard County to Fanny Bozarth. On July 13, 1839, he bought forty acres of Jesse

Cornelius and his wife Sarah—land that lay not far from the Boone County line, and there he seems to have resided the rest of his life. On Sept. 8, 1851, he made a will, leaving his property to his wife Fanny; and on Nov. 4, 1851, the will was admitted to probate.

History of Howard and Cooper Counties, St. Louis, 1883, p. 98. Record of Deeds, Howard Co., I:68, 213, 316. Record of Wills, Howard Co., 1849-1855, p. 139. *Missouri Intelligencer,* July 16, 1825; Nov. 30, 1826.

58 The family of Neheriah Todd, like that of many men on the survey, had followed the folk route from Kentucky to Missouri early enough to be enrolled in frontier forts during the War of 1812. David, Jonathan, Elisha, and Levi Todd are all listed at Fort Hempstead in Howard County, and the latter two are also listed at Fort Kinkead. Neheriah, who joined the survey at Franklin, was probably a son of Elisha or Levi. On Dec. 15, 1829, he was married to Minerva Hawker, who bore him at least eight children and outlived him by eight years. He died on Nov. 12, 1886, in his eighty-second year; and his will, admitted to probate on Dec. 1, 1886, shows that he left a substantial fortune.

History of Howard and Cooper Counties, St. Louis, 1883, pp. 97, 120, 158, 177. *History of Howard and Chariton Counties,* St. Louis, 1882, p. 249. Records of Probate Court, Howard County, Mo., No. 801. L. A. Kingsbury, *Index of Graves in Howard County.* Boonville *Weekly Advertiser,* Oct. 12, 1900.

59 Samuel Givens, son of James, went as blacksmith on the survey. After his return from the Mexican boundary, he filed on a quarter section of land on Big Creek, St. Charles County, Mo., and lived there the rest of his life. In the winter of 1835 he returned to Kentucky and married Sarah Simpson Organ. After their honeymoon trip to Missouri on horseback, they settled down in their log cabin. They were the parents of eight children. Mrs. P. S. Cannon of Webster Grove, Mo., and Mr. Charles Richards and Mrs. Fred Justus of Wentzville, Mo., are grandchildren of Samuel Givens. He died on Oct. 7, 1877. Bryan and Rose, *Pioneer Families of Missouri,* St. Louis, 1876, p. 152. *History of Howard and Cooper Counties,* St. Louis, 1883, pp. 240, 547. Conversation with descendants noted above.

60 Thomas Adams, who had been a neighbor of Benjamin H. Reeves in Todd County, Ky., followed him to Missouri and settled in Howard County. As chainman and guard he went with the survey as far as the Mexican boundary and returned with Reeves and Mather in the fall of 1825. He bought land near Fayette, married Miss Frances Cornelius,

and became a man of property and influence in Howard County. E. W. Stephens, *History of Boone County,* 1914, p. 20.

61 The life of Singleton Vaughan has been difficult to unravel. He probably was the son of Thomas Vaughan of the Boonslick, who had been a corporal in Sarshall Cooper's Company of Rangers in the War of 1812, and whose family had sought refuge in Fort Hempstead. On July 24, 1828, Singleton Vaughan married Susannah Cooper, daughter of Sarshall Cooper and sister of Stephen Cooper, and became a resident of Saline County. In 1844, 1848, and 1849 he sold land in Missouri. From Sacramento, California, in 1860 he sold his remaining property in Missouri. Presumably in the forties he had accompanied one of his children to the Far West. He may have gone with Stephen Cooper in 1846. Bancroft lists a William Vaughan in the immigration of 1843.

H. H. Bancroft, *History of Oregon,* I:393. *History of Howard and Cooper Counties,* St. Louis, 1883, pp. 56, 97, 158.

62 Andrew Broadus was undoubtedly the son of Whitefield Broadus, who died intestate in St. Charles County, Mo., in 1818, Catherine Broadus and Richard Gentry being appointed administrators. On Jan. 10, 1821, Andrew Broadus secured judgment against Richard Gentry for $120 and $4.80 damages; and on Jan. 20, 1823, secured judgment against Reuben S. Campbell for $68 for trespass. But Campbell seems to have come off the better in this feud, for in the June term of the Circuit Court in Howard County in 1824, he secured judgment against Broadus for $149.10½.

He earned a more enduring place in the history of the Santa Fe Trail by being the subject of the prairie amputation described in *Kit Carson's Autobiography* and in Dr. Josiah Gregg's *Commerce of the Prairies.* Record of Deeds, St. Charles County, Mo., D 554. Records of Circuit Court, Howard County, Mo., Book 2, pp. 227, 545; Book 3, p. 64. M. M. Quaife, *Kit Carson's Autobiography.* Dr. Josiah Gregg, *Commerce of the Prairies,* 2v., New York and London, 1844, pp. 59-60.

63 The amazing life of Captain Joe Walker, shorn of all detail, is summed up on his tombstone: "Born in Roan County, Tenn. Dec. 13, 1798. Emigrated to Mo. 1819. To New Mexico, 1820. Rocky Mountains, 1832. California, 1833. Camped at Yosemite Oct. 1833. Died Oct. 27, 1876. Ae 77 yrs. 10 ms & 14 ds."

This is the Captain Walker of Irving's *Adventures of Captain Bonneville,* within whose pages is a description of Walker's Expedition to California in 1833. Fur trapping in the Rockies, horse drives from California, many expeditions as guide for explorers and emigants, prospecting for gold and finding it—such is a brief summary of the rest of his life.

64 John Walker, known on the survey as "Big John," was probably another of Joe Walker's brothers, all four of whom were over six feet in height. He had a farm near Fort Osage.

65 Of John S. Davis, the *History of Jackson County* reported that he lived southeast of Independence and was a county judge in an early day.

66 Sibley, St. Louis, May 1, 1825, to Owen [Simpson]. Sibley Papers, Mo. Hist. Soc. St. Louis. See appendix.

67 Benton, St. Louis, June 30, 1825, to Sibley. Sibley Collection, Lindenwood College. See appendix.

68 Sibley, Fort Osage, July 25, 1825, to Josiah S. Johnson. Hist. Soc. of Pa.

69 See pp. 57, 196.

70 See Sibley's Journal, p. 57.

71 Sibley, Santa Fe, Mar. 5, 1826, to Poinsett, Mexico City. Leonard Collection, Mo. State Hist. Soc., Columbia, Mo. A copy.

72 Edward Bates, St. Louis, Dec. 3, 1825, to George Graham, Commissioner of the General Land Office. Retired File, Indian Office. Misc.

73 C. Vanderventer, Washington, Aug. 6, 1825, to Sibley & Reeves. Sibley Collection, Lindenwood College.

74 Reeves and Mather, Walnut Creek, Sept. 29, 1825, to Sibley. Sibley Collection, Lindenwood College.

75 See appendix, pp. 228-230.

76 James Barbour, Washington, Sept. 19, 1825, to Commissioners. Sibley Collection, Lindenwood College.

77 Reeves, Fayette, Mo., Nov. 9, 1825, to Sibley. Same collection.

78 Reeves and Mather, Fayette, Mo., Nov. 9, 1825, to Sibley. Same collection.

79 Reeves to Gamble, n.d. [Spring of 1826]. Leonard Collection, Mo. State Hist. Soc., Columbia, Mo

80 Sibley, Santa Fe, Feb. 7, 1826, to Reeves. Same collection.

81 Sibley, Santa Fe, Mar. 5, 1826, to Poinsett. Same collection.

82 Reeves, Fayette, Mo., Apr. 15, 1826, to Hon. James Barbour. Same collection.

83 Mather, Kaskaskia, Ill., Apr. 22, 1826, to Reeves. Same collection.

84 Reeves, Fayette, Mo., May 12, 1826, to Sibley. Same collection and also in Sibley Collection, Lindenwood College.

85 S. Camacho, Secretary of State of Mexico, May 13, 1826, to Poinsett. Sibley Collection, Lindenwood College. See appendix.

86 Sibley, Taos, May 20, 1826, to Reeves and Mather. Leonard Collection, Mo. State Hist. Soc., Columbia, Mo.

87 Narbona, Santa Fe, June 14, 1826, to Sibley, Taos. Sibley Collection, Lindenwood College. A copy. See appendix.

88 Sibley, Taos, June 19, 1826, to Narbona. Same collection. A copy.

89 Sibley, Taos, Aug. 19, 1826, to Principal Alcalde, Rancho. Ritch Collection, Huntington Library. San Marino, California.

90 Sibley, Taos, Aug. 23, 1826, to Pedro Martinez. Ritch Collection, Huntington Library. A copy in Lindenwood College Archives, written on back of Martinez' letter to Sibley.

91 Reeves, Fayette, Mo., Oct. 12, 1826, to Sibley. Leonard Collection, Mo. State Hist. Soc., Columbia, Mo.

92 Sibley and Mather, St. Louis, Jan. 10, 1827, to James Barbour. Sibley Collection, Lindenwood College.

93 Sibley, St. Louis, Jan. 29, 1827, to Bates. Hist. Soc. of Pa.

94 Reeves, Fayette, Mo., Mar. 10, 1827, to Sibley. Sibley Collection, Lindenwood College.

95 Sibley, Fort Osage, Mar. 23, 1827, to Reeves. Leonard Collection, Mo. State Hist. Soc, Columbia, Mo.

96 See n. 63.

97 Jacob Gregg, born April 9, 1802, in Overton County, Tennessee, was the third son of Harmon Gregg and his wife Susannah Smelser, and therefore a brother of Dr. Josiah Gregg, born four years later. The history of the family is rich in Indian captivities, rescues, and stealthy Indian murders, first on the Illinois frontier and later on the Boonslick frontier of Missouri. According to William Connelley, Jacob, a young man of twenty, was in the first wagon caravan to Santa Fe. Shortly afterward he and his father removed to western Missouri, where they settled four and one-half miles northeast of what within a few years became Independence, the county seat of Jackson County. Jacob became a man of affairs in its history, as constable, commissioner, deputy sheriff, member of the General Assembly, and postmaster at Stony Point. He became the father of six sons and three daughters. In 1881 when the *History of Jackson County* was published, he was still living, a worthy president of the Historical Society of the Old Settlers.

98 Reuben Collins lived in or near Independence. On March 4, 1826, he married Hannah Crisp. In Alexander Majors' *Seventy Years on the Frontier,* there is a fleeting glimpse of Reuben Collins galloping out of Independence to bring help against a Mormon invasion of that county seat.

99　Jonathan Cameron, who joined the survey at Fort Osage as a hunter and chainman, returned from the Arkansas with Reeves and Mather in the fall of 1825. He voted in Independence in August, 1826, and probably was already a landowner in the neighborhood of Fort Osage. On Sept. 7, 1827, Joel P. Walker united him in marriage with Phoebe Connor. In the course of a few years he amassed 960 acres south and west of Fort Osage. In 1841, he was one of the trustees for Six Mile Academy. He died on Feb. 16, 1868, at the age of sixty-six years. His tombstone may be seen in the old cemetery at Sibley, Mo.

100　According to Switzler's *History of Howard and Cooper Counties*, William Baxter was one of the first settlers in the Boonslick country. He came as early as 1812, built a cabin on Thrall's Prairie east of the Moniteau, and raised a crop of corn. When Indian hostility became acute, he took refuge in Fort Hempstead and joined Cooper's Company of Rangers. William and his sons James and Bryant soon moved on to the western frontier of Missouri. All three joined the survey at Fort Osage as hunters and chainmen and returned from the Arkansas in 1825. In the general election of 1828, William Baxter and his sons voted in Independence, and then or shortly afterward were farmers a little northeast of the county seat.

101　Sibley, Fort Osage, Apr. 7, 1827, to Reeves. Leonard Collection, Mo. State Hist. Soc., Columbia, Mo.

102　There were two Carsons on the survey, Andrew and Robert. Andrew, a half-brother of Kit, was born in South Carolina in 1790, the third son of Lindsey Carson by his first wife whose maiden name was Bradley. Robert, a full brother of Kit, was the third child and first son of Lindsey Carson by Rebecca Robinson, his second wife, and was born in Madison County, Kentucky, about 1802. Lindsey Carson had come to Missouri with Colonel Hale Talbot in 1810. After a year on Loutre Island, he moved into the Boonslick country, where he and his sons had to seek refuge in Fort Kinkead during Indian hostilities, and Lindsey and Andrew served in Sarshall Cooper's Company of Rangers.

　　The Carson are part of the history of the Santa Fe Trail. Family tradition, according to E. L. Sabin, insisted that when Kit ran away down the Trail in 1826, he followed on mule-back his brothers William, Hamilton, and Robert, and caught up with them a few miles out of Franklin. Wm. M. Boggs, a son of Lilburn W. Boggs, wrote in his eightieth year: "Andy Carson, a brother of Kit, at one time engaged in Santa Fe trade, and started from my father's house at Independence when I was a six year old boy." Employed as a chainer, etc., he went all the way to Taos with Sibley, spent the winter there, and in the spring of 1826 was one of the party of six sent back to Missouri, who fell among the plundering Pawnees. Andrew Carson had evidently impressed Sibley as being unusually competent. When he was planning correction of the survey in 1827, he wrote Reeves that he wanted Joe Wright and Andrew Carson to go with him if they were available. On this trip Carson went as far west as the Diamond Spring. He was one of the men rather severely injured by the lightning bolt in early July and asked to be allowed to go home. In the fall of 1831, Commissioner Reeves had difficulty getting the signature of Andrew Carson on another set of vouchers. On November 25, he had only then returned from Santa Fe. The land records of Howard County show a good many real estate transactions carried on by Andrew Carson.

Robert Carson, "Old Bob," went to California in 1849 or 1850. The years had not been kind to him. In 1851, he and a nephew needed $5 that Wm. M. Boggs gave him. He was on his way to visit his brother, Lindsey.

Wm. M. Boggs, "Reminiscences of William M. Boggs," *Mo. Hist. Rev.* 6:86-90.

E. L. Sabin, *Kit Carson Days,* New York, 1935, Chapters I-III.

103 Joseph D. Hardin was the son of Samuel Hardin, who helped plat the town of Fayette; and attended the first school in that town. Joseph inherited a farm, a slave, and a wagon from his father. On Jan. 8, 1833, he married Jane Davis, daughter of Edward Davis, and died in February, 1870. William Hardin became the guardian of his minor son John.

104 Christopher B. Richardson was the son of James Richardson, who with Jesse and Silas Richardson, was domiciled in Fort Kinkead during the Indian troubles of 1814. When James Richardson died in 1821, Christopher, aged fourteen, chose David R. Drake as guardian. Of his life between 1827 and his death in 1851, I can find nothing certain. The Jefferson City *Inquirer,* Jan. 11, 1851, carried notice of the death of Chris Richardson in Sacramento, California.

105 Reeves, Fayette, Mo., May 1, 1827, to Sibley. Sibley Collection, Lindenwood College.

106 See Diary of the Resurvey, June 9, 1827.

FOOTNOTES TO SIBLEY'S JOURNAL

1 For account of Benjamin Jones, see n. 36 preceding.

2 James Brotherton, whom George C. Sibley described as "the son of a widow living near St. Louis," became a man of considerable importance between the time he returned from the survey in 1825 and his untimely death on July 31, 1838. He amassed more than a little property and

enough public confidence to be elected sheriff of St. Louis County in 1836. His brother Marshall, who had served as one of his deputies, became sheriff in his place and served several terms. The village of Brotherton which stood on the Missouri river bank opposite St. Charles until the flood of 1883 swept it away, took its name from Marshall Brotherton, who with his brother-in-law, John L. Ferguson, operated the ferry boat connecting the St. Charles Rock Road with the town of St. Charles. J. Thomas Scharf, *History of St. Louis City & County,* 2 v., Philadelphia, 1883, p. 1073. William L. Thomas, *History of St. Louis County, Missouri,* St. Louis, etc., 1911, I:284. St. Louis *Republican,* Aug. 1, 1838, St. Louis Probate File #1395.

3 Ben Robinson, step-son of Ben Jones, died of a sudden illness near St. Fee as he was departing on a trapping expedition with Ewing Young in the winter of 1825.

4 See n. 38 preceding.

5 For account of Brown and Gamble see Introduction, pages 16-20.

6 Robert Bailey, an Englishman, who had married Martha Satchwell in Boston in 1819, bought the Pond Fort farm, twenty miles west of St. Charles, Missouri, from the heirs of Micajah Baldridge. After his death in 1823, his widow set aside her east bedroom for the use of those who went up and down the Boonslick Trail. From Mrs. Ella Bailey Johnson, great-granddaughter of Robert Bailey, St. Charles, Mo.

7 Lemuel Price of North Carolina settled on the Boonslick Road near Camp Branch in 1815. His cabin, which Isaac Van Bibber, Patrick Ewing, Boone Hays, and Lewis Jones assisted in raising, was the first habitation on that creek. Bryan and Rose, *Pioneer Families of Missouri,* St. Louis, 1876, p. 222.

8 Amos Kibbe (more often spelled Kibby or Kibbey) was a brother of Col. Timothy Kibby of St. Charles County, Missouri, and soon after 1822 had settled eleven miles west of Camp Branch, where the Boonslick road and the Cote san Dessein road forked. Lewiston for eight years county seat of Montgomery County, but now for many years only a memory, was laid off on Kibby's farm, a short distance south of present day New Florence. *Ibid.,* pp. 231-233.

9 After Isaac Van Bibber, adopted son of Daniel Boone, had worked for some years as a salt maker at Boone's Lick for the Morrison brothers, he bought, on Oct. 2, 1818, Nathan Boone's claim to Loutre Lick at the foot of Mineola Hill; entertained travelers at first in several log cabins; and in 1822 built his well-known tavern. A story and a half in height, with a porch running the entire length of both front and back, it remained practically unchanged until 1881, when it was purchased by

Charles Mahanes, who tore away part of the original structure. The entire building has now been gone for many years. Oliver Baker, "Danville and Danville Township," *Mo. Hist. Rev.* 7:204-205.

10 Enoch and Alexander Fruite, two brothers from Christian County, Kentucky, settled on Nine Mile Prairie in 1819. Hunters and trappers as they were, each made his civic contribution. Enoch was a member of the the jail and court-house commission of Callaway County, a road reviewer in 1823, a member of the county court in 1824, and a justice of the peace. Alexander was the first postmaster on Nine Mile Prairie. Bryan and Rose, *op cit.*, p. 270.

11 Thomas Harrison took up residence on the Boonslick road in the northern part of Callaway County in 1819. He purchased the holding of Aaron Watson, whose cabin built in 1818 was at that time said to be the only habitation between the Loutre and Cedar Creek. *History of Callaway County*, St. Louis, 1884, p. 217.

12 No one by the name of Regan has left any land record in Callaway or in Boone County.

13 George Sexton lived eight miles west of Columbia, Mo., where the Boonslick road crossed Perche Creek. For twenty-four years he had the contract for carrying mails west of St. Louis; and his carriage, wagon, and harness shops, stables, and granaries were the main enterprises of the now long extinct town of Persia, platted on both sides of the creek. *History of Boone County*, St. Louis, 1882, pp. 133, 1055, 1056.

14 William, James, Thomas, and Samuel Johnston, all from Scott county, Kentucky, were among the first settlers of Columbia, Mo. James A. Wood, "Settlement of Columbia, Missouri," *Mo. Hist. Rev.* 3:169-178.

15 When Franklin, laid out in 1819 on the north side of the Missouri, opposite present-day Boonville, was devastated by the high waters of 1844, its citizens removed to the high land a mile or two to the north and built New Franklin. In its quarter of a century as a river town, Old Franklin was the western outpost of culture and civilization—a point of departure for Santa Fe traders, fur trappers, and explorers of the Upper Missouri.

16 The road from Franklin to Arrow Rock, which in 1825 (as now) ran entirely within the river bottom, had its origin on July 9, 1816, when on petition of twelve or more householders, the Circuit Court of Howard County appointed Benjamin Cooper, Sr., David Kinkaid, and William Thorp to view and mark out a road from the county seat to Cooper's Fort. Record of Circuit Court, Howard County, Book I, pp. 10, 33, 55, 67, 75; Book 2, p. 133.

17 Lewis Rees entered on his quarter section in Miami bottom on June 10,

1819; and with others petitioned for the first road in Saline County, that leading from Arrow Rock to Grand Pass. *History of Saline County, Missouri*, St. Louis, 1881, pp. 160, 194, 199-200.

18 Green McAfferty or McCafferty, surveyor of Saline County, filed on a quarter section on the headwaters of Cow Creek. *Ibid.*, pp. 198, 199, 441.

19 George Davis from Ross County, Ohio, settled in Petite Osage bottom some time between 1818 and 1820, a little north of the present-day town of Malta Bend. He is said to have planted the first orchard in Grand Pass Township, if not in the county. *Ibid.*, pp. 166, 186, 422, 433.

20 John Dustin settled on the Petite Osage bottom about 1815-16, so near the county line between Lafayette and Saline counties that his activities seem to have been divided between them. He was postmaster near present-day Waverly in Lafayette county in 1821, and was one of the three commissioners on March 12, 1822, to select a site for a courthouse and jail, and therefore has the credit for having helped pick out the site of Lexington, Missouri. *Ibid.*, pp. 166, 209, 210, 424.

21 Jonathan Smith Findley, of an eminent Pennsylvania family, came to Missouri from Washington, D. C., where he is said to have edited a Federalist newspaper. After the admission of Missouri into the Union he became registrar of the Lexington Land Office, which he served until within two years of his death on Nov. 1, 1832. He was a delegate to the Missouri Constitutional Convention from Howard County—"a man of fine education, rare intellectual attainments, and high moral principles." Houck, *History of Missouri*, III:259. Floyd C. Shoemaker, *Missouri's Struggle for Statehood*, Jefferson City, 1916, p. 208.

22 "Fountain Cottage" was the name of George C. Sibley's farm one mile west of Fort Osage.

23 This is Joseph Reddeford Walker, afterwards famous scout and explorer. See n. 63 to Introduction.

24 For accounts of John Walker and John S. Davis, see notes 64 and 65 to Introduction.

25 For account of connection of Senators Benton and Barton with the survey see Introduction, pages 3-6.

26 Senator Josiah S. Johnston of Louisiana, brother of General Albert Sidney Johnston, had married George C. Sibley's half-sister, Ann Elizabeth Sibley. Until Senator Johnston's death in a steamboat explosion on Red River in 1833, a spirited correspondence went on between Sibley and his brother-in-law. Part of the Sibley-Johnston letters are the property of the Historical Society of Pennsylvania through the bequest of Ann Elizabeth, whose second husband was H. D. Gilpin of Philadelphia,

attorney-general in the administration of Polk, and benefactor of the American Philosophical Society, the Historical Society of Pennsylvania, and the Chicago Historical Society.

27 Col. Meredith Miles Marmaduke of Saline county was at this time returning from the Santa Fe expedition on which he had started on May 16, 1824, and of which his journal published in the *Missouri Intelligencer* of Sept. 2, 1825, is a partial account. The issue of August 15, 1825, gives a full account of the Indian attack here mentioned by Sibley. Col. Marmaduke became Lieutenant-Governor of Missouri in 1840 and Governor in 1844 upon the death of Governor Reynolds. He was the father of John Sappington Marmaduke, who also was a governor of the state. Both are buried in the Sappington graveyard at Arrow Rock.

28 See n. 65 to Introduction.

29 Abraham's services, rated at $20 per month, earned $288.67 for his master on the first survey, and at $15 per month, $24 on the resurvey. Vouchers in Sibley Collection, Lindenwood College.

30 Where the Lexington-Independence road crossed the Little Blue was the fish-trap of Richard Fristoe, and not far away stood then or a little later the mill of Benjamin Majors. W. L. Webb, *Centennial History of Independence*, n. p., 1927, p. 127.

31 This plantation was undoubtedly the farm of James Shepherd, from which he had to remove when the commissioners chose the site for county seat of Jackson County. The fine spring mentioned is the one known later as the Emigrant Spring. It may still be seen running with a strong flow a little to the west of the Municipal Light Plant in Independence.

32 The life of Joel P. Walker rivals that of his famous brother Captain Joe for its variety of scene and experience. Born in Goochland County, Virginia, in 1797, he campaigned in his teens with General Andrew Jackson against the Creek Indians in Alabama, and though wounded in the Battle of Horseshoe Bend, volunteered for another Jackson campaign—this time against the Seminoles in Florida. After five months service, he rejoined his family who had moved to Tennessee, and decided to leave for the Missouri frontier. Near Fort Osage he rented government land and raised a crop in 1819. After looking Texas over, he returned to the Fort Osage neighborhood in 1821 and settled down for twenty years as farmer and county office-holder. He and Stephen Cooper organized an expedition to Santa Fe in 1823, which for adventure should be made into a hair-raising Western. If one could not check

Joel P. Walker's account against Stephen Cooper's, one might conclude that the fearful sufferings were imaginary.

In 1840, Joel P. Walker with his wife and four children joined a party of three missionaries and their wives for the long trek to the Pacific Coast. They traveled under the protection of an American Fur Company caravan commanded by Captain Andrew Dripps as far as Green River. Under the guidance of Bill Craig, "one of my brother's men," Walker reached Fort Hall, where he decided to go to Oregon instead of California. After a brief sojourn near Salem, he set out for California in the overland party of Lieutenant Emmons. On his return with 1200 head of cattle, 200 horses, and 500 sheep, he had so much trouble with Indians that he was well qualified to write *"Camping Directions for Travelers on the California-Oregon Trail."* in 1848 he moved to California for good and settled down near Napa. He was a member of the Constitutional Convention and the first assessor of Napa County. His final move was into Sonoma County in 1853. There he was still vigorous in 1878 in his eighty-first year. "Narrative of Joel P. Walker" as related to R. A. Thompson of Santa Rosa, Bancroft Library, Cal. M.SS.D. No. 170.

33 John Young's house, according to W. L. Webb, was on a beautiful site in what became southeast Independence. Webb, *Op. cit.,* p. 45.

34 This camp, two miles west of the state boundary, is well defined in Brown's Notes as nine miles from the mouth of the Kansas River and five miles from the crossing of the Big Blue. Sibley indicates that he crossed the Big Blue eight and one-half miles from John Young's house.

35 This camping site, 73½ miles from Fort Osage according to Sibley's calculation and 74 miles according to Brown's, was on the Big Cut-off Crossing of what is known now as the West Fork of Ottawa Creek. The surveying party had camped there on July 23.

36 This was the stream called Mule Creek by Brown, a branch of the Wakarusa. Both Sibley and Brown agree that it was timberless, but differ a bit on how many miles it was from Fort Osage, the former estimating it as 89½ miles and the latter at 86 in Brown's Notes.

37 This creek is hard to identify. Sibley places it 105½ miles from Fort Osage. It may have been Oak Creek, now called 110 Mile Creek.

38 Archibald Gamble had left the party about sixteen miles west of the Big Cut-off crossing.

39 Elk Creek, known now as 142 Mile Creek, is one indisputable point in the survey. Brown's section map places it 140 miles from Fort Osage; Sibley mentions the same distance.

40 "After the completion of this formality, and the Indians had departed

perfectly content, (August 12, 1825) it was suggested by G. C. S. to have the name of the place, as inserted in the treaty, carved in large and legible characters on the trunk of a venerable White Oak tree that stood and flourished near the entrance of our council tent, and also to add the date and distance from Fort Osage. Colonels Reeves and Mather readily assented, and Capt. S. Cooper was directed to have it promptly executed. Capt. C. employed a young man of the party known to be remarkably expert in lettering with his pen knife and tomahawk, by name John Walker, commonly called in camp "Big John," in reference to his gigantic size, who executed the order very neatly and substantially—thus "Council Grove" came to be the name and designation of the place." George C. Sibley, "Route to Santa Fe, Council Grove, &c.," *The Western Journal,* Vol. V, Dec. 1850, pp. 178-179.

On the Main Street of Council Grove may still be seen one of the oaks of the original forest. The State of Kansas and the Daughters of the American Revolution have marked it with the following inscription:

COUNCIL OAK

Aug. 10, 1825

Under this tree the treaty between U. S. commissioners and Osage Indians was signed giving right of way forever through these lands establishing the Santa Fe Trail.

41 This is William Sherley Williams (Old Bill Williams) at a turning point in his famous career. Now aged thirty-eight, he has been associated with the Osage tribe for some twenty odd years; has an Osage wife of the Big Hill band, and two daughters; has been employed as interpreter at both Fort Osage and the sub-factory on the Marais des Cygnes; has interpreted for the missionaries at the Harmony Mission; and with the Osages has ranged far to the West on hunting and trapping expeditions. From this expedition with the surveying party, we see him launch into the southern Rocky Mountain region where memory of him lives in the name of a mountain, a river, and a town.

42 A. P. Chouteau's trading post was on the Marais des Cygnes, a little to the south of the Harmony Mission to the Osages and the sub-factory of Fort Osage, which in 1825, after disestablishment of government factories for Indian trade, was run as a private business by Sibley, Baillio, and Boggs.

43 Lilburn W. Boggs at this time was a partner of Sibley in Indian trade. Boggs had a remarkable career. Born in Lexington, Kentucky, on Jan. 14, 1789, he, at the age of thirteen, served in the forces of Governor Shelby at the Battle of Tippecanoe. Shortly after the close of the War

of 1812, in which he had served eighteen months, he immigrated to Howard County, Mo., and became a merchant in Old Franklin. After various ventures in business, most of them unsuccessful, he moved to Jackson county and in 1836 became governor of the state. His administration was distinguished for its war on the Mormons. In 1846 he took the trail to California, engaged in merchandising at Sonoma, succeeded Nash as alcalde, and was elected a member of the Constitutional Convention. He died in 1861 in Napa, to which he had removed in 1852. The best account of his life is in Lyman L. Palmer's *History of Napa and Lake Counties, California,* San Francisco, 1881, pp. 373-386.

44 Better known as the Diamond of the Plains or Diamond Spring. Cooke wrote of it: "A true 'Diamond of the Desert,' a Pearl of the Prairie— were pearls but as transparent as its cold and crystal waters!" Travelers who visit it now come away in heaviness of spirit. The little wooded cliff is still there; the ruts of the Santa Fe wagons may still be seen, but the free grandeur of the spring is gone. American enterprise moved some past owner of the farm to install a ram in the beautiful spring so that its cool waters might bless house and barnyard. Cement coping and pipes, now useless, make the visitor wish that the Diamond might have a new setting. The most famous spring in Kansas ought to be a state shrine.

45 Ruxton says that antelope were frequently called *goats* by the mountaineers. And Dr. Josiah Gregg called attention to its goat-like appearance: "This beautiful animal, though reckoned a link between the deer and goat, is certainly much nearest the latter. It's about the size and somewhat of the figure of a large goat." *Commerce of the Prairies,* New York and London, 1844, Vol. II, p. 226.

46 This is a definite reference to the company of 105 Santa Fe traders that rendezvoused near Fort Osage in May. Their code of laws was proposed by Messrs. Thompson, Stanley, Emmons, McKnight, and Shackleford. Augustus Storrs was elected captain. *Missouri Intelligencer,* June 4, 1825. The company of 50 which left Franklin the first week in May was probably a part of this caravan. *Ibid.,* May 14, 1825.

47 The trading post of Curtis and Eley was near the junction of the Kansas and the Missouri.

48 Michael Eley at one time had been assistant factor at Fort Osage.

49 It is impossible to find any correspondence between Brown's government map, Brown's Notes, and Sibley's Journal for the country traversed between the Sora Contza and the Arkansas. Brown's map of the Santa Fe road shows the road crossing Dry Creek, Jarvis Creek, Long Branch, and Little Cow and hitting the Arkansas about fifteen miles east of

Walnut Creek. But Sibley's Journal notes that from the crossing of Cow Creek they traveled only four miles to reach the Arkansas, and after coursing up that river for fourteen miles attained a latitude of 38° 11' 29", which undoubtedly is in the vicinity of present-day Sterling. Their mileage counted backward from Walnut Creek shows that they struck the Arkansas thirty-eight miles below that point, i.e. near Nickerson. The key to the discrepancy between Brown's government map and Sibley's Journal lies in the fact that Brown drew the road as he thought it ought to go, not as they traveled it on the way west.

50 Southwest of Sterling.

51 South of Alden.

52 This camp would be in the vicinity of Raymond, probably to the west of it.

53 1800 feet elevation, according to government contour sheets.

54 About two miles east of Ellinwood.

55 None of the waters of Cheyenne Bottoms, nor the waters that flow in, find their way into either the Smoky Hill or the Arkansas. The bottoms operate as a sink.

56 Nathaniel Miguel Pryor, silver-smith and watchmaker, trapper and trader, was a Kentuckian, born near the Falls of the Ohio about 1798. Probably a nephew and namesake of the Sergeant Nathaniel Pryor who went with Lewis and Clark, he is said to have moved to Missouri in 1820, and from there to New Mexico in 1824. It may be that Sibley's record offers the first direct evidence of when he arrived in the Southwest. After various ventures in trapping and mining he arrived in California in Pattee's party in 1828 and took his place in history among the early American citizens in Los Angeles. "In Pryor's house west of Alameda Street" many prominent Americans such as Kearney and Fremont were entertained. He died in 1850. Col. J. J. Warner, "Reminiscences of Early California, 1831 to 1846," *Pub. Hist. Soc. of So. Cal.* Vol. 7, pp. 176-193; Stephen C. Foster, "Los Angeles Pioneers of 1836," *Ibid.*, Vol. 6, pp. 80-81; H. H. Bancroft, *History of California*, II:554, III:163, 168, 178, 393; IV:495 785; James Ohio Pattee, *Personal Narrative, Early Western Travels*, Vol. 18, Edited by Thwaites, Cleveland, 1903.

57 Camp on site of Larned.

58 Six miles east and a little south of Dodge City.

59 Sibley does not mention the Caches here, though Brown's section map indicates it and his Notes describe it: "Some turn off at a place known to the Santa Fe travelers by the name of the 'Cashes,' near to which is a rocky point of a hill at some distance from the river, composed of

cemented pebbles, and therefore called Gravel Rocks." Brown, *op. cit.*, p. 16. There is a very fine description of the Caches in *Down the Santa Fe Trail*, the Diary of Susan Shelby Magoffin, edited by Miss Stella M. Drumm, New Haven, 1926.

60 The 100th meridian passes through the eastern section of Dodge City. Brown at this time was about seven miles west of it. The returning party turned back about seven miles beyond the Caches, somewhere in the neighborhood of present-day Howell.

61 These men disappeared into the West once for all. I can find them neither in California nor in Missouri.

62 Sibley's partner in the fur-trading firm of Sibley, Baillio, and Boggs. Sibley had recommended him for consul in Santa Fe.

63 Augustus Storrs of Franklin, Mo., had established himself as an authority on Santa Fe trade in "Answers of Augustus Storrs of Missouri, to Certain Queries upon the origin, present state, and future prospects of Trade and Intercourse between Missouri and the Internal Provinces of Mexico, propounded by the Hon. Mr. Benton." See Introduction, p. 4.

64 Pryor crossed two or three miles southwest of modern Deerfield.

65 This camp must have been near present-day Ingalls.

66 At Walnut Creek the returning Commissioners met a small group of traders going to Santa Fe, and an hour later were overtaken by the large caravan which had already passed Sibley and his men. Archibald Gamble joined the latter party for a speedier return to St. Louis and published his report of the road survey in the *Missouri Republican,* Monday, Oct. 24, 1825. For his full report, see appendix, pp. 228-230.

67 This camp was near Pierceville, perhaps a little to the west of it.

68 "At this place," notes Brown, "there are no banks on either side to hinder waggons. The crossing is very oblique, landing on the south side a quarter of a mile above the entrance on this side. The river is here very shallow, not more than knee deep in a low stage of the water. The bed of the river is altogether sand, and it is unsafe to stand long on one place with a waggon, or it may sink into the sand. After passing a few wet places just beyond the river, the road is again very good up to Chouteau's Island. Keep out from the river or there will be sand to pass." *Op. cit.*, p. 17.

69 Despite the assertion in W. E. Connelley's "Notes on the Early Indian Occupancy of the Great Plains," Kan. Hist. Coll., 1915-18, Vol. XIV, p. 443, that this island was "just west of Hartland, in Kearney county, Kansas," I believe the location to be about midway between Lakin and Hartland, where the Arkansas flows southwest to northeast. This is in Sections 5 and 6, of Township 25 South, Range 36 West. The high

"nob" or mound standing on the declivity of the high ridge is about ¾ of a mile directly north of the island. This is the only place, according to the Geological Survey maps on this section of the Arkansas, where it could be. There is another "nob" a mile northwest of Lakin, but the maps show no island in this vicinity.

70 "The high plain between the Arkansas and the Cimarron, whose elevation above the sea is about 3,000, is the most desolate part of the whole Santa Fe Road, and the first adventurers in Santa Fe trade stood many severe trials here. Within a distance of 66 miles, from the Arkansas to the lower springs of Cimarron, there is not one water-course or water-pool to be depended upon in the dry season. The soil is generally dry and hard; the vegetation poor, scarcely anything grows there but short and parched buffalo grass and some cacti. Though the horizon is very distant, there is no shrub or tree to fix your eye upon, and no other game attracts your attention except once in a while a wild antelope, which is apt to allure you to a useless chase." Adolphus Wislizenus, M.D., *Memoir of a Tour to Northern Mexico,* Sen. Doc. Misc. 6, 30th Cong., 1st Sess., Washington, 1848, p. 11.

71 This is the course—40 miles from the Arkansas to the Cimarron—recommended by Augustus Storrs in his replies to Benton. Brown's justification for taking the longer and safer route is set forth at length in his Notes. "It would be much nearer to cross the river here (at the South Bend) and ascend Mulberry creek to its source and then go directly to the lower spring; but on trial of the way travelers have discontinued it as unsafe. It is uncommodious of water and timber for fuel, and wants such prominent land marks as will be a sure guide. On this route has been much suffering; in a dry time 'tis dangerous. Some turn off at a place known to the Santa Fe travelers by the name of the "cashes," near to which is a rocky point of a hill at some distance from the river, composed of cemented pebbles and therefore called Gravel Rocks. At about 3 miles southwest from this rock is a place of crossing for those who travel the lower route, or directly to the aforesaid Semaron Spring, but this (though in a less degree) is subject to the same objections as that directly from the south bend. The road this way is good, and in the spring and early summer, to those who may be acquainted with it or may have a compass to direct them, it is about 30 miles nigher than the upper route." *Op. cit.,* p. 16.

72 "Lower Semaron Spring is at the west edge of a marsh green with bullrushes. The marsh is north of the creek and near it. The spring is constant, but the creek is sometimes dry until you ascend it ten or twelve miles, where it will be found running. The stream is bolder and

the water better as one travels up it. It is the guide to the traveler until he reaches the upper spring near eighty miles." Brown, *op. cit.*, p. 18.

73 "Middle Spring," writes Brown, is "near half a mile from the creek, on the north of it, near a mile below a sort of rock bluff at the point of a hill. Above this middle spring the road is in the creek bottom, which in places is very sandy. One must pick the firmest ground, and for this purpose must cross the creek occasionally, which may be done almost anywhere, as the banks are commonly low and the bed sandy." Brown, *ibid.*

74 37° 4' 2" is about five miles northeast from the southwest corner of Kansas.

75 "The road leaves the creek and continues in a southwestwardly direction to a patch of timber, which may be seen from the hill (near this timber) on the south of the creek. At the patch of timber is a spring, called the upper Semaron Spring, and around it are some mounds of coggy rock several hundred feet high." Brown, *ibid.*

76 Sibley means that the party will now have to cross from the Cimarron to the Canadian fork of the Arkansas.

77 Mt. Dora.

78 Called Mire Spring in Brown's *Notes.*

79 This is a reference to the large party of 105 men, 34 wagons, and about 240 horses and mules encamped near Fort Osage on May 16, 1825, preparatory to getting under way to Santa Fe.

80 "From this to Turkey Creek," says Brown, "and from thence to the Rabbit Ears creek, the routes are various, agreeably to the traveler's notions. There is some sand (I may say sand hills) to pass from this to Turkey creek. The road as here laid down continues up a small fork of Louse creek, on the south side of it, which runs into the creek a mile or more perhaps above the camp, and from the head of this fork passes over to Turkey creek which is near. Perhaps a better way would be to turn up a valley nearly south, which will be seen after leaving the camp a mile or two, continue in the valley a mile or more, perhaps, until the general direction to Pilot Mountain may be resumed. The sand will then be on the right hand. The road is tolerably good." Brown, *op. cit.*, p. 19.

81 This camp is easily identified from its being 1½ miles above the junction of Turkey creek (Alamos) and Rabbit Ear Creek (Cieneguilla) in New Mexico.

82 "From about this place will be seen many small mountains on the right at ten or fifteen miles distance, extending to the southwest; the ex-

tremity of which is called the Point of Rocks, to which the road leads, at first bearing more southward to avoid sand." *Ibid.*

83 On set of small maps Sibley indicated this camp as Travellers' Cache where their horses were stolen.

84 Branch of Carrizo Creek, about five miles east of King.

85 "From the Point of Rocks the traveler will proceed a little south of west, as indicated by the map, leaving a higher swell of the plain or a little hill a fourth or half a mile to the left, and will proceed until at the brow of the high tableland on which he will find himself to be. Looking across the valley before him, through which a small creek flows to southwest, he will see the southern point of a similar highland to that on which he is, a little beyond which is the Canadian river. The road passes as near the south of it as is convenient and continues forward to the Canadian." Brown, *op. cit.,* p. 20.

86 This guide is Francisco Largo, the Comanche who guided Joseph R. Walker's party in 1823 from Taos to the caches they had made on the Arkansas the previous fall. Paul Baillio, in account with the Mexican Road Commissioners, paid $20, "price agreed on," to "Francisco Largo (a civilized Comanche Indian) for his Services as a guide to conduct the Waggons across the mountains to San Fernando in October 1825."

87 Sibley's wagon road into Taos is not exactly the route of any modern highway. Cutting southeast from the Taos Gap, by which he evidently means Cimarron Canyon, he passed the neighborhood of Vallejo and around the point of mountains where the Oñate Creek issues from the range. The guide led him up the Oñate, and over the dividing ridge between the Oñate and Coyote creeks. The Valley Springs noted in the map are evidently the ones around Black Lake (not the town). And from the valley of Coyote Creek, Francisco Largo led him over the dividing ridge by Osha Pass. Thence by the little valley of Tienditas he descended to the Rio Fernandez and so to Taos.

88 "San Fernando, the principal village in Taos. This being the nearest of the Mexican settlements, the most northern and the most abundant in provisions for man and beast, determined the survey of the road hither, although the way to Santa Fe by St. Miguel is said to be somewhat better and equally high. From Taos, which is in latitude 36° 24' 00" to Santa Fe, in latitude 35° 41' 15", the distance as traveled is about 70 miles, and with a little labor a good waggon road may be had. The course is about south-southwest. The Rio del Norte, 7 or 8 miles west of Taos, and about twice that distance west of Santa Fe, is about three chains wide and has many ripples and places to hinder navigation. The road leading from one place to the other falls on the river and continues

along it a few miles. Between these two places are some half dozen villages, or more, the chief of which is Santa Cruz, about 22 miles above Santa Fe and in sight of the river." Brown, *op. cit.*, p. 21.

89 Antonio Narbona served as governor of New Mexico from Sept. 13, 1825, to May 20, 1827.

90 See n. 41 *ante.*

91 For copy of Sibley's letter, Nov. 12, 1825, to Reeves and Mather, see appendix, pp. 226-228

92 The section map received by Reeves is now in the Leonard Collection, Missouri State Historical Society, Columbia, Missouri, and is the basis for the map in this book.

93 Dispatch of Richard Brannin to make arrangements for Sibley's removal to Santa Fe and the title *Captain* which Sibley always attaches to him seem to indicate that Brannin was one of the two men in the party who had been to Santa Fe before.

94 This fortunate sale and arrangement is, of course, between partners in the firm of Sibley, Baillio, and Boggs.

95 Sibley's references to Ewing Young in these diaries corroborate the account of George C. Yount and William Wolfskill as to his trapping activities in 1825-26 and contribute a few useful dates. Young's trapping expedition that Ben Robinson joined left Taos on Sunday, Nov. 27, expecting to return some time in February. That Ewing Young became ill as Wolfskill said may account for his slightly advanced return to Taos on Jan. 22, 1826. A letter of Reeves to Sibley shows that Young left Franklin for Santa Fe about May 20, 1826, in company with Baillio and Tom Boggs.

96 Probably by Mora.

97 "A wagon road of some difficulty has been opened from Taos through the southern spur, which leads to Santa Fe, though the communication is usually kept up by the shorter mule-road, over the highest point of the spur." Emory, *Notes of a Military Reconnaisance*, Ex. Doc. No. 41, 30th Cong. 1st Sess., p. 458. See also Ross Calvin, *Lieutenant Emory Reports,* University of New Mexico Press, 1951.

NOTES TO SIBLEY'S DIARY NO. 4
October 12 to December 31, 1825
and DIARY NO. 5
January 1 to March 31, 1826

The Sibley diaries of Oct. 12, 1825, to Mar. 31, 1826, appeared in a badly garbled version in A. B. Hulbert's *Southwest on the Turquoise Trail,*

1933. The copy used by Dr. Hulbert was made by student typists unacquainted with the script, the places, persons, and events mentioned, and abounds in errors and omissions that minimize its value. It was never compared with the originals and never corrected. No editorial policy is discernible. If the ideal was a verbatim text, there are 22 errors in capitalization and punctuation in the first twelve lines. (Pages 133-134.)

Identity of place is lost when *Louse* Creek appears as *Lower Creek*, p. 134; when *Semerone* is omitted, p. 136; when *ridge to Taos gap* becomes *ridge four gaps*, p. 140; when *San Miguel* is *Lavmigure*, p. 168; and *Sonora* is *Louon*, p. 164.

Identity of person is lost when a Baca is turned into *Bacon*, p. 148; when Genl. Wm. Clark is made a *Clerk*, p. 161; when Thomas Mather becomes a *Mathew*, p. 146; when the eminent fur trader Mr. Pratte is Mr. *Prate*, p. 162; and the U. S. consul, Augustus Storrs, is Mr. *Sterns*, p. 148. The Missouri mule trade of the Switzlers is turned over variously to Mr. *Levetser*, Mr. *Lwitzler* or John *Levitsler*, pp. 154, 156. One might guess that Mr. *Charles* was Mr. Charless, St. Louis editor, but who on earth would ever recognize Thomas Hart Benton, promoter of the road to Santa Fe, as *Colonel Bruton?* These are but samples of the name-mangling that abounds.

All the errors cannot be charged to student typists. The caption *General Sibley's Diaries* indicates that the editor himself confused George C. Sibley, Indian factor and Commissioner, with his nephew, Brig.-Genl. H. H. Sibley, who campaigned in the Southwest during the Civil War. When one reads on page 101 that marking of the route to Santa Fe was made by "a squad, consisting of Benjamin H. Reeves, George C. Sibley and Thomas Mather," one begins to doubt that the editor had even so much as read the diaries.

KATE L. GREGG

98 Called Louse Creek by surveying party; McNee's by Wislizenus; and North Fork of Canadian, or Corrumpa, by modern geographers.

99 Called Turkey Creek by surveying party; Cottonwood Branch by Wislizenus; and Alamos Creek at present.

100 The observation that Mound No. 3 is on the south side of the creek definitely establishes it as Mt. Dora.

101 Sibley also applies the name *Shining Mountains* to this range in the Commissioners' Report.

102 Now called Cimarron Creek, of which Rio Ponil is a northern tributary. In the journal Sibley called it Rio Pone.

103 San Fernandez in 1825 must have looked very much as Albert Pike saw it seven years later: "Directly in front of me, with the dull color of its mud buildings, contrasting with the dazzling whiteness of the

snow, lay the little village, resembling an oriental town, with its low, square, mud-roofed houses and its two square church towers, also of mud. On the path to the village were a few Mexicans, wrapped in their striped blankets, and driving their jackasses laden with wood toward the village. Such was the aspect of the place at a distance. On entering it, you only found a few dirty, irregular lanes, and a quantity of mud houses." Albert Pike, *Prose Sketches and Poems, written in the Western Country*, Boston, 1834, p. 137.

104 This Smith may have been Thomas L. Smith, "Peg-Leg," known to the Indians as *Terry-Oats-at-an-tuggy-bone*. He had gone out to the Southwest in LeGrand's expedition. "While the wagons proceeded by way of San Miguel to Santa Fe, Smith and a few others took their pack-horses and goods to San Fernandez." After trapping on Smith's Fork, a branch of Grand River, for part of the winter of 1824, he returned to Taos and in partnership with James Baird, Samuel Chambers, and Stevens, set up a distillery in a canyon near San Fernandez. In February, 1825, St. Vrain outfitted him for a trapping expedition on other branches of Grand River. Eleanor Meyer, *"The Old Spanish Trail from Santa Fe to California,"* University of California, 1930, p. 11. Also "The Story of an Old Trapper," San Francisco *Daily Bulletin*, Oct. 26, 1866. "Sketches from the Life of Peg-Leg Smith," Hutchings, *California Magazine*, Vol. 5, No. 5, Nov., 1860, pp. 198-206.

105 Cf. n. 93.

106 Sibley, enroute from Taos to Santa Fe on Feb. 24, 1826, met Bill Williams returning from his trapping expedition. Cf. also entry for March 9, 1826, Diary No. 5.

107 Mr. Anderson in Ranchos de Taos may be Paul Anderson who had been elected 1st Lieutenant of LeGrand's company that went from Franklin, Missouri, to Santa Fe in the spring of 1824. *Missouri Intelligencer*, Mar. 20, 1824. Or he may have been William Anderson of McGunnegle, Anderson, & Co., trading out of St. Louis with Santa Fe. *Niles National Register*, Jan. 15, 1825, pp. 313, 315; and *St. Louis Enquirer*, Nov. 10, 1823.

108 "It is a strange sight—a Spanish fandango. Well dressed women— (they call them ladies)—harlots, priests, thieves, half-breed Indians—all spinning round together in the waltz. Here, a filthy ragged fellow with half a shirt, a pair of leather breeches, and long dirty woollen stockings, and Apache moccasins, was hanging and whirtling round with the pretty wife of Pedro Vigil; and there, the priest was dancing with La Altegracia, who paid her husband a regular sum to keep out of the way,

and so lived with an American. I was soon disgusted;—" Pike, *op. cit.*, p. 138.

109 San Juan de Ulluo surrendered to the Mexicans on Nov. 18, 1825.

110 Of the firm of Thomas H. Boggs and James Dempsey trading out of Franklin, Missouri.

111 Bartolome Baca had served as governor of New Mexico in 1824 and until Sept. 13, 1825.

112 Cf. n. 95.

113 Benjamin Robinson, from St. Louis County, was a stepson of Ben Jones.

114 Sibley to Reeves, Santa Fee, 7th Feby., 1826:

"I send you also a little Book, containing a Map of the road from Ft. Osage to Taus, which I think you will find useful and convenient on your journey. I do not think there can be any reasonable doubt but the Semaron Creek is a principal branch of the Grand Saline.

"I am quite satisfied that our Road must cross the Arkansas a little above the South Bend, at or near the *old Caches,* and from thence strike the Semaron some 10 or 15 Miles below the Lower Spring. I am assured that there are *no* Sand Hills to cross on that route, and that it is not more scarce of water and fuel than the usual route by Chouteau's Island, which is probably full 30 Miles farther round.

"I am entirely of opinion now sir, that we may complete this Road with the fund already at our disposal, that is to say, upon the Route already Surveyed and examined; making such corrections as now obviously appear proper, and some further examination of the Semaron, in doing which we may afford to occupy a Month if necessary. But to keep safely within the $30,000 it will be absolutely necessary to use economy in our expenses. By sending you in Six of my men & some good Mules, and making Sale of three or four Waggons for pretty good prices, I save nearly $1000 of expense I believe. These Men having all traveled the whole route are now much better qualified for our Service than almost any other men, and I am sure that you & Col. Mather cannot find any more suitable for your Service on the journey out. I have no fault to find with any of them. Master Jo. Reynolds is, to be sure, a little wild, but he is for all that, a good hand, and I would not like to exchange him for another. We shall have no manner of use for Capt. Cooper at $50 a month. In fine Sir, it is my firm opinion that no other Men than those I now send in (or others in their stead if they decline the service) ought to be brought out by you. If you come out with the caravan, as I presume you will."

. . . . "I have suggested to the Governour here the propriety of establishing two Military Posts east of the Mountains for the purpose of giving protection to the Road, &c.; He is greatly in favour of the project, and has advised his govt. to have it carried into effect; and I have little doubt but it will be done soon. . . . .

"I shall look for you early in July, and with the most restless anxiety." Mo. State Hist. Soc., Columbia, Mo. Leonard Mss., Santa Fe Folder, No. 16.

115 Mary Easton Sibley, eldest daughter of Rufus Easton, first postmaster of St. Louis, territorial delegate of Missouri Territory, and first attorney-general of the State of Missouri, was born on Jan. 24, 1800, and educated in St. Louis and in Lexington, Kentucky. She was married to George C. Sibley on Aug. 10, 1815, and accompanied him to Fort Osage in 1816, where they lived until their removal to St. Charles after the survey of the Santa Fe road. There she and her husband developed a School for Young Ladies, which in 1853 was incorporated as Lindenwood College, and to which they gave all their property as an endowment. It has prospered through the years and is today a handsome memorial to their interest in the education of women. Mary Easton Sibley died on June 20, 1878, and was buried beside her husband in the little cemetery on the Lindenwood College grounds.

116 John and Lewis Switzler were two brothers who carried on trade with the Southwest out of Old Franklin, Missouri.

117 Elisha Stanley at this time was conducting a mercantile business in Santa Fe. As noted before, he had gone out in the spring of 1825, in the company of which Augustus Storrs was elected captain. Dr. Josiah Gregg at the beginning of *Commerce of the Prairies* "makes acknowledgement to Elisha Stanley, Esq. and Doctor Samuel B. Hobbs and David Waldo, whose names have been long and favorably associated with the Santa Fe Trade."

118 Sibley was boarding in the home of Juan Baca. Cf. entry for Tuesday, Nov. 29.

119 February 2nd is Candlemas Day, for the blessing and distribution of candles preparatory to the Feast of St. Blase on Feb. 3rd, when after morning mass and at three in the afternoon the throats of children are blessed.

120 Cf. n. 114.

121 Extract from Sibley's letter to J. S. Skinner, Editor of the St. Louis *Enquirer*, were given in the *Missouri Intelligencer*, July 13, 1826. Sibley pointed out that the wheat was an extraordinary kind, introduced recently from Sonora, where it had been known only a few years. It grew well in poor soil to a height of five or six feet, and produced a very

large bunch, each with 20 or 30 flat heads, each head with many branches all filled with grain. He was, he wrote, trying to obtain seed of a mammoth kind of onion.

122 Dr. Pryor Quarles was a brother-in-law of Sibley, having married Joanna Abby Easton, daughter of Rufus Easton.

123 General Thomas A. Smith was registrar of the land office at Franklin, Missouri.

124 Major Jonathan Smith Findlay was registrar of the land office at Lexington, Missouri. Cf. n. 18.

125 Col. John Thornton of Clay County was an eminent member of the lower house in the General Assembly of Missouri for many years. He served as speaker through 1828, 1829, and 1830. Eight children were born to him and his wife, Elizabeth Trigg. His daughter, Jane, on Dec. 21, 1837, was married to General A. W. Doniphan. W. M. Paxton, *Annals of Plate County Missouri,* Kansas City, 1897, p. 549.

126 Dr. Robert Simpson, born in 1785 in Charles County, Maryland, studied medicine in Philadelphia; in 1809 became assistant surgeon in the United States Army, and as such was in the company of the 1st Infantry that helped establish Fort Madison in the winter of 1808-09. He began the practice of surgery and medicine in St. Louis in July, 1812, in the house adjoining that of Manuel Lisa, and in partnership with Dr. Pryor Quarles is said to have established the first drug-store in that city. He held many offices of public trust—postmaster, collector, sheriff, city controller, member of the State Legislature. He died in 1873 in his 88th year. J. Thomas Scharf, *History of Saint Louis City and County,* 2 vol., Philadelphia, 1883, p. 1520.

127 Rev. Nathaniel B. Dodge, director of the Harmony Mission to the Osages on the Marais des Cygnes, had been sent to his missionary field by the United Foreign Missionary Society of New York. Born at Winchester, N. H., June 5, 1781, he had departed from New York City to establish his mission on Feb. 12, 1821; had arrived on the Marais des Cygnes on Aug. 8, 1821, and along with the twenty odd persons who accompanied him, had almost perished from fevers and agues before they could build shelter against the storms of winter. The career of the Mission was a stormy one, full of bickerings and recriminations, and withal a short one; for the Rev. Mr. Dodge had to sever his connection with the school in 1829. For a time he took up residence near Independence. On Mar. 12, 1830, he was at Boudinot; from Sept. 17, 1832, to May 26, 1833, he visited the East; and on March 24, 1836, was released from missionary service.

The connection of Sibley with the Harmony Mission had been close from the time when he helped the missionaries pick the site for their establishment in the fall of 1821. Mrs. Sibley helped nurse them through their bouts of fever, and George C. Sibley helped to keep them from starving by sending wagon-loads of potatoes. And in this very winter of 1825-26 when Sibley was writing the Rev. Mr. Dodge from Santa Fe, the missionaries were urging the appointment of Sibley as Indian Agent to the Osages in place of A. P. Chouteau, whose quaint establishment, charming though it was to Washington Irving, outraged the sensibilities of pious New Englanders, Rev. Joseph Tracy, Rev. Solomon Peck, Rev. Enoch Mulci, Rev. Wm. Cutler, Rev. Enoch Mack, *History of American Missions to the Heathen from their Commencement to the Present Time,* Worcester, 1840, pp. 340-341.

128 John Hardeman of Howard County, Mo., had developed on the banks of the Missouri, opposite the entrance of the Lamine River, the famous Hardeman Gardens.

129 *Herga* appears as *jerga* in Spanish. It is a coarse woolen cloth for saddle blankets and like purposes.

130 The Journal of one hundred pages here mentioned is the one published in this volume.

131 Joseph Charless Sr. born in Westmeath, Ireland, July 16, 1772, emigrated to the United States in 1796 and found employment in Philadelphia as a printer with the publisher Matthew Carey. In 1800 he moved to Lexington, in 1806 to Louisville, and in 1808 to St. Louis, where he established the *Missouri Gazette,* reputed to have been the first newspaper published west of the Mississippi River. He died in 1834 at the age of sixty-one, leaving a widow and four children, of whom Joseph Charless Jr. was most illustrious. J. Thomas Scharf, *History of St. Louis City and County,* Philadelphia, 1883, pp. 1390-1392.

132 Major Richard Graham was Indian Agent at St. Louis.

133 John C. Sullivan of St. Louis, had been a collector of federal revenue for Missouri in 1814, a member of the Constitutional Convention of 1820, and for five successive terms representative to the General Assembly of Missouri.

134 William C. Carr, born in Albemarle County, Virginia, on Apr. 15, 1783, came to St. Louis in 1804, at the age of twenty-one. In 1826, he was appointed a judge of the Circuit Court, a position he retained for eight years. He died on March 31, 1851, at the age of sixty-eight. He may be said to have married into the fur trade, for he married a daughter of Silas Bent, Sr., and became a father-in-law of William H. Ashley. Scharf, *op. cit.,* p. 1453.

135 See Sketch of Joseph C. Brown, pp. 15-19 of Introduction.

136 More than a quarter of a century later another explorer said of the New Mexican wheat: ". . . . and the Taos wheat, originally obtained from the wild wheat growing spontaneously on the Santa Clara and the Rio de la Virgin, has obtained a wide reputation." Guinn Harris Heap, *Central Route to the Pacific,* Philadelphia, 1854, p. 62.

137 J. R. Poinsett, Legation of U. S., Mexico, Dec. 3, 1825, to George C. Sibley:

"Sir,

I have this instant received your letter of the 12th Ulto. and as the communication between the capital and New Mexico is not very frequent hasten to reply to it by the courier which leaves to night.

"I have hitherto failed to induce the President of these States to take any part in the Survey of the proposed road until after we shall have concluded our Treaty of limits.

"As there has been lately a change in the administration I have again renewed the negotiation and will inform you of the result by the earliest opportunity. Your account of the route is highly satisfactory, and will I hope aid me in to bring this affair to a favorable conclusion. I have the honor to be with great respect Sir

Yr Obt Servt

J. R. POINSETT

State Historical Society of Missouri, Columbia, Mo., Leonard Collection, Santa Fe Folder, No. 17.

138 James Baird, one of the Robert McKnight party arrested in Santa Fe in 1812 and imprisoned in Chihuahua for nine years, had on his release come back to St. Louis to engage again in Santa Fe trade. On his way west with a stock of goods in the fall of 1822, an unusual blizzard snowed him in at the crossing of the Arkansas, but with spring he resumed his way to Chihuahua, sold his goods advantageously and, in 1825, with Peg-Leg Smith, Samuel Chambers, and one Stevens, erected a distillery in a canyon a short distance from San Fernandez. Judge W. B. Douglass in his edition of General Thomas James' *Three Years among the Indians and Mexicans* observes that Baird died in El Paso during December, 1826; but Edwin Le Grand Sabin in *Kit Carson Days,* notes: "In the San Francisco region Carson had found an old mountain-man and fellow Taosan, Jacob Beard, who had gone to ranching." On the following page, he adds, "Beard returned to New Mexico, and lived there for many years afterward." *Kit Carson Days,* New York, 1835, pp. 636-637.

139 This may be the Douglass mentioned by Wislizenus as having been sent

from Chihuahua to Cosihiuriachi at the time of Doniphan's occupation of northern Mexico. Wislizenus, *op. cit.*, p. 32.

140 This probably is the copy of Dr. John H. Robinson's map purchased by Joseph C. Brown for $10 just previous to his departure from St. Louis to go on the survey.

141 George C. Sibley, Santa Fe, New Mexico, March 5, 1826, in answer to Poinsett's of Dec. 3, 1825: An extract:

"The delay on the part of the Mexican Government in yielding its assent to the Survey and marking the western section of the proposed [Road] from the Missouri to this frontier, is a circumstance that was entirely unlooked [for by] the Commissioners. To me it appears the more extraordinary our Government does not ask of the Mexican Govment any participation in the expense; and I am confident that the Road when completed, will be infinitely more advantageous to this country than to the western parts of the United States.

"Unless the consent of the Mexican Government is obtained in Season to reach my colleagues in Missouri via the City of Washington early in May, I should be very apprehensive that they may decline coming to join me here in June agreeably to our arrangement, that the completion of the Road will be obliged to be defered another season, and which will be worse, we shall have incurred a heavy expense unnecessarily, in consequence of our reliance upon the ready assent of this Government to permit the U. States to open the Road at our own expense.

"If this assent can be had and communicated to me here by the 20th of June, or even by the 15th of July, I might perhaps, be able to obviate the most of the above difficulties, and finish the Road by the Setting in of Winter, whether my Colleagues join me *here* or not.

"I enclose you a copy of a communication that I made to the Governour of New Mexico on the 5th of January. *Possibly* you may find it of Some use." State Historical Society of Missouri, Columbia, Missouri, Leonard Collection, Santa Fe Folder, No. 17.

142 This could have been Senor Juan B. Vigil of Santa Fe, custom officer and postmaster, who by the time Albert Pike visited the city in 1833, had for peculation and fraud, "been deprived of office, citizenship, and the privilege of entering a church," but who, Pike observed, lived very comfortably upon his booty, had a church of his own, and got along very well without the citizenship. Pike, *op. cit.*, p. 169. Or it might have been "my friend, the worshipful Don Pedro Vigil, who, owning the best house, the best horses, and prettiest wife in the valley of San

Fernandez, had kindly supplied us with mules and a guide." Pike, *op. cit.*, p. 95.

143 Sketches of Old Bill are full of his gambling exploits. Archeleta recorded: "One night he lost over a thousand dollars in playing seven-up at Maxwell's ranch." In "The Story of Bill Williams," St. Louis *Daily Globe-Democrat*, Dec. 24, 1911, p. 6, Micajah McGehee, who also knew him personally, wrote, "He had no other care for the gains of his labors than as a means of affording him a 'big spree,' and enabling him to procure more powder and lead. It is told of him that he once came into Taos and spent on one spree six thousand dollars, the result of a season of trapping, and then left the place in debt." "Rough Times in Rough Places," *Century Magazine*, March, 1891, Vol. XIX, n.s., pp. 771-772.

144 See n. 138.

145 Cf. Pike, *Prose Sketches and Poems*, Boston, 1834, p. 187: ". . . . he had even been an Alcalde, which title generally implies a greater knave with a better opportunity, and a wider flight for his genius." Also Dr. Josiah Gregg, *Commerce of the Prairies*, 2 vol., New York & London, 1844, Vol. I, pp. 233-234.

146 The diary of Joseph C. Davis, assistant surveyor of the expedition, was in two volumes, the second of which in the possession of Mr. Lionel Davis of Fayette, Missouri, is the only one extant. A photostat copy of this is available in the State Historical Society at Columbia, Missouri.

147 The camp of August 23 had been in the vicinity of present-day Ellinwood, Kansas.

148 "The Commissioners in going out, struck the Arkansas lower down than the road is expected to cross that river; they followed it up to the boundary line of the U. S. in lat. 37° 47′ 37″. and on their return will correct the road back, so as to leave the Arkansas at the mouth of Walnut creek (the North Bend)." "Report of Archibald Gamble," *Missouri Republican*, Oct. 24, 1825.

The letter of Reeves, Fayette, Missouri, Nov. 9, 1825, to Sibley, all of it descriptive of the return trip and the corrections made is here reproduced entire:

"Dear Sir,

I have the pleasure of informing you of our safe arrival here, all in good health. Cap. Gamble left us at Walnut Creek & pass'd on to St. Louis. Col. Mather Sets out in a few days for Kaskaskia. We met with no difficulty on our Retur [Sic] except the loss of two or three of our Horses, untill we arrived in the neighborhood of Lexington where we lost three or four more of our Horses, which I hope we shall be able to Reclaim, they have[ing] Strayd of. We commenced a correction of the Road at our first encampment below Walnut Creek where we threw up a large mound, aimd at going direct to Cottonwood Grove. For two days travel the way was excellent, from that on the waters of the Kansas & Arkansas interlocked so as to make that Route very objectionable. The proper Route ought to be from the lone Hackberry our Second encampment below Walnut creek, passing the head of the sand hills and intersecting our old trace at or near where Williams brot the Kaw Indians to us. At Cottonwood grove we met Becknal, as he supposed with instructions, copys of all of which we have forwarded to you. Should we not join you in the spring which is believed to be doubtful I would be glad if you would examine the Route from the lone Hackberry & mound or mark as you return, that being the only part of the route that needs or requires much marking. Cap. Gamble wrote you from Walnut creek & no doubt informed you of the death of Gov. Bates & Judge Pettibone. . . ." Collection of Sibley Mss., Lindenwood College, St. Charles, Mo.

149 William Becknell was associated with the famous Boon's Lick spring in Howard County, Missouri. In the *Missouri Intelligencer* of June 25, 1819, he advertised for 500 cords of wood, at 50¢ a cord, to be delivered to the salt works at Boon's Lick; and in the issue of Aug. 27 of the same year was notice that Wm. Becknell and James Morrison were making salt at the spring formerly worked by Daniel, Jr., and Nathan Boone.

He was a candidate, in 1820, for representative from Howard County to the first General Assembly of Missouri, but was not elected.

On Aug. 21, 1821, a week after he had been elected captain of the first trading venture to Santa Fe, and just previous to his setting forth, he bought half a section of land in western Howard County. The story of his two historic trading expeditions to the Southwest is well known. He was elected representative from Saline County, Missouri, in 1830, and in the Black Hawk War was a captain of a company from that county.

In the *Diary and Letters of Dr. Josiah Gregg,* recently published, Gregg notes Becknell's Prairie in Texas: "The same Wm. Becknell who was the first Santa Fe pioneer Commissioner; who has lived in the edge of this prairie since 1835." Vol. I, p. 86.

150 "Frederick Bates, governor of Missouri, died of pleurisy at his residence at Bonhomme on Tuesday last." *Missouri Republican,* Monday, Aug. 8, 1828. Cf. account of Reeves in Introduction, p. 8.

151 Becknell is wrong.

152 This pocket diary, six by four inches, with seventeen manuscript pages

within, is preserved in the Leonard Collection in the Missouri State Historical Society, Columbia, Missouri.

153 This diary, *Notes on Resurvey*, is a small leather-bound book, 5½ by 7½ inches, preserved in the Sibley Collection at Lindenwood College. It gives details of the first part of the road, otherwise lacking, because of the speed with which Sibley had hurried in the summer of 1825 to overtake the party, and because of the green fly pest which necessitated travel in the night. Cf. *Report of the Commissioners*, pp. 198, 203.

154 "Fountain Cottage," one mile west of Fort Osage.

155 For copy of contract with the men, see appendix, pp. 224-225.

156 Cf. n. 64 to Introduction.

157 Cf. n. 97 to Introduction.

158 Cf. n. 102 to Introduction.

159 For sketch of Baxters, see n. 100 to Introduction.

160 For sketch of Jonathan Cameron, see n. 99 to Introduction.

161 For sketch of Joseph D. Hardin, see n. 103 to Introduction.

162 For sketch of Kit Richardson, see n. 104 to Introduction.

163 For sketch of Collins, see n. 98 to Introduction.

164 At crossing of the Little Blue.

165 The chief renown of Benjamin Majors is that he was the father of Alexander Majors of Russell, Majors, & Waddel of the Overland and Pony Express. Born in North Carolina in 1794, Benjamin Majors at the age of twenty-nine moved to the Missouri frontier near Fort Osage and became the owner of 240 acres in Blue Township. When he hired himself to Sibley in the summer of 1827 and rented him the use of two cows, he did not accompany the survey party very far, for he earned only $19. He probably had to make an early return to get in his trip to the Rocky Mountains in search of a lost silver mine.

In 1833, he became captain of a company to drive the Mormons out of Jackson County. He was one of three commissioners from Independence to draft the conditions under which the Mormons left. Alexander Majors, *Seventy Years on the Frontier*, Chicago and New York, 1893. *History of Jackson County*, Kansas City, 1881, pp. 129, 166.

166 Joe Walker and his brother Joel had accompanied Hendley Cooper and William Becknell in taking relief to the returning party in October, 1825. For sketch of Joe Walker, see n. 63 to Introduction, and for sketch of Joel P. Walker, see n. 32 *ante*.

167 John Cook had settled southwest of James Shepherd, who had to move when the Commissioners hit upon his land as a site for the county-seat, Independence.

168 All these creeks are branches of Coal Creek, a tributary of the Wakarusa.

169 Creeks that the Commissioners called Waggon, Murder, Willow, and Elm now are known as a branch of Soldier Creek, branch of Elm, Chicken Creek, and Elm.

170 Sibley in an article, "Route to Santa Fe, Council Grove &c.," *Western Journal,* Dec., 1850, adds some interesting details concerning Diamond Spring: "On the 10th and 11th June, 1827, I encamped here with my party. During our stay I made requisition of "Big John" and his carving implements once more, to inscribe on the stooping Elm "Diamond of the Plain"—which was promptly done. The tree has since been cut away I believe."

171 "Walker found the spring on the 13th of June, 1827, brought me some of the water (our camp was near by) and asked me what name it should have. I directed him to cut in large letters "Big John's Spring" on a Big Oak that grows near it. He laughed, and with his knife and hatchet soon performed the work in excellent style. This Spring is on Gravel Creek, short of two miles easterly from Council Grove. It was discovered on my return from my correcting tour, after we had been *sixteen miles* beyond the Grove." *Ibid.*

Unfortunately, the marker by Big John's Spring now records that it was discovered by Captain John Charles Fremont, and so denies to Big John Walker a fame that is justly his.

172 The creek that Sibley called Locust was probably a headwater of Hickory or Bluff Creek, the only one that is seven miles from Rock Creek.

173 Pat's Creek is undoubtedly the stream also called Waggon Creek, because Garrison Patrick had broken a wagon-tongue there on the way out in 1825. It is probably the one now called Soldier Creek.

174 A short distance to the west of Olathe, Kansas.

175 For correspondence between officials of Mexico, New Mexico, and the United States, see appendix; also William R. Manning's article, "Diplomacy concerning the Santa Fe Road," *Miss. Valley Hist. Rev.,* I:516-531.

Bibliography

DIARIES CHRONOLOGICALLY ARRANGED

Sibley, George Champlin—Journal of Expedition to survey and mark a road from the Missouri frontier to the settlements in Mexico. St. Louis, June 22, 1825, to Santa Fe, Dec. 1, 1825. Book of 104 pages, 12 x 14 inches, in National Archives Building, Washington, D. C.

Reeves, Benjamin H.—Booklet No. 3, May 5, 1825, to Nov. 29, 1826. Pocket diary of memoranda. Not much value. Leonard Collection, Mo. State Hist. Soc., Columbia, Missouri.
Booklet No. 1. June 30 to July 17, 1825. Pocket diary. Slight value. Leonard Collection, Mo. State Hist. Soc., Columbia, Missouri.
Diary of return of part of the expedition from the Mexican boundary to Fort Osage, Oct. 8 to Oct. 25, 1825. Leonard Collection, Mo. State Hist. Soc., Columbia, Missouri.

Davis, Joseph S.—Diary or Survey of Santa Fe Road in 1825. Vol. II, Oct. 1 to Oct. 23, 1825. Description of return of part of the expedition from the Mexican boundary to Fort Osage. Diary in possession of Mr. Lionel Davis, Fayette, Missouri

Sibley, George Champlin—Diary No. 4. From near Turkey Creek, Oct. 12, to Santa Fe, Dec. 31, 1825. Small pocket diary 6 x 4 inches, in pencil. Lindenwood College Collection, St. Charles, Missouri.
Diary No. 5, Santa Fe, Jan. 1, to March 31, 1826. Small pocket diary, 6 x 4 inches, in ink. Lindenwood College Collection, St. Charles, Missouri.
Booklet, 4 x 7 inches, containing Way Bill of route from Fort Osage to Taos, with maps. Leonard Collection, Mo. State Hist. Soc., Columbia, Missouri.
Diary No. 8, Fort Osage, May 12 to Oct. 27, 1827. Sibley's straightening of the road, return home, and making the report. Leather bound book, small octavo. Lindenwood College Collection, St. Charles, Missouri.
Field notes of resurvey, 1827. Five pages. Lindenwood College Collection.
Report of the Commissioners in Diary No. 8.

LETTERS, VOUCHERS, ETC.

Lindenwood College Collection, St. Charles, Missouri. 212 items.
Leonard Collection, Missouri State Historical Society, Columbia, Mo. 74 items.
Sibley Collection, Missouri Historical Society, St. Louis. 8 letters.
Office of Indian Affairs, Washington, D. C. Retired Files. 14 letters.
Pennsylvania Historical Society, Philadelphia, Pa. 9 letters.
Chicago Historical Society, Chicago, Illinois. 1 letter.
Huntington Library, San Marino, California. 3 letters.

CHRONOLOGICAL SEQUENCE OF IMPORTANT LETTERS

The collection is indicated by symbols in the margin: LW for Lindenwood, LD for Leonard, IO for Indian Office, PA for Pennsylvania Historical Society, MH for Missouri Historical Society, CH for Chicago Historical Society, and H for Huntington.

IO Mar. 8, 1825—Benton's estimate for laying out the Santa Fe Road.

LW Apr. 12, 1825—Benton to Sibley. Instructions for noting geographical detail—navigability of streams, fertility of soil, etc.

IO Apr. 15, 1825—Reeves to John Scott. Indians on Santa Fe Road.

MH Apr. 24, 1825—Silas Bent to Sibley. Wants to be surveyor.

LD Apr. 25, 1825—Sibley to Reeves. Commissioners ought to meet right away.

MH May 1, 1825—Sibley to Owen Simpson. Account of Santa Fe trade and appointment as commissioner to survey the road.

IO May 4, 1825—Menard to Sec. of War. A flowery letter of regret.

LD May 5, 1825—Reeves' account of his own activity.

LW May 25, 1825—Reeves to Sibley on character of men he has chosen. "They are men who have not participated largely in the dainties & Luxuries of life—have lived and led a life of enterprise & Industry, and in my opinion of a noble dareing."

LD May 25, 1825—James Logan to Reeves. Wants to go as volunteer.

LD May 29, 1825—Sibley to Reeves. Tells of men he has employed. "Mr. Jones is a great acquisition; he is the man who piloted W. P. Hunt & party from the heads of the Yellowstone to Ft. Osage, and was formerly the compeer & favorite of the celebrated Trader and Indian fighter, Robt. McClellan." Boggs row.

LW June, 1825—Sibley's contract with the men.

LW June 9, 1825—Reeves to Sibley. Gray Bynum cannot go as leader of the men; Mr. Emmons has gone to Santa Fe; and Reeves has employed Stephen Cooper as pilot.

MH June 23, 1825—Sibley to Owen Simpson. Good on Sibley's plans.

LW June 30, 1825—Benton to Sibley. "The main idea is thoroughness, for it is not a county or state road,—but a highway between nations." $30,000 not necessarily the limit of expense.

LW July 16, 1825—Gamble to Benton[?] Wm. Becknell will run express to the commissioners with government mail.

PA July 25, 1825—Sibley to Johnston. Fine statement of Sibley as he goes on arduous trip from which he may never return.

LD Nov. 12, 1825—Sibley to Reeves. Sibley's arrival in Santa Fe and plans for meeting commissioners the following spring. Williams gone trapping. Mr. Young will start for Missouri in February.

IO Dec. 3, 1825—Edward Bates to Geo. Graham on Sibley's financial affairs.

LD Feb. 7, 1826—Sibley to Reeves. Sends description of road to Taos with maps. Sends in 6 men. Has suggested to Mex. govt. in Santa Fe two military posts on the Santa Fe road

LD Feb. 26, 1826—Poinsett to Sibley. No success yet in getting Mexican Govt. to do anything about the road. Hopes something from new administration. '

LD Mar. 5, 1826—Sibley to Poinsett. Hopes for assent of Mexican govt. & news in S. F. by July 15.

LD Apr. 15, 1826—Reeves to Sec. of War. Tells of six men returning robbed by 200 Pawnees.

LD Apr. 22, 1826—Mather to Reeves. Returns from Washington, whither he went with Indian treaties, with no news from Mexican Govt. Duel of Clay & Randolph.

LD May 7, 1826—Reeves to Mather. Agrees that Sibley ought to return.

LW May 12, 1826—Reeves to Sibley. Hopes for Sibley's speedy return.

LW May 13, 1826—S. Camacho, Sec. of State of Mex. to J. R. Poinsett. President of Mexico grants permission to George Sibley to examine road through Mexico but make no cuttings or markings.

LW May 13, 1826—Poinsett to Sibley. With news of permission.

LD May 20, 1826—Sibley to Reeves & Mather. May hear from Mexico by three mails before July 1. Commissioners ought to meet in Taos early in July.

LW June 14, 1826—Narbona to Sibley. Grants Sibley permission to proceed with examination of the road

LW June 19, 1826—Sibley to Poinsett. Restrictions will not hamper proper survey & accurate map.

LW June 19, 1826—Sibley to Narbona. Waits arrival of the commissioners.

LD June 19, 1826—Reeves to Mather. Wrote by company leaving on May 20, urging Sibley to come home as soon as possible. Wished they had corrected survey on way home from boundary

H Aug. 19, 1826—Sibley to Alcalde, Rancho de Taos. Hasn't any time to appear before him. The Spaniard who took Sibley's horse and attacked the man sent to get him deserved the beating he got.

LW Aug. 22, 1826—Pedro Martinez to Sibley. Commands Sibley to appear and answer questions before his departure.

LW & H Aug. 23, 1826—Sibley to Martinez. Sibley is on govt. business; his dealings must be with alcalde's superiors and not with him. Has permission of Mex. govt. to proceed with survey. Will go ahead tomorrow under armed escort.

LD Oct. 12, 1826—Reeves to Sibley. Is glad that Sibley is safely home. In July wrote Mather that they ought to meet Sibley at Walnut Creek and make necessary corrections. No reply until too late.

LD Oct. 17, 1826—Sibley to Reeves. Sibley suggests that Mr. Brown be instructed immediately to prepare 5 copies of the field notes and 5 handsome maps and have them ready as soon as possible.

LD Oct. 21, 1826—Reeves to Sibley. Reeves & Mather have decided to put off report until corrections are made next spring.

PA Jan. 23, 1827—Sibley to Johnston. Ideas on where to station regiments along the road. Expects soon to set off on resurvey.

LW Jan. 10, 1827—Sibley & Mather to Sec. of War. Have nearly completed survey. Corrections yet to be made.

LW Jan. 20, 1827—Commissioners resolve to hand over settlement of accounts to Sibley.

PA Jan. 27, 1827—Sibley to Bates. Offers govt. his lands, 2600 acres.

LD Mar. 23, 1827—Sibley to Reeves. Regrets Reeves's inability to help complete road on account of his wife's illness. Knowing Col. Mather's aversion to making the journey, Sibley will with Reeves's concurrence proceed to complete the road.

LD Apr. 27, 1827—Sibley to Reeves. Has fixed on May 15 to start. Discussion of men and wages—12 men in all. Wants a light prairie hat.

LW Apr. 30, 1827—Reeves to Sibley. Santa Fe adventurers set forth tomorrow or next day

LW May 1, 1827—Reeves to Sibley. Sends compass by Carson.

LD May 18, 1827—Sibley to Abiel Leonard. Complete statement of Sibley's indebtedness to the government on acct of Sibley, Baillio, and Boggs.

CH Sept. 20, 1827—Sibley to Reeves & Mather. Regrets that on account of his own illness cannot meet them in St. Louis. Will meet them in Fayette on Oct. 8.

LW Oct. 13, 1827—Brown to Sibley. Submits summary of field notes.

PA Oct. 27, 1827—Sibley to Johnston. Has just completed report to government.

LW Nov. 20, 1827—Commissioners in acct. with Sibley. Total cost and amount due Sibley

LW Dec. 7, 1827—Sibley to Hon. James Barbour, Sec. of War. Statement of expenditures. Notifies the secretary that he has mailed the map.

LD Aug. 17, 1828—Sibley to Reeves. Govt. has mislaid accts. submitted. Necessary to make them all over again

LW Aug. 26, 1828—Mather to Sibley. On visit to Washington in April found that accts. had been mislaid. Must present duplicates and vouchers again.

LW Oct. 28, 1828—Sibley to P. B. Porter, new Sec. of War. Notifies of report made a year before, showing $1597.54 due the commissioners.

PA Feb. 6, 1829—Sibley to Johnston. Can hardly realize that again he is to be disappointed in receipt of money he so much needs, & that he advanced out of his own pocket to complete work ordered by Congress.

LW May 2, 1829—Reeves to Sibley. Regrets inability to lend Sibley anything until appropriation is made.

LW June 2, 1829—Mather to Sibley. Situation of his own affairs makes it impossible to do anything for Sibley's relief.

LW Aug. 25, 1829—Mather to Sibley. Hasn't any copy of accts. to send Sibley for government, except general acct. with commissioners.

IO Aug. 31, 1829—Thomas L. McKenney to Sibley. Printer and engraver have not yet reported on possibility of printing journal & map for profit's sake. Report was loaned to Col. Sevier. He thinks that Secretary of Senate has it.

IO Sept. 2, 1829—Secretary of Senate to Office of Indian Affairs. The maps alluded to cannot be found.

LW Sept. 12, 1829—Sibley to Mather. Vouchers of his acct. with commissioners just what Sibley wants—and also "any vouchers relating to Benton's d—d Santa Fe road." Sibley going to make complete set of accts. in quadruplicate

LW Dec. 20, 1829—Sibley to Hon. John A. Eaton, Sec. of War. Calling attention to acct. still unsettled.

LD May 28, 1831—Sibley to Reeves. Commissioners now have to readjust accts of disbursements as required by Peter Hagner, 3rd auditor of the Treasury. Bring every scrap of memoranda. Will meet in Eckart's Tavern in St. Charles, June 17

LD Oct. 5, 1831—Sibley to Reeves. Mather thinks that Sibley ought to present accounts in person. Must stipulate for division of expenses.

LD Nov. 29, 1832—Sibley to Johnston. Collection of $1497.54 seems close at hand.

LW July 20, 1834—Sibley to Peter Hagner. Sends his receipt for $1497.54. "So that the whole of this Business of the Road to New Mexico is at length finally and fully settled."

Index

Kibbe, Amos, 51, 248
Kingsley, J., 144, 145

Lelande, Baptiste, 9

McAfferty, Green, 53, 250
McClellan, Robert, 30, 222
Majors, Benjamin, 22, 177, 186, 271
Marmaduke, Col. M. M., 33, 54, 251
Martinez, Pedro, 43
Mather, Thomas, 8, 9
Menard, Pierre, 8, 9
Military Posts, 208
Mire Spring, 95, 96, 258
Moore, James, 32
Mount Clayton, 38, 123
Mount Dora, 38, 94, 101, 258
Mule Trade, 139-140, 146-147, 156, 230, 233
Murphy, Daniel, 30, 50, 221, 239

Narbona, Antonio, 38, 43, 113, 115, 118, 131, 132, 134, 135, 137, 200, 201, 260

Overton, David, 45
Owens, William M., 175, 189

Patrick, G., 32, 241
Pawnees, 156
Poinsett, Joel R., 38, 40, 41, 42, 43, 112, 114, 131, 152, 153, 154, 200, 201, 225, 232, 234
Point of Rocks, 38, 129
Price, Lemuel, 50, 248
Pryor, Nathaniel M., 22, 37, 70, 81, 82, 84, 255
Pyles, Bird, 32, 84, 116, 132, 143, 241

Quarles, Dr. Pryor, 143, 265

Rabbit Ears. 94, 95f, 122
Rees, Lewis, 52, 249
Reeves, Benj. H., 8, 26, 31, and letters in appendix
Reynolds, Joseph, 32, 84, 116, 139, 143, 241
Richardson, Christopher B. (Kit) 46, 175, 180, 189, 247
Robinson, Benjamin, 29, 50, 84, 116, 132, 140, 154, 248, 268
Robinson, Dr. John H., 1, 2, 30

Round Grove, 173, 178, 179, 190

San Fernando, 81, 105, 107, 108, 111, 128, 130, 219-220, 259, 261-262
San Juan d'Ulluo, 135, 137, 263
Sangre de Cristo, 125, 126, 210, 261
Sena, Manuel, 135, 137
Sexton, George, 51, 249
Shining Mountains, see Sangre de Cristo
Sierra Grande, 98, 101, 123
Sibley & Baillio, 149
Sibley family, 1, 2, 11
Sibley, George Champlin, 10-17
Sibley, Mary Easton, 264
Simpson, Dr. Robert, 39, 144, 265
Skinner, J. S., 143, 264
Smith, Gen'l Thomas A., 131, 143, 262
Stanley, Elisha, 140, 142, 143, 254, 264
Storrs, Augustus, 4-5, 81-82, 118, 134, 254, 256, 257
Switzler, John, 140, 142, 143, 264
Switzler, Lewis, 264

Taus Gap, 38, 105f, 126
Thompson, 254
Thorp, John, 141
Thornton, Col. John, 144, 265
Todd, Neheriah, 50, 242
Travelers' Cache, 101, 259

Van Bibber, Isaac, 51, 248
Vaughn, Singleton, 32, 84, 105, 106, 107, 116, 126, 127, 128, 243
Vigil, Pedro, 154, 268

Walker, Joel P., 21, 33, 36, 55, 167, 178, 186, 249-252
Walker, John, 32, 45, 53, 68, 84, 105, 106, 107, 108, 116, 126, 127, 139, 143, 147, 175, 244
Walker, Joseph R., 21, 32, 36, 53, 173, 177, 178, 243, 250
West, George, 22, 30, 50, 81, 153, 256
Williams, William Sherley (Old Bill), 21, 33, 37, 57, 59, 61, 69, 75, 84, 114, 132, 152, 155, 253, 262, 279
Wells, James, 29, 50, 221
Wool trade, 2-5, 85, 141

Young, Ewing, 22, 116, 140, 227, 260
Young, John, 33, 37, 55, 174, 252